International Political Economy Series
Series Editor: **Timothy M. Shaw**, Visiting Professor, University of Massachusetts Boston, USA and Emeritus Professor, University of London, UK

The global political economy is in flux as a series of cumulative crises impacts its organization and governance. The IPE series has tracked its development in both analysis and structure over the last three decades. It has always had a concentration on the global South. Now the South increasingly challenges the North as the centre of development, also reflected in a growing number of submissions and publications on indebted Eurozone economies in Southern Europe.

An indispensable resource for scholars and researchers, the series examines a variety of capitalisms and connections by focusing on emerging economies, companies and sectors, debates and policies. It informs diverse policy communities as the established trans-Atlantic North declines and 'the rest', especially the BRICS, rise.

Titles include:

Greig Charnock, Thomas Purcell and Ramon Ribera-Fumaz
THE LIMITS TO CAPITAL IN SPAIN
Crisis and Revolt in the European South

Felipe Amin Filomeno
MONSANTO AND INTELLECTUAL PROPERTY IN SOUTH AMERICA

Eirikur Bergmann
ICELAND AND THE INTERNATIONAL FINANCIAL CRISIS
Boom, Bust and Recovery

Yildiz Atasoy (*editor*)
GLOBAL ECONOMIC CRISIS AND THE POLITICS OF DIVERSITY

Gabriel Siles-Brügge
CONSTRUCTING EUROPEAN UNION TRADE POLICY
A Global Idea of Europe

Jewellord Singh and France Bourgouin (*editors*)
RESOURCE GOVERNANCE AND DEVELOPMENTAL STATES IN THE GLOBAL SOUTH
Critical International Political Economy Perspectives

Tan Tai Yong and Md Mizanur Rahman (*editors*)
DIASPORA ENGAGEMENT AND DEVELOPMENT IN SOUTH ASIA

Leila Simona Talani, Alexander Clarkson and Ramon Pachedo Pardo (*editors*)
DIRTY CITIES
Towards a Political Economy of the Underground in Global Cities

Matthew Louis Bishop
THE POLITICAL ECONOMY OF CARIBBEAN DEVELOPMENT

Xiaoming Huang (*editor*)
MODERN ECONOMIC DEVELOPMENT IN JAPAN AND CHINA
Developmentalism, Capitalism and the World Economic System

Bonnie K. Campbell (*editor*)
MODES OF GOVERNANCE AND REVENUE FLOWS IN AFRICAN MINING

Gopinath Pillai (*editor*)
THE POLITICAL ECONOMY OF SOUTH ASIAN DIASPORA
Patterns of Socio-Economic Influence

Rachel K. Brickner (*editor*)
MIGRATION, GLOBALIZATION AND THE STATE

Juanita Elias and Samanthi Gunawardana (*editors*)
THE GLOBAL POLITICAL ECONOMY OF THE HOUSEHOLD IN ASIA

Tony Heron
PATHWAYS FROM PREFERENTIAL TRADE
The Politics of Trade Adjustment in Africa, the Caribbean and Pacific

David J. Hornsby
RISK REGULATION, SCIENCE AND INTERESTS IN TRANSATLANTIC TRADE
CONFLICTS

Yang Jiang
CHINA'S POLICYMAKING FOR REGIONAL ECONOMIC COOPERATION

Martin Geiger, Antoine Pécoud (editors)
DISCIPLINING THE TRANSNATIONAL MOBILITY OF PEOPLE

Michael Breen
THE POLITICS OF IMF LENDING

Laura Carsten Mahrenbach
THE TRADE POLICY OF EMERGING POWERS
Strategic Choices of Brazil and India

Vassilis K. Fouskas and Constantine Dimoulas
GREECE, FINANCIALIZATION AND THE EU
The Political Economy of Debt and Destruction

Hany Besada and Shannon Kindornay (editors)
MULTILATERAL DEVELOPMENT COOPERATION IN A CHANGING GLOBAL ORDER

Caroline Kuzemko
THE ENERGY- SECURITY CLIMATE NEXUS
Institutional Change in Britain and Beyond

Hans Löfgren and Owain David Williams (editors)
THE NEW POLITICAL ECONOMY OF PHARMACEUTICALS
Production, Innnovation and TRIPS in the Global South

Timothy Cadman (editor)
CLIMATE CHANGE AND GLOBAL POLICY REGIMES
Towards Institutional Legitimacy

Ian Hudson, Mark Hudson and Mara Fridell
FAIR TRADE, SUSTAINABILITY AND SOCIAL CHANGE

Andrés Rivarola Puntigliano and José Briceño-Ruiz (editors)
RESILIENCE OF REGIONALISM IN LATIN AMERICA AND THE CARIBBEAN
Development and Autonomy

Godfrey Baldacchino (editor)
THE POLITICAL ECONOMY OF DIVIDED ISLANDS
Unified Geographies, Multiple Polities

Mark Findlay
CONTEMPORARY CHALLENGES IN REGULATING GLOBAL CRISES

Helen Hawthorne
LEAST DEVELOPED COUNTRIES AND THE WTO
Special Treatment in Trade

Nir Kshetri
CYBERCRIME AND CYBERSECURITY IN THE GLOBAL SOUTH

International Political Economy Series
Series Standing Order ISBN 978–0–333–71708–0 hardcover
Series Standing Order ISBN 978–0–333–71110–1 paperback

You can receive future titles in this series as they are published by placing a standing order.
Please contact your bookseller or, in case of difficulty, write to us at the address below with
your name and address, the title of the series and one of the ISBNs quoted above.

Customer Services Department, Macmillan Distribution Ltd, Houndmills,
Basingstoke, Hampshire RG21 6XS, England

The Limits to Capital in Spain

Crisis and Revolt in the European South

Greig Charnock
Lecturer in International Politics, University of Manchester, UK

Thomas Purcell
Visiting Scholar, Universitat Oberta de Catalunya, Spain

Ramon Ribera-Fumaz
Senior Lecturer in Economics and Business, Director of the Urban Transformation in the Knowledge Society Research Programme of IN3, Universitat Oberta de Catalunya, Spain

First published 2014 by
PALGRAVE MACMILLAN

Palgrave Macmillan in the UK is an imprint of Macmillan Publishers Limited, registered in England, company number 785998, of Houndmills, Basingstoke, Hampshire RG21 6XS.

Palgrave Macmillan in the US is a division of St Martin's Press LLC, 175 Fifth Avenue, New York, NY 10010.

Palgrave Macmillan is the global academic imprint of the above companies and has companies and representatives throughout the world.

Palgrave® and Macmillan® are registered trademarks in the United States, the United Kingdom, Europe and other countries.

ISBN 978–1–137–31993–7

This book is printed on paper suitable for recycling and made from fully managed and sustained forest sources. Logging, pulping and manufacturing processes are expected to conform to the environmental regulations of the country of origin.

A catalogue record for this book is available from the British Library.

A catalog record for this book is available from the Library of Congress.

Typeset by MPS Limited, Chennai, India.

Contents

List of Boxes and Tables

Boxes

Table

Acknowledgements

Research for this book was conducted with financial support from the Spanish Ministry of Innovation and Science (award CSO2010-16966) and the Spanish Ministry of Education (award SB2010-0060). Pau Subirós provided excellent assistance in researching material that appears in Chapter 4. Work in progress for the book was presented at the June 2012 meeting of the Northern IPE Network in York; the July 2012 RGS-IBG conference in Edinburgh; the 'Urban Transformations from the Grassroots' seminars in Barcelona in July 2012; the September 2012 meeting of the Critical Political Economy Research Network, also in Barcelona; a meeting of the Global Political Economy Cluster at The University of Manchester in May 2013; and a Jean Monnet Centre of Excellence and Politics sponsored international day conference, in June 2013, on 'The European Crisis: Alternative Responses', also in Manchester. Our thanks go to the respective panel and seminar organisers, as well as to those participants who gave us constructive feedback. Werner Bonefeld, Paul Cammack, Brett Christophers, Miren Etxezarreta, Nicolas Grinberg, Guido Starosta, and Japhy Wilson generously read and commented on various early drafts, for which we remain very grateful (the usual disclaimers apply). In addition, several people gave valued encouragement and advice at different stages of the project. Specifically, we would like to thank Marc Badia-Miró, Josep Lladós, Hug March, Dimitris Papadimitriou, Hugo Radice, Magnus Ryner, Ivan Serrano, Stuart Shields, and Erik Swyngedouw. Finally, we are also very grateful to Tim Shaw and to Christina Brian and Amanda McGrath at Palgrave Macmillan for their enthusiasm for the project, and for their assistance in helping us to realise it.

List of Abbreviations

15-M	Movement of the 15 May (2011)
ANC	Assemblea Nacional Catalana (Catalan National Assembly)
AR	Absolute Ground-Rent
BBVA	Banco Bilbao Vizcaya Argentaria
BSCH	Banco Santander Centro Hispano
CAD	Computer Aided Design
CC.OO	Comisiones Obreras (Workers' Commissions)
CiU	Convergència i Unió (Convergence and Union)
CSE	Conference of Socialist Economists
DR	Differential Ground-Rent
DRY	¡Democracia Real Ya! (Real Democracy Now!)
EC	European Communities
ECB	European Central Bank
EEC	European Economic Community
EMS	European Monetary System
EMU	Economic and Monetary Union (of the European Union)
ERM	Exchange Rate Mechanism
ETA	Euskadi Ta Askatasuna (Basque Homeland and Freedom)
EU	European Union
FASA	Fabricación de Automóviles SA (Automobile Factory (of Valladolid))
FDI	Foreign Direct Investment
FIAT	Fabbrica Italiana Automobili Torino (Italian Automobile Factory of Turin)
FMS	Flexible Manufacturing Systems
FROB	Fondo de Reestructuración Ordenada Banacaria (Fund for the Orderly Restructuring of Banks)
GDP	Gross Domestic Product

IBEX	Índice Bursátil Español (Spanish Stock Exchange Index)
ICF	Institut Català de Finances (Catalan Finance Institute)
IMF	International Monetary Fund
INE	Instituto Nacional de Estadística (National Institute of Statistics)
INI	Instituto Nacional de Industria (National Institute of Industry)
IPE	International Political Economy
ISI	Import Substitution Industrialisation
M5S	Movimento 5 Stelle (Five Star Movement)
NIDL	New International Division of Labour
OECD	Organisation for Economic Co-operation and Development
PAH	Plataforma de Afectados por la Hipoteca (Platform for the Mortgage Affected)
PAI	Planes de Actuación Integrada (Integrated Action Plans)
PCE	Partido Comunista de España (Communist Party of Spain)
PP	Partido Popular (Popular Party)
PSOE	Partido Socialista Obrero Español (Spanish Socialist Workers' Party)
R&D	Research and Design
SEA	Single European Act
SEAT	Sociedad Española de Automóviles de Turismo (Spanish Touring Car Company)
SEPI	Sociedad Estatal de Participaciones Industriales (State Society for Industrial Participations)
TNC	Transnational Corporation
UCD	Unión de Centro Democrático (Central Democratic Union)
UGT	Unión General de Trabajadores (General Workers' Union)
UK	United Kingdom
US	United States of America
VCF	Value Capture Financing

Introduction

In 2006, on the twentieth anniversary of Spain's accession to the European Communities, the President of the Government of Spain wrote:

> Twenty years is a sufficiently long period to enable us to take stock of what has been achieved. It has undoubtedly been a positive experience for both Spain and for what is now the European Union. As far as Spain is concerned, it is difficult to find in our modern history a period of political stability, economic growth and social welfare such as the one we have experienced since 1986. There is no question that Spain today is more modern, more prosperous and more united than the Spain that joined the European Communities twenty years ago ('Letter from José Luis Rodríguez Zapatero', in Elcano Royal Institute, 2006: 9).

Back in 2006, Zapatero's pride in his country's development might have been forgivable. At this time, Spain was the eighth largest economy in the world. In the preceding decade, the country had experienced growth rates higher than the European Union (EU) average;[1] had created more jobs than any other European country; had witnessed huge infrastructural investment; had achieved nominal convergence in per capita incomes with the rest of the EU; and had seen the emergence of internationally successful and high-profile Spanish banking, utilities, and construction firms – global brands such as Banco Santander, Banco Bilbao Vizcaya Argentaria (BBVA), Telefónica, Endesa, Ferrovial, and the high street fashion retailer Zara. Spain, it was said, was 'one of the great success stories' (Chislett, 2008: 61).

Yet just three years after Zapatero penned his letter, Spain was in deep recession – the deepest since its democratic transition in the late

1970s. Between 2008 and 2009, total employment fell by 7 per cent (Meardi, Martín and Lozana Riera, 2012: 12), and by the end of 2010 Spain's unemployment rate was more than double the eurozone average (Rico, 2012: 219).[2] After first attempting to buck the recession with an economic stimulus package, Zapatero's government took a u-turn in 2010 and introduced a spate of austerity measures aimed at reducing the country's fiscal deficit – measures that failed to prevent a second slump into recession in 2011.

Immediately after assuming office in late 2011, Mariano Rajoy's Partido Popular (PP) government introduced its own package of additional austerity measures aimed at a fiscal adjustment worth €150 billion, or 15 per cent of annual gross domestic product (GDP), in accordance with EU budget pledges (Benoit, 2012). By April 2013, unemployment had risen to 27.16 per cent (over 6.2 million out of work) – the highest level in Spain since the 1970s – with youth unemployment rising to over 57 per cent (INE, 2013: 5).[3] The draconian public spending cuts had not assuaged fears that Spain would require a European Central Bank (ECB) bailout of the kind that had effectively brought down governments in Greece, Ireland, and Portugal in recent years. The European Commission warned that the country's public debt could surge to 97.1 per cent of GDP by 2014, while experts reported to Rajoy's government that the country would remain blighted by 'chronic' problems for some time to come: 'entrenched unemployment, a large mass of small and medium enterprises with low productivity, and, above all, a constriction in credit' (*Economist*, 2013a).

Crisis and revolt in the European South

Spain is by no means the only country to have suffered crisis and austerity in recent years. Since 2008, the streets and plazas of Southern European cities, especially, have become sites of mass, often spontaneous, revolt against crisis and austerity – more often than not by young people. In Greece, they called them the '700 euro generation'. Many of them were university educated, and they were, it was observed, the daughters and sons of the Greek 'middle class'. On 6 December 2008, they became enraged. The murder of a 15-year-old boy by the Special Guard in a district of Athens provoked a spontaneous uprising, which very quickly spread to other cities. The riot – on a scale not seen in Greece since the last months of a military dictatorship that ended in 1974 – was, of course, partly understood in terms of public anger at the tragic death of Alex Grigoropoulos. But, as Kaplanis (2011: 224) observed, the principal grievance of the young people who took to the streets was perhaps more deep-seated: 'the youth in Greece share a common present and future – the deterioration of their employment prospects; and this unifying element was reflected vividly in December'.

The events made it abundantly clear that all was not well in Greece, despite a sustained 14-year period of economic growth that exceeded the EU average by the mid-2000s. Yet by 2007, youth unemployment stood at 22.9 per cent – the highest in the EU at the time – and unemployment remained high among more highly qualified people aged 20 to 29. It was also noted in December 2008 that a likely global recession – sparked by the collapse of the fourth largest investment bank in the US in September 2007 – might only make matters worse in Greece (Margaronis, 2008). Indeed it did. By May 2010, thousands were again taking to the streets in protest, this time against draconian public spending cuts announced by the socialist government. The national debt then stood at 115 per cent of GDP, and in late April of that year, Greece's debt had been downgraded to 'junk' status by the ratings agency Standard and Poor's, prompting fears of a default that could threaten the very future of European Monetary Union (EMU).[4] In return for a record €110 billion bailout from the EU and International Monetary Fund (IMF) (worth 49.5 per cent of GDP), the government announced a parliamentary vote on three-year austerity package amounting to public budget cuts of €30 billion. Somewhere between 30,000 and 50,000 people marched in Athens on 5 May, the day of a national 24-hour strike against the package. Some attempted to storm the Greek Parliament. In the midst of the chaos, the Prime Minister, George Papandreou, made clear to the people of Greece the (non-) choice that lay before them: 'Today things are simple ... Either we vote and accept the deal, or we condemn Greece to bankruptcy' (quoted in O'Grady and Lichfield, 2010).

The other European countries had little choice but to agree to bail Greece out in 2010. According to the Bank for International Settlements, a Greek default threatened those French and German banks, especially, that held a combined total of US$123 billion worth of Greek government bonds (O'Grady and Lichfield, 2010). Europe's politicians also feared the prospect of 'contagion' – that other vulnerable countries within the eurozone would catch 'Aegean flu' and run into their own debt servicing crises should international investors stop providing credit to national banking systems that were in desperate need of liquidity. Their fears were not unfounded. First came Ireland, the first EU country to enter recession in 2008 and the second country to secure an EU bailout in November 2010 (to the tune of €85 billion, 47.5 per cent of GDP). The recession exposed the vulnerability of the Irish banking sector, as well as the state's deteriorating budgetary situation (see Kirby, 2010).[5] A bailout was secured in return for the Irish government's promise to make €10 billion worth of public spending cuts and €5 billion worth of tax increases by 2015.[6] Then Portugal needed an EU-IMF bailout, secured in May 2011, to the tune of €78 billion. And then Spain: in June 2012, the government secured EU assistance worth €100 billion to 'recapitalise' its banking system and save it from imminent collapse.

But then came the 'indignant ones' (*'indignados'*) – a mass movement in Spain that brought together a broad spectrum of society in protest, and which as if from nowhere led to the occupations of the country's most iconic public spaces on 15 May 2011 – including Puerta del Sol in Madrid and Plaça de Catalunya in Barcelona. Spain's equivalent of the 700 euro generation (the *'mileuristas'*) were also enraged, and understandably so given that youth unemployment was high and escalating. Perhaps the most emblematic grouping among the '15-M movement' was Juventud Sin Futuro (Youth with No Future). Their bright yellow T-shirts and banners defiantly proclaimed: 'NO HOUSE, NO JOB, NO PENSION ... NO FEAR'. But other groups came together as part of the 15-M movement as well: the anti-globalisation organization ATTAC España, the civic platform ¡Democracia Real YA! (Real Democracy Now!), and a movement that campaigns against the growing number of forced housing evictions in Spain – Plataforma de Afectados por las Hipotecas (PAH) – to name but a few.

Spurred on by events in Spain, Greece's own 'indignant citizens movement' occupied Syntagma Square, outside the Parliament in Athens. Their rage had deepened. By April 2011, unemployment stood at 15.8 per cent, with youth unemployment up to 43.1 per cent (*Guardian*, 2011). Some 21.4 per cent of the population was deemed to be at risk of poverty and 15.2 per cent was classified as 'severely materially deprived' according to Eurostat (2012a), prompting commentators to wonder whether the situation in Greece could qualify as a 'humanitarian crisis'. Yet the recession endured into 2012 and has since only worsened in terms of its social impact.[7] Meanwhile, the threat of default once again began to panic the wider European banking system. In February 2012, a second Greek bailout was agreed with the so-called 'Troika' (the European Commission, the IMF and the European Central Bank, or ECB), this time worth €130 billion (67.1 per cent of GDP). In return for a further €23.3 billion in public spending cuts between 2012 and 2014, a relatively new 'government of national unity' led by a former Governor of the Bank of Greece and Vice-President of the ECB negotiated an additional debt write-off of around €107 billion in a record-breaking restructuring deal.[8]

In November 2011, Mario Monti – another highly experienced EU technocrat – was appointed to lead a non-partisan government in Italy after the collapse of the governing coalition led by Silvio Berlusconi. While commentators considered Italy – Europe's third largest economy – to be a lesser candidate for an outright crisis (see Benedikter, 2012), by 2011 Italian national debt did stand at some 119 per cent of GDP.[9] And, after 14 years of near zero growth and a double-dip recession in 2007, the people of Italy also had to face austerity. Monti's newly inaugurated government immediately announced a €30 billion austerity package and sought to implement further reforms in areas such as labour markets and pensions. But this depended upon the parliamentary backing of other parties – Berlusconi's included. When the latter withdrew his party's support in late 2012, the way was paved for fresh elections that delivered no clear winning party and an extended period of political uncertainty. One notable development in these elections was the rise of the anti-austerity Five Star Movement (M5S). Founded in 2009, and nominally led by the comedian Beppe Grillo, the M5S called for a referendum on Italy's future involvement with the euro. For the February 2013 elections, the self-proclaimed 'non-party' M5S selected its candidates in an online ballot and managed to win a quarter of the national vote – only to refuse any part in a governing coalition.

Like that of Monti, the technocrat-led government in Greece lasted only a short time. Two general elections were held in 2012. In these – and over two years on, as Papandreou offered the people of Greece the aforementioned (non-)choice – the dilemma facing the population appeared starker still. As a *Guardian* editorial (2012a) in the UK put it: 'The Greeks reject the strangulation of livelihood that they can see all around them, but are also determined to cling to the euro and avoid lurching back to a Balkan past'. As in Italy, these most recent elections saw significant popular support go to radical anti-austerity parties. On the one hand, the left-wing party SYRIZA became the main opposition party, while on the other, the far-right Golden Dawn won just under 7 per cent of the national vote. With this in mind, Bonefeld's (2012a: 446) reminder of what's at stake in contemporary forms of crisis and revolt in Europe is incisive: 'The struggle against austerity ... can be expressed in all sorts of different forms, including communism and socialism, and also nationalism and barbarism'.

The limits to capital

> The *true barrier* to capitalist production is *capital itself*
> (Marx, 1981: 358).

The crisis that has engulfed Spain and much of what we will call the 'European South' has been attributed either to collective human frailty (from the greed of bankers, property developers, and consumers to the self-aggrandising behaviour of politicians) or to institutional failure (regulation was poor, the labour market not flexible enough, and the retirement age was set too low).[10] 'Bad policies' led to 'imbalances', 'skews', and 'distortions' in the economy (see, for example, OECD, 2010) – the non-tradable sector, particularly housing construction, was allowed to become too dominant, while bankers were left unsupervised and free to engage in an orgy of financial speculation.[11] Imbalances and distortions can, implicitly, be redressed – bad policies and institutions can be made good. However, in the context of EMU (which precludes devaluations of the national currency) and monetary governance by the ECB (which is committed to price stability, by design), eurozone governments have little other choice but to restore balance and growth by slashing public spending, increasing regressive taxation (such as VAT), and undertaking further rounds at labour market reforms – a process of so-called 'internal devaluation'. In order to get better, the patient must take more of the same austerity medicine – however much it prolongs the agony.[12]

There has been an explosion of scholarly and public debate about austerity and possible alternatives to it since 2008. In our view, too much of the debate fails to capture what is essentially at stake in this crisis. In contrast to approaches that maintain that balance and unity can be restored in the face of catastrophe,[13] we maintain that in order to analyse the current crisis – to ask what is a crisis of, how it was brought about, and what its economic, social, and political results might be – one must first try to engage in a critique of the immanently processual, fluid, contradictory, dynamic, and transformative character of the social form of production called 'capitalism'. Our own understanding of capitalism has developed out of a value-theoretical tradition that began with Marx's critique of political economy. Lamentably, it is safe to say that Marxian critique has had an uneasy relationship even with(in) international political economy (IPE) – despite the latter representing a collective scholarly endeavour ostensibly oriented toward understanding and debating what 'capitalism' is and how it relates to political authority.[14] Encouragingly, however, there appears to have been a resurgent interest in exploring critical approaches to IPE generally

(Shields, Bruff, and Macartney, 2011), with noteworthy texts engaging with or advancing Marxian approaches being published within this very book series (for example Bieler, Bonefeld, Burnham, and Morton, 2006; Rogers, 2012). With our book, we supplement but also advance some way beyond these recent contributions by providing a Marxian analysis of the crisis in the European South, focusing on Spain. In doing so, we necessarily cast light upon developments and issues beyond Spain: from the contradictions of European integration, in general, to the relation between Spanish transnational corporations and the Global South.

Our overarching argument, put simply, is that crisis is a *necessary* and *periodically recurring* feature of a capitalistically constituted form of social reproduction. The challenge for us, therefore, is to investigate the same crises and sequence of events described earlier, but to expose the inherent contradictions of capitalist development where others resort to largely contingent phenomena to explain crisis and cling to the prospect of bringing 'balance' back to economy and society. We meet this challenge by means of pursuing a Marxian approach to understanding crisis developed in the UK since the 1970s and within the Conference of Socialist Economists (CSE). Closely associated with Simon Clarke and the proponents of 'open Marxism' (see Bonefeld, Gunn, and Psychopedis, 1992; Bonefeld, Gunn, Holloway and Psychopedis, 1995; Bonefeld, 2008), the approach has contributed much to the advancement of a critique of the state and of the social power of money – especially since the crises that engulfed most of the capitalist world market in the 1970s. Detractors of the approach have argued, however, that the critique developed by these scholars has too often remained at too high a level of abstraction. In maintaining that 'whatever the specific form of capitalism, the law of value remains, as does the law of capital and its state' (Bonefeld, quoted in Bieler and Morton, 2006: 197), the approach has been criticised for overlooking significant structural changes that differentiate the forms taken by capitalism over space and time. We take this accusation seriously, and in this book, we have sought to move some way toward providing an analysis that is consistent with the critique of the state and the social power of money developed by CSE scholars, but which can better account for the uneven development of global capitalism and the formal differentiation of national and regional spaces of accumulation – specifically within the EU. We do this by drawing mainly upon work by the geographer David Harvey, and an approach to the critique of political economy associated with the work of Juan Iñigo Carrera. Both of their approaches are broadly consistent with the CSE approach's analysis of the *global overaccumulation of capital* – a central theme of this book – but also explore the role played by ground-rent, as discussed by Marx in Volume III of *Capital* (1981), to theorise the uneven development of capitalism at global, national, regional, and urban scales. We suggest that to draw upon insights from all three sources, and associated literatures, provides an illuminating analysis of the crisis-ridden historical development of capitalism in Spain, the contradictory process of European integration, and the cycle of boom and collapse that has resulted in the present catastrophe.

Outline of the book

Throughout this book, our focus is very much on Spain. We have tried wherever possible to indicate parallel developments across the European South, and to refer the reader to literatures that offer comparative insight into the development of other national forms of accumulation at key world-historical junctures (usually in Notes, where relatively lengthy or tangential discussion would otherwise disrupt the flow of our analysis). The book contains five chapters. It is organised in such a way as to first prepare the reader with an understanding of our general theoretical approach and how it relates to political, economic, and social transformations and crises in world historical terms. We then move on to develop more specific theoretical insights into the experience of relatively late industrialising countries, and to show how these cast light on the development of capitalism in Spain. Our analysis is presented diachronically in that we provide a historically unfolding account of the development of capitalism in Spain over Chapters 2 to 5; and synchronically in that we shift perspective on the respective limits to European integration, urbanisation, and the state within the same analytical timeframe in much of Chapters 3 to 5.

In Chapter 1, we outline the basis of our theoretical approach – focusing on the Marxian theory of value, the global overaccumulation of capital, and transformations in the international division of labour since the 1960s. In terms of analytical scope, Chapter 1 makes a series of claims about the crisis-ridden development of global capitalism since the 1970s that is theoretically consistent with the CSE approach, and which shares its empirical concern with the advanced capitalist economies. With Chapters 2 and 3 of the book, we shift our focus to ask how Spain was transformed from a backward, isolated, and civil war-ravaged society in 1936 to a liberal, cosmopolitan stalwart of the EU by 2006. Chapter 2 introduces the advancements offered by Iñigo Carrera and others regarding the theorisation of import substitution industrialisation (ISI), before analysing the development of capitalism in Spain under fascist rule and the material bases for rapid industrialisation and the expansion of the domestic market in the 1960s. Many existing literatures recognise that the economic management of the Spanish economy from the 1940s took the form of ISI, but we suggest from a value-theoretical position that ISI in Spain differed fundamentally from its counterparts in Latin America and elsewhere. In Latin America, ISI would later sustain accumulation in spite of the absence of competitive world market industry because of the magnitude of ground-rent that could be appropriated by capital in these countries. In Spain, however, and in the absence of such a magnitude of ground-rent, ISI could only be sustained for a limited period in the 1960s – first on the basis of wage repression and through securing new sources of international aid, but then because of the transformation of world market conditions that brought opportunities for the accumulation of capital through the appropriation of new sources of revenue in the form of remittances, mass tourism, and foreign direct investment (FDI). Ultimately, these were insufficient to sustain the expansion of the market beyond the 1960s, meaning that Spain was susceptible to balance of payment problems and suffered heavily in the global crisis of overaccumulation that erupted after 1973. The limits to ISI in Spain therefore found their political expression in the crisis of the fascist form of state and its transformation after the death of Franco toward a liberal-democratic state-form.

Put simply, our analysis reveals that ISI in Spain was never capable of developing an industrial base that could sustain the expansion of the market on the basis of its capitals' part in the production of relative surplus value – a process discussed in Chapter 1. In Chapter 3, we explain how the crisis of ISI prefigured the cycles of economic development under the liberal-democratic state that not only exacerbated the underdeveloped character of Spanish industry but were also marked by the disproportionate expansion of key sectors – principally banking, tourism, and construction. This is explained in the context of successive crises of global overaccumulation since the 1970s – the principal characteristic of which, generally, has been the massive expansion of debt to fund social consumption in societies where industrial production has been transformed on the basis of its operation on a reduced scale and upon the fragmentation of labour. We argue that European integration became the means of, and cover for, this transformation in Spain and in the European South. And, while the particular circumstances in which Spain liberalised its market in the context of European integration meant that it could enjoy a sustained period of accumulation and expanded social consumption between 1997 and 2008, they also meant that fundamental contradictions within the development of Spanish industry, and therefore of the economy more generally, simultaneously deepened. By 2008, and after a decade-long boom, the limits to European integration were revealed in a profound crisis that today still threatens not only the economic and political stability of Spain but also the very form of European integration itself.

Chapters 4 and 5 explore the process of crisis formation in Spain in more empirical depth and the various forms of revolt against – and coping strategies to deal with – state austerity since 2008. Chapter 4 builds upon the analysis of the structural weaknesses of capitalism in Spain in Chapter 3 so as to explain the specific manner in which urbanisation and the development of a spatial division of labour built around the coercive laws of competition between cities and urban regions mediated the possibilities for a decade-long boom and in the context of the contradictions outlined in Chapter 3. We provide a materialist analysis of why and how the expansion of credit in the last boom period sustained social consumption and capital accumulation well beyond the limits set by the evolution of real earnings and personal savings, focusing on the significance of Spanish real estate market and construction sector for the wider eurozone. In summary, we argue that the characteristics of the Spanish economy other commentaries identify as imbalances – the concentration of economic activity in non-tradables, real currency overvaluation, rising inflation, a growing current account deficit, and a dependence upon money capital from outside Spain (in the main, savings from Germany circulating as interest-bearing capital) – were but the expressions of the historical and crisis-ridden development of capitalist production in Spain, and of the uneven development of capitalism in Europe more generally.

Chapter 5 examines the depth of the crisis in Spain in greater detail. We ask after the possibility of a political crisis of the state, looking at the relationship between the state and various forms of revolt against state austerity and the political management of the crisis. We focus on perhaps the two most significant mass movements across Spain: the *indignados* and the PAH. We then examine the significance of the resurgence of nationalism, particularly in Catalonia, where a mass independence movement threatened the very form of the Spanish state from 2012. All three movements, we argue, express the struggle against the imposition of state austerity and internal devaluation, and the subordination of social reproduction to capital. The book concludes by summarising our argument, and by reflecting upon the broader significance of our analysis for the European South.

1
The Limits to Capital

This chapter lays the theoretical groundwork for the analysis that follows in the next four chapters. In it, our overriding concern is to explain the *necessity of crisis* in capitalism, the periodic appearance of crisis in the form of the overaccumulation of capital, and the relation between crises of overaccumulation and the transformations in production and patterns of social reproduction witnessed across much of the world since the 1970s – culminating in the current crisis. The chapter is organised as follows: First, we elaborate upon Marx's analysis of capital as a process – one of self-expanding value – and the importance of inter-capitalist competition as a 'coercive law' that results from the formation of the general rate of profit across different branches of production. Competition impels individual capitalists to play their part in the continuous, 'leapfrogging' technological and organisational revolutions characteristic of capitalist production, a process marked by the uneven development of the forces of production. We explain why there is a general tendency toward overproduction in capitalism, and the relation between money, the credit system, and crises of overaccumulation. We then introduce our understanding of the social constitution of national states that together mediate the global unity of capitalist production. Here, we develop the notion that the national state itself should be understood in processual terms, and as an active 'moment' in the global accumulation of capital and in crisis formation and management. We follow this with a discussion of the uneven development of global production, the general tendency toward a new international division of labour since the 1960s, and how cycles of overaccumulation and crisis since then have been characterised by the spectacular expansion of credit and debt on a global scale. Throughout this chapter, our analysis remains at a relatively general and abstract level. In Chapter 2, we shift our focus to the specificities of capitalist development in relatively late industrialising countries, and Spain in particular.

The accumulation of capital and the 'coercive laws' of competition

Since the emergence and consolidation of the capitalist mode of production on a world scale, the general mode by which social-ecological processes combine to reproduce the means of human social reproduction itself has had its basis in a material process – that of the *production of commodities*. As Marx explains in the infamously difficult opening chapter of *Capital* (1976), a commodity is the embodiment of two potentialities: that of being socially useful and of being exchangeable for other such commodities for the right price. The secret to the commensurability of the exchange value of commodities lies in their being forms of (or the mode of appearance of) *value*. Value mediates the unity of all concrete, independent, and private acts of social labour within the capitalist mode of production, and therefore social-ecological metabolism in general. Marx names the substance of value *'abstract labour'*, since the expenditure of concrete labour time by so many individuals appears as the same general and undifferentiated social labour time – congealed in the form of commodities as the products of that social labour. The magnitude of value is determined by the socially necessary labour time for its production – the average measure of the entirety of private and independent concrete acts of productive activity required to produce the (material and moral) means of human social reproduction. Value therefore has no corporeal materiality; one cannot touch it, as it were. Rather, value is expressed in its most developed concrete form as *money* (Starosta, 2008: 310). As such, money is 'the most abstract form of private property' – 'the supreme social power through which social reproduction is subordinated to the reproduction of capital' (Clarke, 1988: 13–14).

But what is *'capital'*, in this sense? The private and independent manner in which commodities are produced is a general organisational principle that is historically specific to capitalism (Iñigo Carrera, 2008: 10–11). In capitalism, the production process itself generally consists of a series of transformative moments in which money is invested in a labour process (specifically to purchase means of production and labour-power) with the motive of exchanging the commodities produced for the original sum outlaid plus a surplus which is realised once they are sold in their intended market. The capitalist, as proprietor of the means of production, receives the original money outlaid plus a *profit* (an outcome which appears as if it were entirely down to her or his own ingenuity and effort). It follows from Marx's analysis of production that *capital* ought to be properly conceptualised not as a thing or a 'factor' of production – as is the case in neo-classical economics – but as a *process* (Harvey, 1982: 20); capital is value-in-motion, or 'self-valorising' value (Marx, 1976: 994).

The various metamorphoses of value-in-motion can be represented in the formula for the circuit of capital:

$$M\text{–}C <^{LP}_{MP} \ldots P \ldots C\text{–}M + \Delta M$$

In this, 'M' is money; 'C' is commodities; 'LP' is labour-power; 'MP' is means of production; 'P' denotes the combination of LP and MP in production; 'M' is the original money outlaid; and delta (Δ) denotes a surplus that accrues to the capitalist in the form of profit.

Harvey's distillation of Marx's analysis of this circulation process into ten core features, summarised in Box 1.1, suffices for now to present the fundamentals of Marx's analysis of it, as it unfolds in the course of the three volumes of *Capital*. It attests to how Marx's analysis of commodity production first necessitates the discovery through dialectical analysis of the value-form, and therefore how it penetrates the categorical presuppositions and fetish character of classical political economy and neo-classical economic theory, *avant la lettre* (Heinrich, 2012: 33). Crucially, of course, Marx also explains how the source of profit (ΔM) for the industrial capitalist is *surplus value*: the appropriation of unpaid labour time from the workforce. So, we can explain how the production of value in the process of circulation requires a class society consisting of buyers and sellers of *labour-power* – the only commodity, peculiar to the capitalist mode of production, whose specific use-value is the capacity to produce more value than it itself costs to produce – a surplus of value. And, further, that the total surplus value available to the capitalist class is derived from the realisation of the surplus labour time produced over and above the necessary labour time expended by social labour. We can then draw out the necessary but contradictory and 'irrational' features of the production of value, the necessarily accumulative character of the circulation of capital, and of capitalists' relentless pursuit of profit.

Marx shows how the production of a particular form of *relative* surplus value is key to understanding not only the historical and territorially expansive development of capitalism but also its inherent tendency

Box 1.1   Ten Core Features of the Circulation of Capital (from Harvey, 1985a: 129–32)

1. *The continuity of the circulation of capital is predicated upon a continuous expansion of the value of commodities produced …*
2. *Growth is accomplished through the application of living labour in production*
3. *Profit has its origin in the exploitation of living labour in production …*
4. *The circulation of capital, it follows, is predicated on a class relation …* [between] those who buy rights to labour power in order to gain a profit (capitalists) and those who sell rights to labour power in order to live (labourers) …
5. *This class relation implies opposition, antagonism, and struggle.* Two related issues are at stake. How much do capitalists have to pay to procure the rights to labour power, and what, exactly, do those rights comprise? Struggles over the wage rate and over conditions of labouring (the length of the working day, the intensity of work, control over the labour process, the perpetuation of skills, and so on) are consequently endemic to the circulation of capital …
6. *Of necessity, the capitalist mode of production is technologically dynamic.* The impulsion to fashion perpetual revolutions in the social productivity of labour lies, initially, in the twin forces of inter-capitalist competition and class struggle …
7. Technological and organisational change usually requires investment of capital and labour power. This simple truth conceals powerful implications. *Some means must be found to produce and reproduce surpluses of capital and labour to fuel the technological dynamism so necessary to the survival of capitalism.*
8. *The circulation of capital is unstable. It embodies powerful and disruptive contradictions that render it chronically crisis-prone […]* Growth and technological progress, both necessary features of the circulation of capital, are antagonistic to each other. The underlying antagonism periodically erupts as fully fledged crises of accumulation, total disruptions of the circulation process of capital …
9. *The crisis is typically manifest as a condition in which the surpluses of both capital and labour, which capitalism needs to survive, can no longer be absorbed.* [This is] a state of *overaccumulation.*

10. *Surpluses that cannot be absorbed are devalued, sometimes even physically destroyed.* Capital can be devalued as money (through inflation or default on debts), as commodities (unsold inventories, sales below cost price, physical wastage), or as productive capacity (idle or underutilised physical plant). The real income of wage labourers, their standard of living, security, and even life chances (life expectancy, infant mortality, and the like) are seriously diminished, particularly for those thrown into the ranks of the unemployed. The physical and social infrastructures that serve as crucial supports to the circulation of capital and the reproduction of labour power may also be neglected.

to enter periodic crises. It is therefore worth considering how this form of surplus value is produced. Relative surplus value is a counterpart to *absolute* surplus value. The latter is produced by the extension of the working day beyond the socially necessary period required to produce the use values necessary for the reproduction of the average labourer and therefore of their labour-power.[1] Relative surplus value, on the other hand, arises most effectively out of enhancements in the productivity of labour-power achieved through technological innovation and its application to the labour process, and by investing in the increased scale of production. Such enhancements in the *forces of production* increase the mass of use values produced in a given period of labour time, thereby making innovation attractive to individual capitals seeking to realise surplus profits by producing a greater mass of commodities than their competitors, and in the same timeframe. But, given that one turnover of capital results in a fresh surplus (ΔM) – which must be reactivated as capital if more surpluses are to be accumulated and if the capitalists are to reproduce themselves as such – the development of the productive forces depends less upon the volition and entrepreneurial spirit of the capitalist than upon the competitive pressures on their rate of profit as other capitalists adopt similar technological and organisational forms of production (Clarke, 1994: 238; Harvey, 2010a: 165–9; Heinrich, 2012: 106–8). Marx's original contribution here was to reveal that constant revolutions in the development of the forces of production are *necessary* to the process of the *accumulation of capital* as undertaken by the capitalist class: 'the development of capitalist production makes it necessary constantly to increase the amount of capital laid out in a given industrial undertaking, and competition subordinates every individual capitalist to the immanent laws of capitalist production, as external and coercive laws' (Marx, 1976: 739).

To sum up, the Marxian theory of value explains how the imperative to enhance the productivity of labour-power under the control of individual capitalists – and therefore to produce more cheaply than their competitors – is 'hard-wired' into capitalist production; and, concomitantly, the competitive pressure to match, or indeed better, the productivity of those innovating capitals on the part of those left behind cannot be withstood if the latter wish to remain profitable and, ultimately, in production. As Marx puts it: 'The law of the determination of value by labour-time makes itself felt to the individual capitalist who applies the new method of production by compelling him to sell his goods under their social value; this same law, acting as a coercive law of competition, forces his competitors to adopt the new method ... Capital therefore has an immanent drive, and a constant tendency, towards increasing the productivity of labour, in order to cheapen commodities and, by cheapening commodities, to cheapen the worker himself' (Marx, 1976: 436–7). This adjustment process on the part of individual capitalists is the source of crisis in capitalism, since, as Clarke (1990/1: 454–5) underlines: 'The drive to increase the production of surplus value, although imposed by capitalist competition, is not confined within the limits of the market but is subject to its own laws, which determine the tendency to expand production *without regard for the limits of the market*. These laws are defined not by the subjective irrationality of the capitalist, but primarily by the *uneven development of the forces of production* as capitalists struggle for a competitive advantage'.

The tendency toward overproduction, the necessity of crisis and cycles of overaccumulation

Since money *appears* in capitalist societies as some-'thing' that stands apart from other commodities and which bridges the gap between different moments of capital accumulation – sale and purchase, production and circulation; there always exists a formal *possibility* that the metamorphosis of capital might breakdown, and that capitalists might not realise the value of the commodities that they have produced (see Burnham, 2002: 125–6). Capitalists engage in production in a private and independent manner so as to realise profit (i.e., surplus money – ∆M), and the tendency of capitalist production is to develop the productive forces without limit. Therefore, there is no guarantee that supply will be met with proportionate demand. Indeed, the tendency inherent in the capitalist mode of production is toward the overproduction of commodities – a tendency borne out of the uneven development of the productive forces within and between different branches of production and, under the circumstances, imposed by competition (Clarke, 1990/1, 1994). This explains the enduring insight of Marx and Engels' early depiction in the *Communist Manifesto* of capitalism as an inherently expansive system of production, forcing the opening up of new markets abroad by the compulsion of capitalists to overcome barriers to profitability experienced as competition in existing markets (Cammack, 2013; Harvey, 1988). Such endeavours – along with the aforementioned development of the productive forces – can historically explain boom-like periods of growth and expansion within and across different national capitalist societies. Yet the tendency toward overproduction is never overcome. It is evident that in the competitive struggle between capitalists, those which are unable to maintain the pace and scale of technical and organisational change will find it harder to turn a profit – their eventual liquidation leading to the further concentration and centralisation of capital in progressively fewer hands.

All capitalists experience overproduction in the form of intensified competition, as each one struggles to maintain profitability in the face of a downward pressure on prices and the devaluation of their stock and means of production. Some capitalists will invest in further technological and organisation change; others will switch their capital into new productive or speculative ventures in the hope of making profits elsewhere (as we will see in our analysis of 'capital switching' into Spanish real estate in Chapter 4); and the capitals left behind by the pace of technological change will look to a variety of 'adventurous paths', such as borrowing and even swindling, so as to guarantee their survival (Marx, 1981: 359). In each scenario, the capitalist looks to sustain her or his own reproduction regardless of the limits of the market and, in turn, plays her or his part in the extension of generalised overproduction that sooner or later presents itself to all capitalists as a limit to accumulation (usually when banks restrict loans, as we explain in further detail next). In such circumstances, profitability will only be restored through a *crisis* – in which, for instance, backward capitals are liquidated, stocks and machinery are devalued or scrapped, and workers are laid-off and forced to re-enter the labour market to look for jobs on new contractual bases (perhaps with lower pay or fewer guarantees regarding the terms and conditions of work). This will be illustrated in our analysis of industrial restructuring and the fragmentation of labour in Spain in the 1980s, in Chapter 3.

Given the inherent tendency to develop the productive forces without limit, and therefore toward generalised overproduction, we can therefore insist that crisis is not only a formal possibility in capitalism, but that crisis plays a *necessary* role in re-limiting accumulation within the confines of the market and restoring the conditions for capital accumulation. Within a mode of production in which 'the *true barrier* to capitalist production is *capital itself*' (Marx, 1981: 358), crisis obtains as the 'irrational rationaliser' (Harvey, 1982: 305). Crisis 'is not a pathological phenomenon appearing on the surface of capitalist society, but the normal and regular means by which prices and production are adjusted in order to make possible the renewed reproduction of capital ... *"Crisis* is nothing but the forcible assertion of the unity of the phases of the production process which have become independent of each other"' (Clarke, 1994: 196, quoting Marx).

The credit system

The theory of overproduction and crisis as presented up to this point is, in itself, insufficient (it is merely a 'first cut', to borrow from Harvey, 1982). Specifically, we need to explain two recurrent phenomena: first, the periodicity of such crises; and, second, why crisis usually appears in the first instance as a crisis of money rather than of production (as a so-called 'credit crunch' – see Chapter 5). This requires that we integrate our consideration of development of the forces of production with an understanding of the role of *credit* (which circulates as *interest-bearing capital* – a circuit represented in the form M ... ΔM). There are practical reasons why credit must be made available to capitalists, and on the basis of imminent need rather than the part particular capitals have played in the production of surplus value in the past. For example, industrial capitals must periodically – and subject to the 'coercive laws of competition' – undertake expensive and speculative investments in organisational and technological changes to improve their competitiveness and maintain profitability. Such investments often require that surplus money-capital with no material basis in production be made available to them in credit form. And, since the sustained accumulation of capital requires expanding *social consumption* on the part of workers and other capitalists, interest-bearing capital might also be thrown into circulation whenever workers' and capitalists' abilities to consume commodities is disproportionate to the production of commodities (Harvey, 1982: 95). We will address the relation to monetary policy and political struggles over the reproduction of capital and labour later in this chapter.

Harvey (1982: Chapter 8) discusses the first example in some detail, looking to establish a relation between credit and the circulation of another form of capital – *fixed capital*.[2] We have seen how the most potent means of producing relative surplus value is to raise the productivity of labour-power. Historically, the necessary innovations in the organisational and technological form of the labour process to this end have entailed the development of large-scale industry. The development of the forces of production requires raising large sums of money to invest in fixed capital – plant, machinery, and so on – that might not be amortised for long periods of time; fixed capital, in other words, that effectively acts as a 'prison' for value since, in practice, it takes the form of large-scale, often immovable physical installations. An increasingly more complex system of finance, with significant global reach, has therefore developed historically within and across national spaces of accumulation and as a necessary means of helping to smoothen the temporal unevenness of the depreciation and investment in fixed capital that is central to the accumulation process (Clarke, 1994: 273), and so that capital may circulate at optimal velocity (regulated by a suitable rate of interest and meeting at least, what Harvey terms, 'socially necessary turnover time').[3] 'Necessarily', then, 'the competition between capitalists to establish surplus profits is conducted at the level of access to credit' (Fine, 1979: 246).

The credit system provides a 'temporal fix', in other words, to the potential barriers and blockages inherent to the accumulation process within large-scale industry, allowing competing individual capitals to maintain the pace of technical change. Of course, the expansion of the credit system to finance the expansion of fixed capital means that credit 'obtains as a mortgage on the future, a speculative gamble on the future exploitation of labour' (Bonefeld, 2000: 56). In this sense, credit money therefore circulates as 'fictitious capital', and, as such, relates to productive capital in terms of laying a claim to the *appropriation* of a portion of surplus value.[4] This claim is inherently uncertain, since future surplus value production varies according to the state of competition, the rate of exploitation, and so on (Harvey, 1982: 267). Historically, various means of engineering a credit system that can absorb risk and adjust to prevailing conditions in production have produced complex financial systems – incorporating stocks and shares, state money and government debt that can themselves be traded as claims on the appropriation of surplus value – and which are increasingly global in scope. The credit system therefore elevates the contradictions inherent to the accumulation of capital discussed previously to 'a higher plane'

(Harvey, 1982: 238): 'credit does not resolve the contradictions of the commodity form, it merely generalises them' (Clarke, 1994: 274). An understanding of the role of the credit-system also illuminates a significant historical dimension to the theorisation of crisis formation in capitalism, since 'experimentation' in terms of creating new financial instruments and institutional configurations 'lays the material basis for later phases of accumulation' (Harvey, 1982: 326), but have done so at the risk of intensifying cycles of overaccumulation and of making crises ever more destructive (Clarke, 1988: 110). Note that this will have particular relevance for our analysis of speculative urbanisation in Spain, in Chapter 4.

The periodicity of crisis

While the development of the credit system introduces no new determinations to the accumulation process, it does mediate, and at times exacerbate, the cyclical character of accumulation and the uneven development of different branches of production, but also the periodicity of crises in capitalism.[5] In earlier phases of growth, credit expands to meet the requirements of individual capitals undertaking investment in new technological and organisation forms of production, and it serves to promote the free flow of capital between different branches of production so that the pace of technological change in the most dynamic sectors dictates that of less dynamic ones. Credit therefore helps individual capitalists to maintain profitability, but does so by extending the life of smaller, more technologically backward, capitals in less dynamic branches of production. In general, credit therefore intensifies the tendency to develop the forces of production beyond the limit of the market. Sooner or later, this confronts even the more dynamic capitals as pressures on profitability. This means that capitalists respond not by cutting back the scale of production but by looking to reduce costs of production further still or looking for new markets, thereby intensifying the pressures of competition and the thirst for credit (Clarke, 1994: 282). In response, credit is expanded to further prolong the agony of less dynamic capitals, to allow others to buy up liquidated assets from those capitals that cannot maintain competitiveness and profitability, or to fund investment in new speculative ventures. The accumulation cycle is therefore not determined by the limit to the market, but – fed by the expansion of fictitious capital – it pushes well beyond such a limit. The expansion of credit fuels the boom, while compounding the likelihood that when such speculative investments can no longer lay claim to the appropriation of surplus value, the crisis of overaccumulation will be more destructive. 'Such a state of over-production of capital is called the *overaccumulation of capital*' (Harvey, 1982: 192, emphasis added).[6]

It follows, therefore, that when crises periodically erupt in the course of the development of capitalism, they appear not as crises of production but as crises of money. Or, put another way, as a crisis of the command of money over the exploitation of labour. The crisis confronts society as a need to restore the quality of money to a more stable basis. As we explain in the next section, the crisis – and its resolution – therefore becomes a political matter.

The state, money, and the national processing of global class relations

For most of Marx's *Capital*, the analysis rigidly remains at a 'level of generality within a purely functioning capitalist mode of production' (Harvey, 2012: 36). Yet already at this high level of abstraction, we can begin to outline a Marxian theory of the state (as does Harvey, 1976). As Harvey summarises, there are several essential conditions for capital accumulation that make certain forms of state action necessary and permanent feature in the development of capitalism. Harvey (1976: 83) writes: 'The capitalist state must, of necessity, support and enforce a system of law which embodies concepts of property, the individual, equality, freedom and right which correspond to the social relations of exchange under capitalism'. He goes on to add: 'The guarantee of private property rights in means of production and labour power, the enforcement of contracts, the protection of the mechanisms for accumulation, the elimination of barriers of mobility of labour and capital, and the stabilisation of the money system (via central banking, for example), all fall within the field of action of the state' (p. 84). He also suggests: 'The state should, in fact, be viewed as a *relation* ... or as a process' (p. 87). This latter point is somewhat underdeveloped in Harvey's 1976 piece on the Marxian theory of the state, and indeed in his subsequent writings. It is more developed in the writing of scholars working within the 'CSE approach', since they have contributed to a Marxian understanding of, first, why and how the capitalist form of state stands in separation from civil society (see Clarke, 1988: Chapter 5); and, second, why and how states mediate the global accumulation of capital by means of 'the national processing of global class relations' (Burnham, 1996: 94; see also Clarke, 2001).

First, and in a similar vein to Harvey, Bonefeld (2006: 206) makes clear the class character of the state in capitalism:

> In sum, the critique of political economy amounts to the critique of the form of the state: the form of the state does not stand outside of history [as in political economy and political theory] but is rather the organization form of a capitalistically producing and bourgeois (*bürgerlich*) constituted society. The form of the state, as Marx put it in the *Grundrisse*, is the concentration of bourgeois society. The state, then, is the political form of bourgeois society; it is the form in which the safeguarding of the equality of rights is focused politically. The law of the (labour-) market presupposes, as its condition, the capitalist state that protects the inequality in property through the safeguarding of the equality of rights, of abstract equality.

In this approach, therefore, 'the state' is very much understood in relational, processual terms: it denotes the continuous struggle to impose the conditions for the accumulation of capital through money and law, as well as the continuous struggle to limit the demands made by capitalists and workers to secure their social reproduction within the confines of stable capital accumulation and in the context of the tendency toward overaccumulation that is inherent to the capitalist form of social production (see Bonefeld, 1992; Clarke, 1992; Holloway, 1992).[7] We return to concrete instances of such struggles in Spain in Chapter 5 of this book.

Second, the 'CSE approach' insists that the state should be understood not primarily in terms of its constitution on a national basis, but as a differentiated moment – or 'political node' – within a global totality (Burnham, 1994; Clarke, 1992). To the uninitiated scholar of IPE that first encounters it, the Marxian understanding of international relations can appear be counter-intuitive: 'the world', suggests Holloway (1996a: 124) for example, 'is not an aggregation of national states, national capitalisms or national societies: rather the fractured existence of the political as national states decomposes the world into so many apparently autonomous units'. The key to decoding this argument is to return once more to the question of capitalists' pursuit of profit. In Volume III of *Capital*, Marx explains how profit is distributed among different industrial capitals as aliquot parts of the total social capital (see also Arthur, 2002; Guerrero, 2003; Moseley, 2002 and 2009). Competition between capitals operating in different branches of production within the international division of labour has the result of equalising rates of profit in those branches, and thus averaging out to form an average world market rate of profit.[8] In effect:

> This equalisation 'compares' the productive labour set to work within industry with the productive labour of all other industries, leading to the determination of an average rate of profit. This average rate of profit obtains as the average world market rate of profit. This equalisation and averaging entails the unleashing of the 'heavy artillery' of cheaper prices (cf. Marx and Engels, 1997: 17) upon national states should the exploitation of labour within their jurisdiction fall below the average world market rate of profit. This heavy artillery makes itself felt through pressures on the exchange rate, the accumulation of balance of payments deficits and drains on national reserves. It is through the movement of money capital that the global conditions of accumulation impinge on 'national economies'. World money is not only a means of exchange or a means of payment; it obtains, fundamentally, as a power that polices the effectiveness of the 'domestic' exploitation of labour. (Bonefeld, 2000: 38)[9]

National states are therefore confronted with a dilemma, as Burnham (1996: 105) explains:

> To increase the chances of attracting and retaining capital within their boundaries ... national states pursue a plethora of policies (economic and social policy, co-optation and enforcement, etc.) as well as offering inducements and incentives for investment. However, the success of these national policies depends upon re-establishing conditions for the expanded accumulation of capital on a world scale. The dilemma facing national states is that while participation in multilateral trade rounds and financial summits is necessary to enhance the accumulation of capital on the global level, such participation is also a potential source of disadvantage which can seriously undermine a particular national state's economic strategy.

Burnham goes on to elaborate on the historical evidence for the playing of this tension in the post-1945 international system, and, for our purposes, it is worth bearing this insight in mind as we consider the fate of particular national states within the project of the European common market and, later, EMU – a central theme in Chapters 3 to 5 of this book.

We do not suggest that all states should be treated as merely identical when it comes to political and economic analysis: 'although all national states are constituted as moments of a global relation, they are distinct and non-identical moments of that relation' (Holloway, 1996a: 125), and 'their development is the outcome of a history of class struggle *in and against* the institutional forms of the capitalist mode of production, whose historical resolution is always provisional' (Clarke, 1988: 16, emphasis added). Let us expand on this. After due consideration of the historical development of international and national institutions adequate to a system of global trade and finance, we can generally claim that in a crisis of overaccumulation, central banks are confronted with a drain on reserves with which to support the exchange rate. The crisis therefore appears to the state, as backer of the central bank, 'in the form of a balance of payments deficits, over-ridden by a claim on tax revenue by creditors, and in the form of a threat to the convertibility of currency in commodities on the world market, over-ridden by speculative pressure on the exchange rate' (Bonefeld, 1996a: 198). The state must therefore impose control over the money supply so as to restrict credit in the national economy as a means of retaining 'credit-worthiness' in international financial markets. 'In other words, it involves a policy of state austerity' (Bonefeld, 1996a: 199). This much has a general resonance in the experiences of crisis in recent decades. Yet, in any given crisis, the state also becomes the object of class struggle, as capital and the working class confront it as a barrier to their own social reproduction (Clarke, 1988: 16). The politics of economic management therefore consists of negotiating the contradictory political pressures to re-establish the conditions for expanded accumulation on a global scale by confining growth within the limits of the market, on the one hand, and pressures to pursue expansionary (and therefore inflationary) policies to support growth and rising standards of living – regardless of the limits of the market – on the other.[10] The outcomes of a given crisis – mediated by the competitive strategies of capitalists and state policies – are never predetermined, although we can claim, as Harvey does, that the manner in which one crisis is managed politically lays the material basis for the next accumulation cycle and therefore for the 'objective' viability of some forms of state action over others. This will become clearer as we trace the development of capitalism in Spain and the European South in the coming chapters of this book.

In the next section we delineate the process of the transformation of the international division of labour during the latter half of the twentieth century, precisely to arrive at a more specific understanding of the spatially differentiated results of transformations in the development of capitalism on a world scale. In it, we bear in mind that the 'CSE approach' points forcefully at understanding state action as being essentially oriented toward the permanent management of the process of overaccumulation and of the threat of crisis. And, of course, it also suggests that the state's management of economic policy always entails significant risk, since the state's effectiveness in guaranteeing the validity of speculative claims on the production of surplus-value can only be sanctioned *post hoc*, rather than *ex ante* (Bonnet, 2002: 121). Kerr's (1998: 2282) analysis of the private finance initiative in the UK in the 1990s has a generalisable resonance in this regard: 'the *necessity* for state restructuring and its general *form* (i.e. state austerity) was constituted outside of the limits of the national state (and its policy-making processes). But the particular *ways* in which that restructuring occurred ... were the result of a trial-and-error response by the political administration of its own "domestic" context ... and as it confronted the resistance of its own labour process and that of the market' (see also Clarke, 1990: 194).

It is worth reiterating, in general terms, that the Marxian theory of value illuminates how, *in essence*, all forms of state – whether individually, regionally or through their international relations with other states – must exert a significant degree of direct control over the quality of money within their jurisdiction, the education of the workforce, the 'freedom' for (national and foreign) workers to enter and leave the labour market, the efficiency of infrastructural arrangements (transport networks, for example), and so on (see Bonefeld, Brown, and Burnham, 1995: 29). Later, we explain why in recent decades we have witnessed the ascendancy of money as the ultimate arbiter of state policies under increasingly intense cyclical conditions of the global overaccumulation of capital.[11] Equipped with such insights, we will go on, in subsequent chapters, to explain the recent development of capitalism in European countries such as Spain – not in terms of political agency, institutional autonomy, and national self-determination but in terms of the permanent necessity for national states to secure a stable footing within the international division of labour, and to manage the threat of devaluation that confronts them in the form of external, coercive pressures on exchange rates, balance of payments deficits, and so on. The creation of a currency union in Europe in the 1990s marked an attempt to create a zone of monetary stability after two decades of crisis: 'EMU amounts to an institutional attempt at buttressing domestic policies of austerity with a supranational anchor and the establishment of an anti-inflationary police force that seeks to protect member states from speculative runs by securing the right of private property' (Bonefeld, 1998: PE55). The purpose and contradictory constitution of EMU has been vividly demonstrated in the current crisis and is a central theme in Chapters 3 to 5 of this book. But before addressing this theme, we must first broach the theorisation of the uneven global development of production in recent decades, and as a means of analysing the crisis-ridden development of capitalism in Spain prior to the process of European economic integration from the 1980s (our aim in Chapter 2).

The tendency toward a new international division of labour

In Volume III of *Capital*, Marx sustains the argument that individual industrial capitals can only remain viable for as long as they 'progressively tend to conform with the capitals of mean composition under pressure of competition' and therefore 'tend to realise in the prices of their commodities ... the average profit' (Marx, 1981: 274). 'Mean', or 'normal', industrial capitals are therefore categorised as those which achieve a degree of average concentration that allows them to put into action the productivity of labour corresponding to the determination of the value of commodities, to play an active role in the formation of the general rate of profit at the level of the world market, and, therefore, to claim their due share in the distribution of surplus-value (Iñigo Carrera, 2008: 3).[12] As cycles of overaccumulation proceed, the survival of the mass of '*small* industrial capitals' (those which fail to maintain the degree of normal concentration, and which are therefore unable to valorise at the average rate of profit for their specific branch or sector) is put into question.[13] This, surmises Marx (1981: 359), forces small capitals down 'adventurous paths: speculation, credit swindles, share swindles, crises' – paths taken as means to avoid being liquidated and made available to normal capitals as fresh capital (and thereby feeding the process of the centralisation of capital in progressively fewer hands; see Harvey, 1982: 139). Harvey characterises this explanation on the part of Marx as some kind of 'equilibrium' theory of 'the organisation of production – expressed in terms of size of firm, degree of vertical integration, level of financial centralisation or whatever – that is consistent with capitalist accumulation and the operation of the law of value' (Harvey, 1982: 140).[14] In this, normal industrial capitals are those which can constantly enhance the productivity of labour under their control in step with the average levels of productivity in their respective branches of industry. And, where such branches of industry consist of capitals competing across international jurisdictions – that is, on the world market – such capitals therefore play an active role in the formation of a general (or average world market) rate of profit.

Iñigo Carrera (2008: 59) explains how from through the nineteenth century and for much of the first three quarters of the twentieth century, the development of capitalism within Western Europe and the United States took this precise form.[15] This is to say that, in their pursuit of profits from production for the world market, industrial capitals within countries such as Germany and the UK tended to develop the productivity of labour through organisational and technological innovations associated with the development of large-scale industry and, from the nineteenth century, the system of 'machinofacture'.[16] Harvey (1982: 148) uses the historical examples of vertically integrated large corporations that developed in the US from the 1920s, such as General Motors, to illustrate this tendency. Elsewhere (Harvey 1990: 127–40), he argues that the spread beyond the US of these organisational and technological forms of production – together with associated forms of the reproduction of labour-power, culture, morality and so on – was a possibility only after the Second World War. Previous forms of skilled craft industries in Europe – such as automobile manufacturing – were, by the 1950s, exposed to competition from new systems of machinofacture, such as that in the Ruhr-Rhineland region, which adopted new organisational forms and technologies and began to benefit from larger economies of scale. Rising demand for cars, shipbuilding, steel, petrochemicals, 'white goods', and other manufactured commodities was fuelled by the growth in these industries' own workforces, as well as the expansion of state spending across North America and Europe (in post-war reconstruction, and in infrastructure and housing construction, for example).

The unique and uneven manner in which different national states adopted modes of management of labour markets, fiscal policy, and welfare and infrastructure spending was given a degree of cogency through the Bretton Woods monetary system. Established in 1944, this established the convertibility of the US dollar to gold, made the dollar the world's reserve currency, limited fluctuations in international exchange rates, and allowed national states an unprecedented degree of monetary independence. The content of Bretton Woods, for Hampton (2006: 152–3), was to allow for the national processing of class relations 'in the form of a conflict between internal and external equilibrium', granting the national state a measure of control in 'recalibrating the balance between necessary and social labour' by permitting 'a gentle decline in the value of money as the costs of de-valorising capital and labour power were "socialised", while productivity gains fuelled wage rises'.

US firms benefited from European national states' opening of their economies to foreign investment and trade after 1945. When, by the 1960s, the West European and Japanese post-war recovery was complete, their leading industrial capitals also had to respond to the problem of overproduction in their internal markets – in short, 'the drive to create export markets for their surplus output had to begin' (Harvey, 1990: 141). Yet the need to create and access new markets was only part of the story. The global accumulation of capital from the 1960s onwards has to be understood in the context of a significant reconfiguration of the international division of labour.

By the mid-1970s, Fröbel, Heinrichs and Kreye (1978: 849) had already identified that 'industrial capital can now earn extra profits through a suitable reorganisation of production into fragmented tasks, which enables it to exploit the worldwide reserve army with the help of a highly developed transportation and communication system'. This was an insightful, but partial, observation that captured the form taken by the *new international division of labour* (NIDL), without uncovering its general content as lying in the computerisation and robotisation of the production processes of large-scale industry (Grinberg and Starosta, 2013). From the 1960s onward, this latter content underpinned the spread into Western Europe of broadly 'Fordist' techniques of fragmenting labour processes into a series of elementary operations. On the basis of automation and spatial relocation, industrial capitals in the classical countries could relocate moments of the production process to factories in countries that, at that time, possessed low-cost labour surpluses and with relatively little resistance from local trade unions. This also explains moves by late industrialising European states toward an uneven process of partial liberalisation of economic policy and toward allowing the entry of FDI, as we show was the case in Spain at this time in Chapter 2; as well as the process through which the 'classical' European countries began a process of transferring in workers from abroad to work under different national variants of the West German *Gastarbeiter* system (Fröbel, Heinrichs and Kreye, 1978: 851) – many of whom came from Southern Europe.

Also of crucial importance in understanding this period were the systems of industrial relations between capital and labour that were established in many industrialising countries, since they allowed for rising standards of living for many workers. As Clarke (1992: 144–5) confirms: 'Political stabilisation depended on the systematic and political integration of the working class through industrial relations, social reform, and the franchise. The condition for such integration was the sustained accumulation of productive capital, within the context of the sustained accumulation of capital on a world scale'. The problem was that forms of Fordist production and 'Keynesian' economic management could guarantee neither.[17] Indeed, by the 1960s, the process of the global overaccumulation of capital intensified pressures upon states to pursue further expansionary, and inflationary, policies. This, along with the adoption of Fordist methods of production across much of the advanced industrial countries, served to set the scene for new patterns of class struggle in the factories and against the state. Harvey (1990: 137–8) highlights new forms of resistance to deskilling and the routinisation imposed by machinofacture; opposition to the formation of a 'competitive' labour market outside of the relatively privileged 'monopoly' sectors (in which the exclusive development of the latter consisted of low-wage, precarious jobs filled by women and racial and ethnic minorities); and struggles within the trade union movements themselves as they clashed with management, their own rank and file, and militants (as within the British shop-steward movement, for instance).

In sum, as Harvey (1990: 141) argues, 'the period 1965 to 1973 was one in which the inability of Fordism and Keynesianism to contain the inherent contradictions of capitalism became more and more apparent'. The tendency toward the NIDL – which consisted of transformations in the labour process oriented toward increasing the rate of valorisation for global capital as a whole – was itself the result of the tendency to develop the forces of production without limit and was mediated by the competitive strategies of the most dynamic industrial capitals – the transnational corporations (TNCs) – and political strategies of states looking to secure a stable basis for accumulation in the context of generalised overproduction. The resultant rise in FDI from advanced to less developed countries, the establishment of agreements between late industrialising states and foreign TNCs, and the search to find low cost, more disciplined labour-power from the late 1960s onward (see Fröbel, Heinrichs and Kreye, 1980) all signalled a looming global crisis of overproduction as well as the basis for a global recovery in the longer term that would be fraught with contradiction (Iñigo Carrera, 2008: Chapter 6).[18] As we will see in Chapter 2, the upshot of the early tendency toward the NIDL for countries like Spain, which had yet to develop an industrial base that could compete beyond the restricted domestic market and which was already facing a crisis by the 1960s, was that a lifeline was offered to them. The arrival of FDI meant new flows of revenue to the state, the chance to upgrade production processes in manufacturing, and a means of prolonging the life expectancy of its many small capitals. The combination of automation-based technological change and spatial relocation that characterises the NIDL meant that Spain, as a late-industrialising economy in immediate proximity to the major Western European markets, offered low production costs and a competitive location for TNC investment in the late 1960s and 1970s. However, as we will explain further in Chapters 2 and 3, this form of integration into the NIDL was partial and of an intermediate character, a fact that was expressed in the incapacity of the industrial base to absorb future labour surpluses and underpin the expansion of social consumption for generations to come – a trait which is at the root of the experience of Spain and other relatively late industrialising countries within Europe.

Cycles of global overaccumulation and crisis since the 1970s

By 1974, the world was experiencing 'a classic overaccumulation crisis' (Clarke, 2001: 86), as the limits to the post-war boom confronted the classical capitalist countries, such as the US and UK, in the form of an inflationary crisis. The immediate political response to the crisis was to defer a policy of austerity and the destruction of productive capital across much of the advanced industrial countries. In Spain, as we will see in Chapter 3, this decision was made in the context of a transition from a fascist to a liberal-democratic form of state. Most national states adopted expansionary policies in the midst of the 1974 crisis, initiating a global period of stagflation that lasted until a sharper recession in 1979, when the US responded to rising commodity prices and speculation against the dollar by restricting the money supply (the so-called 'Volcker shock'). It was not until the global recession of 1979–81, then, that states responded to crisis through a deflationary policy of austerity – the imposition of tight money; the accelerated destruction of commodity capital and of small, technologically backward capitals; and the ideological propagation of a new 'social realism', most emblematically expressed in Margaret Thatcher's dictum 'there is no alternative' (see Clarke, 1988: 348–9).

In the context of low profitability, recession, and austerity from the 1970s, capitals in world market–oriented branches of production sought to drive production costs down further still – thereby intensifying the tendency toward the NIDL. In the classical countries, and by then in Japan, industrial capitals with excess capacity sought increasingly to rationalise, restructure, and intensify control over labour as a means of restoring profitability. By the 1980s, 'Technological change, automation, the search for new product lines and market niches, geographical dispersal to zones of easier labour control, mergers, and steps to accelerate the turnover time of their capital surged to the fore of corporate strategies for survival under conditions of deflation' (Harvey, 1990: 145). The outcome of this was twofold: first, the fragmentation of the working class intensified, as those workers in increasingly competitive labour markets were exposed to even greater 'flexibilisation' and deskilling (see Standing, 1997); while second, and relatedly, production on an international basis was further reconfigured so as to consist of entirely new organisational forms – operating on smaller scales of production – or the integration of networks of small capitals (many of which are disciplined by familial and kinship responsibilities) into existing forms of production on a 'sub-contracting' or 'outsourcing' basis (Harvey, 1990: 152–6).[19] Such a spatial reorganisation has been deemed appropriate to the 'lean', small-batch form of 'just-in-time' production – or 'systemofacture' (Kaplinsky, 1989) – that, for instance, was the basis of Japanese capitals' overtaking of US capital's dominance in the global automobile manufacturing industry after 1982 (Sturgeon and Florida, 2004).

In the 1980s, then, governments across the world responded to a severe recession by means of a state-orchestrated assault on the working class in a deflationary attempt to confine the latter's reproduction within the limits of profitability. The product of this reconfiguration of the international division of labour – in which it *appears* as if capital has transcended the regulatory capacities of national states (Bonefeld, 2000; Clarke, 2001) – has *not* been a more 'disorganised' capitalism. On the contrary, 'capitalism [was] becoming ever more tightly organised *through* dispersal, geographical mobility, and flexible response in labour markets, labour processes and consumer markets, all accompanied by hefty doses of institutional, product, and technological innovation' (Harvey, 1990: 159). In other words, part of the 'rationality' of 'industrial restructuring' was to recover rates of profit in industry (as it would turn out, with much lower rates than in the post-war period),[20] through technological innovations and novel organisational forms. Thus, through the NIDL 'capital has been increasingly able to disperse the different parts of the labour process globally according to the most profitable combinations of relative costs and productive attributes of the different national fragments of the global labour-force' (Grinberg and Starosta, 2009: 772). This process has also served to further undermine the bargaining strength of trade unions in key industries – a necessary response to the political crisis across much of the industrialised world (on both sides of the 'iron curtain') from the late 1960s and into the 1970s (Harvey, 2005: 15; Holloway, 1996b: 22–8; Radice, 2010).

Yet the post-1982 recovery was *not* founded upon the imposition of tight money, however attractive the monetarist notion of restoring profitability by subordinating the social reproduction of the working class to money – and within the limits of profitability – might have been for proponents of the new social realism. Rather, the recovery was based upon the dramatic expansion of credit.[21] Of crucial importance in this was the earlier collapse, in 1973, of the Bretton Woods system, under the weight of its own contradictions, and its replacement by a 'non-system' – an irredeemable, paper-money standard that would permit the dramatic expansion in the speculative buying and selling of debt in years to come (see Hampton, 2006). Indeed, what emerged after 1982 was a 'juxtaposition' of two seemingly contradictory developments: on the one hand, the expansion of credit throughout the global economy (made possible by the collapse of Bretton Woods); on the other, the imposition of austerity upon social relations (Bonefeld, 1996b).[22] The boom of the 1980s was marked by intense speculative fever, fed by high interest rates. This resulted in the dramatic rise of stock markets as a highly profitable sphere of investment. Such developments only intensified the tendency toward the global overaccumulation of capital – the effects of the stock market crash of 1987 being attenuated only by a reflationary response that ultimately failed to prevent the onset of a severe global recession by 1990.[23]

The next global cycle of accumulation was to last some fourteen to fifteen years. Crucially, for our analysis in this book, it encompassed the creation of the EMU as an ill-fated supranational policy response to the previous cycles of crisis and intensified global competition. It ended with the collapse of high-profile investment banks in the US, in 2007, the onset of the longest and most destructive global recession since the 1930s, and a crisis of 'European integration'. It had been punctuated by several partial crises, affecting specific sectors, countries, and regions of the world. Of crucial importance to our argument in Chapter 4, for example, will be the impact of the so-called 'dotcom crisis' of 2000. International stock markets grew spectacularly after 1995, spurred on in the US by the rapid development of electronics and Internet-based companies concentrated in and around the Bay Area of San Francisco.[24] The bubble burst in 2000, with the US-based NASDAQ alone losing some 77 per cent of stock values by October 2002 (Walker, 2006: 120). The crisis provoked flight from stock markets as investors searched for a 'safe haven', such as the Spanish real estate market as discussed in Chapter 4. In short, 'hyper-speculation' in the home mortgage market was to compensate for the bursting of the stock market bubble (Foster, 2008; see also Christophers, 2011; Duménil and Lévy, 2011: 177–8; Fox Gotham, 2009; Harvey, 2010b: 29; Rutland, 2010: 1173). By 2005, leveraging in the US banking system had reached debt-deposit ratios of 30:1 (Harvey, 2010b: 30). When the US housing bubble burst in August 2007 – the first sign being the so-called 'subprime' mortgage crisis – de-leveraging in the US banking sector sparked huge defaults and the state-coordinated bailouts of investment banks that were previously considered 'too big to fail' (see Dymski, 2012). This heralded a profound global crisis of overaccumulation from which much of the world is yet to recover.

In summary, the current crisis was born out of the immanent tendency in capitalism to develop the productive forces without regard to the limit of the market. The more recent development of capitalism has a certain specificity, however – in that periods of sustained accumulation since the 1970s have been conditional upon the global expansion of debt (and, indeed, the spectacular increase in its trading as an asset).[25] Iñigo Carrera (2008: 86) stresses that, as a counterpart to the reconfiguration of the NIDL, the 68 per cent increase in production by the world's leading economies since 1973 had been sustained by a 156 per cent increase in public and private indebtedness from then until 1992; while, in the subsequent period to 2000, total GDP grew a further 26 per cent, with a further 48 per cent increase in indebtedness. Harvey (2010b: 30; also 1990: 160–8) similarly places great import upon the global expansion of credit and of it being 'born out of necessity' since 1973. He has pointed out, for example, that 'the US\$40 trillion annual turnover in 2001 compares to the estimated US\$800 billion that would be required to support international trade and productive investment flows' – highlighting the apparent disunity in the global expansion of speculative finance capital relative to that of industrial production that has characterised the development of global capitalism in recent decades.

Part of the reason for this expansion of fictitious capital has been the funding of social consumption. The global reorganisation of production associated with the NIDL has allowed capital in the classic countries to exploit increases in productivity garnered from automation and the cheapening of globally differentiated labour power. However, across the advanced capitalist countries, the slow growth in the demand for labour due to the global dispersion of the production process has resulted in a greater proportion of the workforce in these countries being pushed into lower-wage, less-skilled jobs, or into the ranks of the unemployed.[26] In such national contexts, the expansion of fictitious capital in the form of credit has been central to the maintenance of social consumption well beyond the levels determined by the evolution of real earning and personal savings – as we will show in Chapters 3 and 4, with specific reference to Spain.[27]

Conclusion

The impact of the global crisis that erupted in the UK and the US in 2007 has since been devastating for several late industrialising countries in the European South. The challenge we have set for ourselves in this book is to explain the specific role played by Spain in the more general developments that we have outlined earlier: the consolidation of a NIDL since the 1960s; the sustained expansion of the scale of production beyond the immediate confines of social consumption since the 1980s; and the incredible expansion of debt on a global scale. But in order to fully address this challenge, we must first examine the specific basis for accumulation in Spain in the period immediately preceding its insertion within the NIDL and the process of European Integration. We must analyse the limits to import substitution industrialisation.

2
The Limits to Import Substitution Industrialisation

Chapter 1 of this book outlined a relatively general and abstract theoretical approach to understanding the crisis-ridden development of global capitalism – largely from the perspective of the advanced or 'classical' capitalist countries. With this chapter, then, we begin our more focused examination of the development of capitalism within Spain. Our aim is to explain why the crisis that erupted in 2008 has deep historical roots. We make clear the link between Spain's relatively 'backward' industrial status within Europe by the end of the 1970s and the subsequent cycles of growth, overaccumulation, and crisis from the 1980s onward. This requires that we now recognise – and briefly theorise – the specificity of national forms of capitalism in certain parts of the world, which cannot adequately be explained with recourse to the general approach provided in Chapter 1, while also maintaining that the Spanish state had its own part to play in the processing of global class relations and in relation to the emerging NIDL from the 1960s.

After offering a brief theorisation of ISI, and some background on Spain's historical economic 'backwardness', we explain the material bases upon which Spain witnessed rapid economic development after the 1950s. We suggest this development was limited in key respects, and that it depended upon the mediation of state policies as a means of sustaining capital accumulation in the context of low productivity in agriculture and the weak development of the forces of production in industry. By the 1960s, the Spanish state was able to defer a serious crisis by being able to offer previously excluded foreign firms the opportunity to enter Spain and to enhance their profitability – and that of some Spanish industrial capitals – under the conditions peculiar to import substitution industrialisation (ISI). Concurrently, the Spanish state also managed a mass emigration of Spanish workers whose remittances took on an important compensatory function; and the state was also able to benefit from Spain's increasing significance as a tourist destination for northern Europeans. By 1974, however, Spain eventually did experience the onset of a global crisis of overaccumulation in the form of a crisis of ISI and of the fascist state. A full-fledged strategy of austerity and industrial restructuring was deferred until after the transformation to a liberal state form and the election of the first Socialist government in 1982. In making this argument, we lay the groundwork for Chapter 3 insofar as it should become clear as to why the project of European integration from the 1980s became a significant means of, and cover for, the state's attempt to re-confine accumulation within the limits of the market by deflationary means.

Theorising the limits to import substitution industrialisation

In Volume III of *Capital*, Marx provides a theory of landownership and ground-rent in capitalism that stems from the observation 'that certain persons enjoy the monopoly of disposing of particular portions of the globe as exclusive spheres of their private will to the exclusion of all others' (Marx, 1981: 752). In order to gain access to non-renewable natural resources attached to such portions of land, or to non-replicable locations, capitalists must, Marx argues, cede a portion of surplus value. The resulting income for the landowner 'is known as ground-rent irrespective of whether it is paid for agricultural lands, building land, mines, fisheries or forests' (Marx, 1981: 755–6). Marx originally focused his discussion in *Capital* upon 'differential' and 'absolute' forms of ground-rent in the context of agricultural production, in an attempt to disentangle the complex conditions that impact upon the flow of surplus-value between and within sectors (such as location, fertility and technological development).[1] Marx's advance over classical political economy, and Ricardo especially, was to show how even marginal landowners could claim a rent without resorting to selling agricultural products at prices above their value, and, in so doing, was able develop a theory of ground-rent that was consistent with his labour theory of value.

The Marxian theory of ground-rent as an appropriation of surplus value provides a basis for explaining the development of national forms of accumulation in certain parts of the world. As the 'classical' international division of labour developed from the sixteenth and into the twentieth centuries, Latin American countries, in particular, assumed a position within it precisely based upon their 'resource rich' agrarian and mining export sectors (Grinberg and Starosta, 2009). In short, the appropriation of the ground-rent contained in primary materials exports became the basis upon which countries such as Argentina and Brazil established their inter-national relations; while the late development of industry in such countries (until the arrival of foreign TNCs from the 1960s) proceeded only on the limited basis of the reproduction of small, local industrial capitals producing on a scale specifically restricted to the scale of the domestic market (usually for basic wage-goods) (Iñigo Carrera, 2008: 156). During the great depression of the 1930s, when demand for primary commodity exports from Latin America fell, many states in the region introduced economic policies designed to boost the production capacities of domestic capitals producing basic manufactured goods. After the Second World War, ISI became a consolidated economic strategy in Latin America, boosted by European demand for primary imports required for post-war reconstruction. In post-war Europe, isolated national states such as Greece, Portugal and Spain similarly embarked upon ISI, introducing a raft of tariffs, duties and import quotas (Maravall, 1997: 42). In so doing, and in contrast to the classical countries, those countries closed off their domestic market to the world market and therefore to the processes that 'normally' regulate the valorisation of capitals.

The reproduction of national societies based upon production by small industrial capitals restricted to the scale of the domestic market can be explained with reference to the Marxian theory of value. Such capitals can, of course, valorise on the basis of the systematic maintenance of low wages relative to the value of labour-power. That is, for a limited period, capitals can appropriate even a portion of the socially necessary labour time pertaining to the reproduction of labour-power in that specific labour market at a given time. Alternatively, the valorisation of small industrial capitals can be sustained and expanded through *ad hoc* state policies that are common to ISI. The principal means by which the reproduction of a mass of small capitals has historically transpired in Latin America is explained in Box 2.1

Later in this chapter, we explore the degree to which the high levels of growth that Spain enjoyed in the 1960s were based upon the reproduction of small industrial capitals that produce for the domestic market. In the absence of a large magnitude of inter-sectoral transfers from primary materials exports that sustained ISI in Latin America, for example, the Spanish state found that it could only sustain ISI beyond the 1950s due to three developments. First, the inflow of remittances from millions of Spaniards that left the country to work abroad. This had the effect of

Box 2.1   Ground-rent, ISI, and the differentiation of national processes of accumulation within the NIDL

Iñigo Carrera (2007; 2008: Chapter 5) argues that the specificity of capital accumulation in many ISI countries and regions is defined by the valorisation of capital through the appropriation of ground-rent. This has historically been the case in Latin American countries that are 'resource rich' (see also Grinberg and Starosta, 2009). The appropriation of ground-rent is mediated by state policies and institutions that transfer resources from the primary sector to the rest of the economy in three interconnected ways. First, the overvaluation of the currency and export taxes have allowed the transfer of ground-rent by setting the price of raw materials and wage goods below international levels, which cheapens the value of labour-power and reduces production costs for industrial capitals. This also allows the state to facilitate the import of cheapened means of production (machinery, patents, and so on). Second, the state can also use the additional resources appropriated from the primary sector – for example, through unusually high import taxes or export taxes on ground-rent bearing commodities – to provide services, subsidised credit, and prices and to fund the expansion of public sector employment, thereby increasing the size of the domestic market. Third, the protection of domestic markets (through tariffs and quantitative restrictions on imports) allows industrial capitals to appropriate ground-rent when selling their commodities domestically (see Iñigo Carrera, 2007: Chapter 3). The fundamental significance of national accumulation processes based on the appropriation of ground-rent is that the development of the forces of production proceeds on a limited, 'backward', basis relative to world market norms. The appropriation of ground-rent compensates for higher production costs incurred by backward capitals, so they can nonetheless valorise at the general rate of profit.

With the development of the NIDL, TNCs entered Latin American countries whose national process of accumulation was based on the appropriation of ground-rent on a specific material basis. In general, *'fragments'* of normal capitals have been put into action operating as small capitals of a magnitude specifically restricted to the scale of the internal market. In so doing, they are able to compensate for increased production costs and for not reaching the scale required to produce at world market prices of production by continuing to indirectly appropriate ground-rent. And, as such, they do not contribute to the development of the forces of production in step with world market norms. This marks out the specificity of capital accumulation in Mercosur countries such as Argentina and Brazil within the NIDL (Iñigo Carrera, 2006; Grinberg, 2008).

The systematic reproduction of a mass of industrial capitals of a restricted magnitude on the basis of the appropriation of ground-rent, together with the existence of fragments of foreign capitals, has resulted in the limited development of the productive forces in Latin America and the periodic dependence upon international credit when fluctuations in the price of primary materials remove the capacity to sustain accumulation. A contrasting example is South Korea (Grinberg and Starosta, 2009; Grinberg, 2013), where the magnitude of ground-rent circulating in the economy by the 1960s was insufficient to sustain ISI to the same extent as in Latin American countries. As a result, and despite the relatively inferior level of development of industry, capital in South Korea was able to take advantage of the release of a large surplus population from agriculture after the abolishment of landlordism. Thus South Korea's emergent position within the NIDL was based on the exploitation of a work force that was more easily adaptable to large-scale labour processes and which was more easily habituated into labour-intensive work in harsh conditions. This made South Korea a profitable source of cheap and disciplined labour-power for world market production and explains the 'jump' that was made to heavy-industry exports from the 1970s.

allowing Spanish families to consume wage-goods even when the state fixed wages below socially necessary levels (to the benefit of the valorisation of industrial capitals).[2] Second, flows of value from outside the national sphere of accumulation that arrived in the form of revenues from mass tourism. These inflows had the combined effect of allowing Spanish workers employed (formally and informally) in the tourism economy to meet their subsistence needs, of expanding the domestic market and, more importantly, of allowing the Spanish state to plug its current account and balance of payments deficits.

The third 'life-line' to Spain was the arrival of restricted flows of FDI. In addition to the lowered costs of production provided by the exploitation of low-skilled, surplus labour in and from late industrialising countries that we discussed in Chapter 1, the rise in FDI from the 1960s can also be explained by the benefits that accrued from the importation of patents and machinery from abroad. States like Spain, as we will see, could establish a basis for the expansion of domestic industries by facilitating the import of technologies that were deemed as obsolete by world market; that is, means of production that could no longer maintain the productivity of labour relative to new means of production and/or in new configurations of the labour process in specific branches of production for the world market, but which still served to raise the productivity of labour within the restricted scale of the protected domestic market and so to raise the rate of profit for those capitals that put them to use in their labour process. And, from the perspective of foreign firms that set up subsidiaries within these restricted markets, this recycling of obsolete and already amortised machinery meant that they could, in short, get more than their money's worth with regard to technologies that were backward in world market terms (Iñigo Carrera, 2008: 157).

The remainder of this chapter traces the development of capitalism in Spain under ISI. The upshot of our discussion is that, as far as Spain was concerned, ISI was always doomed to failure – the forms of compensation that extended the life of ISI in Spain were strongly dependent upon expanding capital accumulation outside of Spain, and in Northern Europe in particular. Therefore, not only did the state's commitment to ISI carry Spain on the path to a severe crisis of overaccumulation by the mid-1970s, but it also prefigured the subsequent paths of both political transformation toward liberal democracy and crisis-ridden integration into the European common market and, later, EMU. And the failure of ISI to develop an industrial base of sufficient scale and competitiveness relative to world market industry meant that capital accumulation in Spain would continue to assume a specific, 'backward' European form from the 1980s. Chapters 3 and 4 will explain this specificity in detail.

The historical roots of Spain's economic 'backwardness'

As with most accounts of Spain's modern development, this chapter focuses on the period following the Civil War that ended with the establishment of a fascist state under General Francisco Franco in 1939. It is first worth noting, however, that enduring characteristics of the Spanish economy that can be identified from this period and into the early twenty-first century have deep historical roots in Spain's colonial past: namely, low agricultural productivity, a relatively weak industrial base, financial oligopoly, and a high dependence on foreign capital. At first sight it is perhaps curious that a country boasting a colonial empire on Spain's scale by the seventeenth century had come to be widely seen as 'backward' by the mid-twentieth century – 'like its neighbour Portugal ... an underdeveloped, stagnant area of western Europe' (Stein and Stein, 2000: 3; see also Harrison, 1985: Chapter 1; Molinas and Prados de la Escosura, 1989). The reasons for Spanish decline in the interim period have been much debated, but what is interesting for our argument in this book is the notion that the *rentier* form taken by Spain's early modern empire during the colonial era can explain its backwardness by the twentieth century (see also Blinkhorn, 1980; Drelichman, 1995; Drelichman and Voth, 2008; O'Brien and Prados de la Escosura, 1998). This will take on an interesting historical parallelism as we examine the form of capital accumulation in Spain and its regions within the NIDL, in Chapters 3 and 4.

A critical survey of the economic-historical literature on early modern Spain suggests that from the mid-sixteenth to the late seventeenth centuries, the development of Castile and the Spanish regions was characterised by two inter-related expressions of dependency: first, upon external markets for, and external suppliers of, commercial goods (Kamen, 1978); and, second, upon the profitability of precious metals and bullion mining in the Americas on the part of the Spanish Crown and its merchant class (Flynn, 1982). In essence, the development of early modern Spain foreshadowed that of the country within the contemporary international political economy:

> While Spain functioned as a periphery to a dominant centre located in Western Europe, Madrid also acted as a dominant centre to its own periphery. There were in this way two tiers of dependence, in which the dominant market within the peninsula was itself dominated at an international level (Kamen, 1978: 46; see also Molinas, 2012).

A good deal of work by economic historians of this period suggests that the *rentier* form of the early modern state, along with its two-tier dependency, was inimical to the development of Spanish industry.[3] By the seventeenth century, Spain was in effect an *entrepôt* – wealth flowed in from the Americas only to flow out again to other Western European economies (Kamen, 1978: 43; Reinert and Reinert, 2011). By the time of Bourbon dynastic rule in the eighteenth century, French economic domination of the peninsular was firmly established. Under the Bourbons, attempts were made to address Spain's perennial balance of trade problems by promoting the production of higher value commodities that had been formerly imported from abroad. In what now appears as a foreboding antecedent of twentieth century industrialisation in Spain, the new royal factories that were established were ill-coordinated, costly, and lacked technologies comparable with other industrialising economies of the period (Clayburn la Force, 1964).[4]

A Spanish export boom did arrive in the early nineteenth century, driven by primary commodities and minerals. This established the initial but transient basis upon which the national economy was inserted into the modern international division of labour: through specialisation in primary goods that were in demand by the industrialising Western European economies. This process was mediated by juridical-institutional changes that for the first time would create capitalistic private property in agriculture; principally, the marketisation of lands confiscated from the Church (*desamortización*), and the dismantling of the prevailing feudal property regime (see Tortella, 2000: 51–8). Together with increasing the scale of cultivation and commercialisation of agricultural products, this process transformed feudal landlords into an incipient capitalist landed oligarchy that was able to take advantage of an over-supply of agricultural labour and to accumulate flows of ground-rent from land that was previously unavailable to them.

The period 1840 to 1890 saw Spain embark on its first significant industrialisation drive, facilitated by successive Moderate and Progressive regimes' liberalisation of the economy (Tirado, Paluzie and Pons, 2002: 345–50). As with changes in agriculture, such reforms were motivated by the necessity to finance a persistent budget deficit. Industrialisation was driven primarily by foreign investment in the new train network and, significantly, by an exporting mineral mining sector financed by British, French, and German capital. European industrialisation in general had given rise to large demand for raw materials, and with its rich reserves of iron, lead, sulphur, copper, and mercury, Spain became one of the world's principal mining nations in the latter half of the century (Harvey and Taylor, 1987: 185). The mining sector accounted for a third of all exports, provided the largest employment base, and stimulated industrial development in the Basque Country, especially, where related industries such as shipping and banking flourished. However, after the liberalisation of the mining sector in 1868, mining profits largely accumulated in the hands of large, vertically integrated foreign companies. When the mineral boom came to an end, from around 1895, industrial development was largely absent outside of the Basque Country and Catalonia; and even in the case of mining, it had not developed to the scale of the most successful mineral-rich European regional economies of that time (Domenech, 2008: 1123).[5] The Spanish domestic market remained small; the majority of the working population was engaged in traditional agriculture, meaning there was low domestic demand for manufactured goods, low levels of urbanisation, and low schooling rates – a pattern replicated across the largely agrarian societies of Southern Europe at that time (Hadjimichalis, 1987).[6] Faced with an agricultural crisis and the threat of rural revolt that had been growing steadily since the *desamortización*, the Spanish state introduced the Cánovas tariff in 1891, thereby commencing an extended period of protectionist isolation for Spain.[7] As Carreras and Tafunell (2003: 126) underline, the degree of openness of the Spanish economy in 1890 was not to be reached again until 1970.

By the early twentieth century, protectionism in Spain was higher than in any other European economy (Fraile and Escribano, 1998: 19, Tortella and Houpt, 2000: 132). Nominal protection increased significantly first in 1891 for textiles, iron, and steel, then for agriculture in 1906, and finally for capital goods from 1926. This permitted experimentations with ISI, especially in the context of the First World War as the disruption of international markets stimulated both domestic production and wartime exports. Large monopolies were formed under the auspices of the state in the iron and steel sectors, along with such capital goods industries as electricity, cement, and mining. The incorporation of foreign technology and large public works undertaken during the Primo de Rivera dictatorship (1923–9) raised productivity, created economies of scale, and supported intra-industry demand. This was partly down to the investments of an increasingly monopolised banking sector into heavy industry; indeed, 'by 1921, directors of the seven largest banks were found on the boards of 274 corporations, whose combined capital amounted to half that of the paid-up capital of all Spanish corporations' (Simpson, 1997: 356). In world market terms, however, the monopoly structure of Spanish industry saw productivity lag behind that of other countries; while, in key sectors such as railways, banking, mining, and steel and iron manufacturing, firms were largely state-owned or foreign-owned.

The crash of 1929 and the onset of the Great Depression brought this period of industrial expansion in Spain to a sharp halt as exports and demand both fell by half (Carreras and Tafunell, 2003: 244). The expansive fiscal policy that had stimulated investment, technological upgrading, and internal demand came under the pressure of an unsustainable current account deficit. Protectionism failed to insulate the Second Republic (1931–5) from the global crisis of overproduction in the 1930s (Comín, 2011). A preeminent historian of that period surmises that the civil war that broke out in 1936 was triggered by a series of reforms deemed necessary by the Republican-Socialist government to improve working conditions and basic pay for the mass of landless seasonal labourers in the midst of the depression: 'given the apparent determination of the working class to introduce major reforms and of the oligarchy to resist them', concludes Preston (1994: 282), 'the failure of legalist tactics could not but lead to a resurgence of the "catastrophist" Right and the imposition of a corporative state by force of arms'.

The limits to import substitution industrialisation under Franco

The destructive impact of the Spanish Civil War (1936–9), the isolation of the Franco regime by the Western allied powers after 1940 (Carrasco-Gallego, 2012), and the lack of external demand for Spanish agricultural exports during the Second World War (Medina Albaladejo, 2010: 419) only exacerbated the country's backwardness. This was compounded by the state's dogged pursuit of economic autarky from 1939. The modest growth of the pre-Civil War period therefore had little bearing on Spain's economic development in the 1940s, when output in agriculture and industry fell, inflation persisted despite government price controls (which led to an extensive black market), the average standard of living declined, and unemployment rose. By 1950, half the working population was employed in an agricultural sector that lagged far behind Western European norms in terms of modernisation, and with seasonal unemployment affecting around one-third of its workforce (Tortella, 2000: 266; Simpson, 1995: 273). At the same time, less than one fifth of Spain's work force was employed in industry – one of the lowest percentages in Europe (Román, 1971: 22). Industry contributed only 22.95 per cent of GDP (Prados de la Escosura, 2003: 584), and the level of industrialisation per head of population achieved in 1930 was not reached again until 1952 (Tortella, 2000: 266, 313). As a comparative measure of Spain's economic development, compound annual growth in the period 1913 to 1956 was a mere 1.6 per cent – a rate bettered by Greece, Italy, and Portugal (Román, 1971: 19).[8]

Most economic histories of Spain divide the period of rule by Franco's fascist state (1939–75) into two distinct periods of economic development: 'the first fifteen years saw economic stagnation and a slow recovery, while the following twenty years saw rapid economic growth, intense industrialisation, and profound social change' (Tortella, 2000: 238). We, however, are wary of drawing too marked a distinction between these periods on the basis of an about-turn in the Franco regime's economic strategy (represented by successive national development plans after 1959) (see Guerrero, 2009). Seen from the long-term perspective of growth rates that take into account the post Franco period (1975), the period of autarky did in fact lay the foundations for Spain's late industrialisation, albeit largely upon the systematic payment of labour below its value for a limited period (Echebarría and Herrero, 1989: 14).[9] The remainder of this section therefore takes into account the material bases that made the Spanish industrial take-off possible after the 1950s.

After the Civil War, the Spanish domestic market was largely closed to foreign imports of commodities in a bid for self-sufficiency. In what amounted to 'a clear policy of import substitution' (Alonso Gil, 1982: 92), the state imposed quantitative restrictions on imports, foreign exchange controls, a fixed and overvalued exchange rate, it controlled capital markets, and centralised the regulation of foreign trade – eventually administering it through a multiple exchange rate system (Donges, 1971: 38–9; Lieberman, 1982: 168).[10] The period 1945–9 unsurprisingly represents the historic minimum of FDI in Spain since 1939 (Catalan, 1995: 121). With such protectionist measures in place, the Franco regime created the Instituto Nacional de Industria (INI) in 1941; a state holding company charged with promoting national industrial development in key sectors – initially energy, iron, and steel production (Chilcote, 1966: 446). Under inflationary-financed ISI, Spain began to industrialise, with average industrial growth rates in the 1950s that was four times higher than that in the 1940s (Barciela López, 2002: 362). By 1960, industry was contributing 30.93 per cent of GDP (Prados de la Escosura, 2003: 584), with the INI having secured state monopoly control in over sixty 'national enterprises' and across a range of sectors by the mid-1960s (Chilcote, 1966: 445), including such new sectors of 'national interest' as automobile manufacturing.

There were, however, clear limits to the development of industry under autarkic ISI – as is recognised by most commentaries on the period. Even by 1960, the top INI-run firms made 'very low profits – if any' (Carreras and Tafunell, 1994: 23).[11] Moreover, Spanish industry remained backward relative to international norms: 'between 1950–1 and 1957–8, the country's export/GDP and import/GDP ratios never exceeded 5 per cent, an extremely low figure for an industrialising nation' (Harrison, 1985: 137). For Carreras and Tafunell (1994: 24), the explanation for this lies in the reality that '"national enterprises" were created to address national problems and not to expand through the world ... they were just the contrary of a "global enterprise"', as attested to by their reporting that Spanish firms were entirely absent from rankings of the world's 497 largest industrial enterprises (in terms of sales) between 1962 and 1967 (Carreras and Tafunell, 1994: 33). Ultimately, the state's commitment to protectionism 'led to a highly overvalued currency, a current account deficit, low reserves of hard currency, inflation (consumer prices increased by an average of 13 per cent per year in the 1940s and 10 per cent in the 1950s), and a small and inefficient industrial sector' (Prados de la Escosura and Sanz, 1996: 368–9). As a consequence, and in 'lacking the capacity to import the necessary technology, [and with] firms suffering from insufficient capital and obsolete equipment', Spanish industry was unable to compete in international markets' (Prados de la Escosura and Sanz, 1996: 369). Indeed, by 1958, small firms comprised 85 per cent of total Spanish industry: 'many of these small industries did not modernise substantially since they were created'; 'considerable shortages in the supply of basic inputs for manufacturing industry [meant] that established firms had to work far below their productive capacities'; and 'industry was unable to hold unit costs in line with international standards, although wages were temporarily kept low by administrative means' (Donges, 1971: 45).[12]

The primary basis for the valorisation of capital in Spain during this period appears to have been the purchasing of labour-power below its value. Molinero and Ysás (2003) report that, while nominal wages increased slowly between 1939 and 1951, the rate of increase was maintained below that of wage-goods prices, resulting in the diminution of purchasing power for the majority of the population. In 1956, for example, the estimated real value of wages was between 15–35 per cent below the pre-Civil War level, with an associated low per capita consumption of sugar, milk, and meat (Lieberman, 1982: 188).[13] A mass exodus of workers from the agricultural to the industrial sector during that decade (about half a million workers according to Román, 1971: 24) helped to maintain a steady supply of low-wage labour-power to industrial labour markets (Barciela López, 2002: 363; Cámara Izquierdo, 2007: 554–5).

In addition to the control of wages in domestic industry, the state managed to secure further means of sustaining the limited development of the economy in the 1940s and 1950s. Bilateral trade and aid agreements were secured with the Perón regime in Argentina in 1947, but the crucial boost to economic growth came with the 1953 Pact of Madrid – an agreement on trade, investment, and credit struck with the US in exchange for the establishment of military bases in Spain (Calvo-Gonzalez, 2007). In addition, toward the end of the 1950s, emigrants' remittances and tourism began to yield incipient inflows of revenue – boons that were to increase in significance during the 1960s, as we explain next (Catalan, 1995: 132; Donges, 1971: 48; Román, 1971: 22).[14] Nevertheless, by the end of the 1950s, the limits to rapid industrialisation on the basis of an extremely restrictive version of ISI were beginning reveal themselves. The state – which had exhausted its foreign exchange reserves – could no longer finance a spiralling budget deficit, nor could it stave off workers' demands for wage increases in the context of high inflation (which reached 15.5 per cent in 1957, according to Salmon, 1990: 3). A political crisis of the state threatened.

The implementation of the 1959 Stabilisation Plan by Francoist technocrats – a turning point for most economic historians of this period – was a necessary response to this looming national crisis. The crisis of 1957–59 took the form of a credit crisis. The ensuing recession and rise in the cost of living led to a wave of strikes in industrialised centres across Northern Spain and, in turn, heightened the sense of a 'mounting political crisis' (Pérez, 1997: 63). Faced with the need to contain the prospect of a popular revolt, the state was left with little option but to try to address the severe balance of payments problem. The Plan therefore consisted of a combination of public austerity to attack domestic inflation, coupled with the controlled liberalisation of imports. Multiple exchange rates were unified and, in Spain's joining of the Bretton Woods monetary system in 1961, the peseta was devalued and became convertible on international markets – thereby boosting the export capabilities of some national industries (Harrison, 1978: 145). Under the Plan, select exporters were further assisted by the state's granting of tax rebates, official credit and insurance (Salmon, 1990: 4). Most significantly, however, new foreign investment regulations permitted up to 50 per cent ownership in Spanish firms, with no limits at all imposed on strategic sectors such as steel, textiles, shoes, leather, machine tools, and construction. As a result, between 1958 and 1972, Spain's most important growth industries boomed, but in turn (with the exception of shipbuilding and electricity sectors) became heavily dependent upon FDI and foreign technologies (McMillion, 1981: 296) – a matter we take up again later in this chapter.

The bases for growth in the 1960s

The availability of cheap labour-power and the arrival of flows of FDI were by themselves not sufficient to account for high levels of growth in Spain in the 1960s, especially given the palpable limits to ISI discussed earlier. A fuller understanding of how demand in the domestic economy expanded during this period involves an appreciation, first, of the development of the mass tourism market in Northern Europe and, second, the increasing significance of remittances from Spanish workers abroad. In anticipation of subsequent chapters, this will provide an appreciation of how the development of capitalism in Spain has long been related to the appropriation of inflows of capital from outside the national economy.

Supported by the devaluation of the peseta in 1959 and the liberalisation of currency exchange, Spain became an extremely attractive destination for the expanding mass tourism market in Britain, France, Scandinavia, and West Germany – with receipts from foreign tourism increasing by 57 per cent in 1960 alone (Pack, 2006: 84).[15] The number of tourists visiting Spain increased from 6 million in 1960 to 34 million in 1973, by which time net tourist revenue amounted to some US$2.8 billion (Wright, 1977: 38). During the 1960s, foreign currency exchange from tourism dominated the Spanish state's receipts in relation to those accruing from the agricultural and manufacturing sectors, and continued to offset deficits in the balance of trade well into the 1970s and beyond (Bote Gómez, 1994: 120; Pack, 2006: 108).[16] The additional revenue from tourism also permitted major public investments in transportation, infrastructure, housing, and nationalised industries (such as automobiles), while the wages associated with the growth of the service sector stimulated domestic demand for wage goods (Anderson, 1970: 219; Bote Gómez, 1994: 126; Wright, 1977: 72). Indeed, Román (1971: 51) argues that an excessive concentration of public investment in infrastructure in the 1960s was to the detriment of the expansion of scales of industrial production, accentuating a growing imbalance in investment in favour of services.[17] This period also marked the first of the three great speculative construction booms in Spain,[18] all of which have been inextricably related to tourism and the disproportionate development of related branches of production, to which we return in Chapter 4.

Although tourism developed into a genuinely competitive tertiary sector, providing 'invisible exports' or exports *in situ* (Bote Gómez, 1996: 6; Pack, 2006: 84), it intensified rather than resolved structural problems in the economy by compensating for the otherwise limited development of Spain's industrial base. Crucially, as Williams (2001: 131) stresses of the 1960s, 'the critical role of the positive tourism and travel account trade balance is it helped to finance imports, including intermediate and capital goods for other economic sectors' (see also Lieberman, 1995: 149; Balaguer and Cantavella-Jordá, 2002). Tourism receipts, in other words, permitted technological upgrading in state-supported Spanish firms – many of which were incapable of doing so on the basis of profitability alone. And in the light of problems facing the numerous small capitals outside of state support, such as restricted access to finance and their reliance upon out-dated means of production, the influx of tourists and associated activities raised domestic demand for goods and services that either could not be imported or were sufficiently protected from foreign competition.

The second principal basis for the development of Spanish industry in the 1960s was an indirect result of a combination of the state austerity program rolled out in 1959 and further developments in Northern European labour markets – namely, a significant rise in emigration.[19] Between 1961 and 1966 around 10 per cent of the Spanish labour force left the country, looking to access employment in northern Europe at wage levels three to four times higher than those in Spain (Román, 1971: 74). Such was the scale of emigration that the state sought to manage remittances back to Spain under the auspices of the Instituto Español de Emigración (Fernández Asperilla, 1998). By 1971, remittance flows covered 40 per cent of the trade deficit (Roman, 2002: 99), while huge sums of money classified by the state as tourism inflows were periodically brought back to Spain by expatriated workers visiting their families, further boosting demand – especially in the housing market – and funding the establishment of many small, family-run businesses (Tamames, 1986: 176).

Together then, tourism receipts, the rapid speculative development of tourism resorts, and remittances underpinned a period of rising demand in the Spanish economy during the 1960s. Meanwhile, Spain remained a relatively closed domestic market – the inflow of tourism and remittance revenues therefore also serving to offset the country's growing trade deficit (Hadjimichalis, 1987: 108; Serrano Sans and Pardos, 2002: 375). At the same time, Spain's agricultural sector was in secular decline – a shrinking labour force and low productivity relative to European norms meant that production declined steadily throughout the 1960s, while prices for domestic food products rose steadily. As a result, food imports rose sharply in the 1960s, causing a deterioration the state's balance of payments over the course of the decade (and notwithstanding the offsetting effects of tourism; Román, 1971: 39). In short, though ISI in Latin America could sustain capital accumulation on the basis of the appropriation of an extraordinary magnitude of ground-rent for years to come, Spain could not. The conditions were ripe, then, for Spain to assume a position within the emerging NIDL based on the conditions already outlined at a general level in Chapter 1: first, that it offered foreign capitals the opportunity to relocate moments of the production process to a relatively low-wage and weakly unionised labour market, in which internal demand was rising, in which obsolete technology and patents could be profitably recycled. Then, in the midst of the crisis of ISI in the early 1970s and after the state's watershed agreement with the Ford Motor Company (discussed next), Spain offered the foreign capitals geographical proximity to the expanding European export market – a development that ushered in a transformation of the material basis of accumulation in Spain that would be completed with the full accession to the European Communities (EC) in 1986.

Industrial development in Spain within the emergent new international division of labour

By 1970, Spain had experienced rapid industrialisation with manufacturing, accounting for over 30 per cent of output (compared with agriculture, then down to 13 per cent; O'Brien, 1975).[20] This year marked the zenith of a period commonly referred to as *'el milagro español'* ('the Spanish miracle'). Under ISI, Spanish industry could be characterised as a 'marginal supplier' of labour-intensive exports to Northern Europe (Donges, 1972) – an appraisal that, we will suggest, retains its relevance today.[21] This much was achieved on the basis of small industrial capitals producing for the protected domestic market – the expanded reproduction of such capitals being possible only due to the arrival of FDI, the largely unplanned tourism boom, and mass emigration. In other words, Spain's late industrialisation was itself dependent upon general transformations associated with the global accumulation of capital. In this section, we focus our attention on the development of those key Spanish industries that managed to transform themselves after the arrival of FDI so as to engage in production for the world market. Our aim is to show how, prior to the mid-1970s, such industries developed only so far as to occupy what some commentators term an 'intermediate' position within the NIDL (see, for example, Molero, ed., 1995). Even the most developed sectors of Spanish industry exhibited low levels of innovation in the organisation and technology of the labour process relative to core European and world market norms by the 1970s. Moreover, the development of Spanish industry to that point was conditional upon foreign investment, technology, and patents (McMillion, 1981; Molero, 1998).

The secret to the sudden take-off of Spanish industry in the 1960s was the rapid diffusion of technology in key mass production sectors (chemicals, automobiles, metallurgy, and food) – albeit technology of almost completely foreign origin (see, for example, Cebrían Villar, 2005; Hidalgo, Molero and Penas, 2010). Until 1969, and under the terms of the deal struck between the INI and the Italian firm FIAT which we discuss next, most foreign technology imports came with contractual restrictions that expressly limited production to sale in the domestic market. By 1970, when Spain's exports increased quite dramatically, 70 per cent of imports of foreign technology was by Spanish firms with foreign equity participation; while almost 50 per cent of these firms were of half or majority foreign-ownership; and, by 1972, 96 per cent of direct payments for foreign technology went to just nine countries (mainly the US, Western Europe, and Italy; O'Brien, 1975). Most of these contracts involved assembly or final product preparation, with very little need to train the workforce to handle more advanced technologies. In short, Spain's insertion into the emergent NIDL was possible only on the basis of the arrival of foreign capital and technology – that is, on a limited and uneven basis that allowed for the rapid development of the productive forces but in such as way as to reproduce the limits to inherent to ISI.

A further characteristic of Spain's industrial development from the 1960s was its marked geographical unevenness. As McMillion (1981: 300–1) noted of the period:

> While the population and employment increased considerably in [Catalonia], Basque-Navarra, and Madrid, in the rest of the country only the Balearic and Canary Islands and Valencia had even moderate growth. Extremadura, Mancha, and Castille-Leon, three of Spain's least densely populated and least industrial areas, lost nearly 15 per cent of their population and 25 per cent of their employment during the period [1955–75]. Andalucia and Aragon also experienced an absolute loss in employment and, together with other regions, had very substantial out-migration. As is usually the case with industrialisation, emigration is primarily of the younger, more productive, and reproductive sector of the population. This elevates the age structure

of nonindustrial regions as it lowers the age structure of industrial regions, implying an even greater disequilibrium in the future and intensifying pressures on social services in congested areas.

We take up an analysis of the uneven geographical development of the Spanish economy in Chapters 4 and 5. For now, however, our discussion remains at the national level so as to further demonstrate how Spain's industrial development was from the outset, of a limited and intermediate character within the context of the development of world market production. No other industry expresses this more vividly than Spain's oft cited 'success story' – its automobile manufacturing industry.[22]

The development of the Spanish automobile industry I: The 1960s and 1970s

Between 1970 and 2000, Spain accounted for 50 per cent of the growth in European car production (Rubenstein, 2001: 344) – the car being, by 1999, the single product with the most market share in world trade and the most important export commodity of most industrialised countries (with almost one in ten jobs within the EU relating to the car industry; Krempel and Plümper, 1999). In 2000 alone, Spain produced three million cars; in 2007, it produced 2.9 million (Ortiz-Villajos, 2010). From our perspective, the analysis of the Spanish automobile industry offers the potential to further illuminate the basis upon which Spain was inserted into the NIDL from the 1960s, since in world market terms this industry has been at the forefront of the development of the productive forces ever since the inception of scientific management approaches to mass production by the Ford Motor Company a century or so ago. By examining the development of the Spanish automobile industry, but in the context of the key technological and organisational changes within an increasingly internationalised global industry, we can shed further light upon the limits to Spanish industrial development within the NIDL.

From the late 1940s, the Spanish car industry was transformed under the auspices of the INI, which established Sociedad Española de Automóviles de Turismo (SEAT) with a 51 per cent capital share in 1948 (the Italian firm FIAT providing the patents in return for a 7 per cent initial share). In 1951, Fabricación de Automóviles SA (FASA) was created in Valladolid with 70 per cent Spanish capital (mainly from Banco Santander), thereby establishing an effective duopoly in Spanish production (Catalan, 2010: 211). By 1962, these firms were specialised in small vehicle production under Italian and French licenses. Both firms fared well in the boom of the 1960s. By 1970, when the European Economic Community (EEC) reduced tariffs on Spanish imports, SEAT was Spain's leading export firm and its flagship 'national champion'. In García Ruiz's (2001) estimate, the development of the car industry was fed by rising internal demand as far as 1967 – the same year in which the state was forced to devalue the peseta in the face of a growing balance of payment deficit, the onset of inflation, and a brief recession that Román (1971: 86) suggests defined the limits of profitability on the basis of production solely for the domestic market.[23]

Realising that the domestic market had reached the limits of its development, FIAT and Renault opted to permit exports of cars from Spain produced under their licence but demanded a greater share of SEAT and FASA, respectively, in return. However, the picture that had emerged by then was one of an industry that was technologically backward and increasingly dependent upon foreign investment and technology. Production by these firms during the 1960s and into the 1970s was characterised by small economies of scale, short production series, high labour intensity, technical backwardness and the manufacture of products that were antiquated in relation to world market standards (see Ramos Barrado, 1986). 'The Spanish market', writes García Ruiz (2001: 145, our translation), 'was filled with old models, "residual technologies", that had become obsolete in their countries of origin, but that were acceptable in a market like Spain, protected, of low purchasing power, and with taste of low sophistication'. Outside the duopoly, the growth of an auxiliary components industry consisting of many small capitals was sustained largely by the state's insistence upon a 90 per cent Spanish-made parts quota.

By the early 1970s, the limits to the ISI-based expansion of the Spanish car industry were being felt. Faced with increasing labour costs, SEAT's profits declined from a 4.2 per cent margin in 1967 to 2.2 per cent in 1971 (Catalan, 2010: 216). At this time, the Ford Motor Company was also in negotiations with the Spanish state to invest US$300 million in a new assembly plant in Valencia, in return for several concessions (Studer-Noguez, 2002: 92–3). By 1972, in what are known as the 'Ford Decrees', the state agreed, among other things, to relax the Spanish-made parts quota, to decrease tariffs on Ford's imports, and to exclude imports from other foreign firms. Ford's aim was to produce technologically backward models in Spain for the EEC market, saving on the cost of producing them in the US in short runs. In effect, this meant that 'Ford could serve the EEC's markets from Spain and still be secure that no other [TNC] would compete with it in Spain' (Doz, 1986: 72–3). Ford began production of its 'Fiesta' in 1976 and in direct competition with SEAT, whose market share in Spain dropped from 51 per cent in 1973 to 26 per cent by 1980 (Catalan, 2010: 222).

The arrival of Ford therefore heralded the transformation the Spanish automobile industry and the transition toward a full insertion of the national process of accumulation into the emergent NIDL; General Motors would arrive in 1979, Nissan and Suzuki would follow from Japan in 1982, and Volkswagen would take over SEAT in 1986.[24] In the context of the industry's response to the crises of the 1970s, such multinational producers restructured the labour process – taking into account the transformations associated with Japanese 'lean' production techniques and innovations in 'systemofacture'. We discuss in further detail the restructuring of Spanish industry from the 1980s in Chapter 3, but here we can highlight how the development of the automobile industry into the 1970s became emblematic of the more general scenario discussed previously: the position of Spanish automobile industry was in a sense 'intermediate' – it was that of a producer and exporter of equipment and components of lower complexity and an importer of components requiring more complex technology (Ramos Barrado, 1986). As we show in Chapter 3, this position was further consolidated from the 1980s and into the twenty-first century.

Summary

Even though the 'productivity gap' with other countries was narrowed as a result of liberalisation and Spain's insertion into the NIDL, Spanish industry continued to rely upon foreign technology, patents, and licenses (Hidalgo, Molero, and Penas, 2010), and outside the foreign-dominated car industry, rarely achieved a degree of concentration sufficient to compete at the level of world market. It is telling that recorded real GDP growth rates of 7.6 per cent between 1960 and 1973 and levels of productivity remained more than 50 per cent below the average in the EEC (Albarracín, 1991: 320). By 1972, 'two-thirds of manufacturing output was still produced by firms with fewer than five workers, so size remained a major shortcoming' (Prados de la Escosura and Sanz, 1996: 371). And, while 'manufacturing performance was impressive, growing at over 10 per cent annually, with an increasing role for producer goods industries ... it depended mostly on home demand (87.6 per cent over 1962–72), with exports accounting for only 22 per cent of the increase' (Prados de la Escosura and Sanz, 1996: 371). Spanish industry in general struggled to compete with those from the most advanced countries, despite lower labour costs – being able to export only some 'capital-intensive' goods to less developed countries (Donges, 1972; Viñas et al., 1979: 357). Such were the limits to ISI in Spain.

Overaccumulation and the crisis of the fascist state

As far as Spain was concerned, if the emergence of some export-oriented industries by the end of the 1960s attested to the rapid development of the productive forces under ISI, the crisis of 1974 revealed that the ISI process had pushed this development well beyond the limits of the market itself. In 1974, Spain actually recorded an annual growth rate that dwarfed that of the OECD countries, but it also had to deal with a precipitous fall in visiting tourists and a net migratory inflow as Spanish workers abroad fled recession-hit Northern Europe (Lieberman, 1995: 155). To make matters worse, the rate of growth of domestic demand contracted sharply – a more serious reduction being mitigated only by rising wages, but which had the effect of increasing inflationary pressures from 1975. By 1975, industrial production contracted, productivity slumped, and weakened exports reduced Spain's imports capacity (Lieberman, 1995: 167). A looming crisis of overaccumulation on a world scale found its expression in the dramatic expansion of the Spanish state's debt and the further deterioration of its balance of payments (O'Brien, 1975). The year 1974 therefore marked the end of the (first) Spanish growth 'miracle'.

Increasingly, then, the struggle waged by the Spanish working class within the institutional form of the fascist state became a broader struggle over the very form of the state – a scenario replicated in adversarial industrial relations and social unrest in other Southern European, fascist-ruled countries (Karamessini, 2008: 513). The development of workers' organisations from the 1950s was of key importance in the state's inability to deal with the limits to ISI after 1967 by any other means than through inflationism and the rapid expansion of its own debt (see González i Calvet, 1991). Under the Franco regime, all workers were obliged to join one official trade union (Organización Sindical Española), and industrial relations were officially conducted through the system of *sindicatos verticales* (vertical trade unions) in which workers' representatives had to be members of the official party of the state, Falange. Although officially illegal, workers' councils were tolerated at company and plant level from 1953 so as to allow for a degree of decentralised negotiations between workers and management, and collective bargaining was introduced in 1958 with wage increases explicitly tied to productivity increases (Lawlor and Rigby, 1986). By the 1960s, however, an extensive network of workers' councils had developed – prompting an explosion in collective bargaining contracts and effectively putting an end to the state's ability to unilaterally control wages (Encarnación, 2003: 87). In addition, the early 1960s also saw the emergence of a clandestine labour movement, centred around and sometimes against the workers' councils, and heightened political agitation – most notably, on the part of Euskadi Ta Askatasuna (ETA) in the Basque Country and regional parties linked to the Spanish Communist Party (PCE) in Catalonia and elsewhere (Martínez-Alier and Roca, 1987; Holman, 1996: 57–8). Although striking was strictly prohibited throughout the Franco era, working class militancy gathered steam throughout the decade and, despite the state's re-intensification of repression against the councils after the devaluation of the peseta in 1967, striking intensified in the early 1970s as workers sought to defend full employment and real wage increases in the face of rising inflation.

By 1974, the dictatorships in Greece and Portugal had fallen and the Franco regime was confronted with a growing political crisis.[25] The regime's response was to attempt to sustain social consumption, and to meet the demands of a politically threatening working class, by agreeing large increases in wages, reducing taxes, and subsidising energy consumption. Inflation soared to 18.5 per cent by the beginning of 1975, while drawing upon international credit became the principal means of footing the bill for this strategy (Lieberman, 1995: 165). As the Eurodollar market expanded in the early 1970s, the Spanish state borrowed heavily – its current account balance shifted from a surplus of US$500 million in 1973 to a deficit of US$3.26 billion in just one year (Lieberman, 1995: 165).

Franco's death in the midst of this crisis, on 20 November 1975, set in motion a process of political transformation toward a liberal-democratic state in Spain – a process that culminated in a referendum on a new constitution on 6 December 1978. The details of this process are covered in detail elsewhere,[26] but what is most important for our argument to come is to take into account the manner in which the timing and pace with which the re-confinement of the aspirations of the working class within the limits of the market was conditioned by the political transition.[27] While the monetarist response to the crisis in the form of a politics of state austerity was not fully imposed in the classical countries until after a period of 'stagflation' and the global recession of 1979, the massive devaluation of capital necessitated by the development of the productive forces beyond the limit of the Spanish market also had to wait for the transition to a liberal-democratic state form. The signing of the Moncloa accords by the major Spanish political parties in 1977 was a key moment in this process. In return for political reforms, the unions were bound to a policy of wage restraint – laying the basis for the 'normalisation' of collaborationist industrial relations during the years of austerity and 'industrial reconversion' that were to follow in the 1980s (Albarracín, 1987: 45–8; Goldner, 2000: 97–107). In short, the accords ensured that the cost of the crisis would be socialised (González i Calvet, 1991: 172), and that burden of making the transition to a fully liberalised market in Spain would be borne by the working class.

Conclusion

In a sense, our primary objective in this chapter has been to lay the basis for our argument that the liberalisation of the market in Spain after the crises of the 1970s was destined for further crises before the process had even started – just as autarky and ISI had been before it. The Spanish case is illustrative of the characteristics of relatively late industrialising European countries that also encountered significant barriers to ISI by the 1970s. Such countries shaped – and were shaped in turn by – the crises of that decade. We will see in the following chapter how the Spanish state played its part in the response to such crises and the national processing of global class relations beyond the 1980s. The degree of historical analysis in this chapter has therefore been necessary, since it allows for a fuller comprehension of how the restoration of profitability and growth across the world market from the 1990s increasingly depended upon the expansion of speculative investment in property and fictitious capital 'on a scale far beyond anything that could be justified by the production and appropriation of surplus-value' (Clarke, 2001: 89–90). And it is also necessary in order to comprehend why the full liberalisation of the Spanish state and market – realised through the Common Market, and later, EMU – amounted to the final consolidation of Spain's position within the European South.

3
The Limits to European Integration

With this chapter, we begin our examination of the uneven development of capitalist production within Spain in the decades following the crises of the 1970s, and its relation within the uneven development of national and regional spaces of accumulation within Europe. In so doing, we endorse the argument that, from the outset, the process of European 'integration' associated with the Common Market, monetary convergence, and of course, European Monetary Union (EMU) reinforced patterns of uneven development that were prefigured in previous cycles of the global overaccumulation of capital (Bonefeld, 1998; Carchedi, 1997; Hadjimichalis, 1994).[1]

The chapter focuses on Spain but in the context of the dramatic transformations associated with the emergence of the NIDL, as outlined in Chapter 1. We explained in Chapter 1 how – in response to the inflationary and political crises of the 1970s – national state governments across much of the world struggled to re-establish a basis for sustained accumulation in the early 1980s and in the context of heightened competition across the world market. The response to the crisis in the classic countries entailed

> the massive devaluation of surplus capital and destruction of surplus productive capacity, escalating unemployment and an intense offensive against the working class on the part of both capital and the state which sought not so much to force down wages, as to restructure the institutional forms of industrial relations and the welfare state through which workers had sought to realise their material aspirations, in order to subordinate the reproduction of the working class to the reproduction of capital. (Clarke, 2001: 86)

This chapter first looks at how the Spanish national state, in particular, responded to the crisis. We explain how the first governments of the post-Franco era imposed deflationary policies aimed at destroying surplus productive capacity and restoring profitability and at placing the burden of this process squarely on the working class as labour markets adjusted to a rapidly changing industrial structure. We examine state-led strategies to concentrate and centralise capital in banking, utility, and energy capitals, and the politics of economic management in the context of deindustrialisation, fiscal expansionism, and the growing intransigence of the main trade unions. Further, we suggest that the particular manner in which Spain entered the European Monetary System (EMS) in 1989 intensified a growing disproportionality (see Clarke, 1990/1; 1994) between the development of different branches of production, a process that would have significant repercussions for the form of capital accumulation in Spain beyond the monetary crisis of 1992.[2]

The remainder of the chapter establishes the basis for arguments that will be further developed in Chapters 4 and 5. We scrutinise the extent to which hyperbole surrounding the last 'Spanish miracle', as already discussed in the introduction to this book, belied the reproduction of profound structural contradictions with historical roots in the development and crisis of ISI and the industrial restructuring of the 1980s. We then further substantiate our endorsement of existing analyses of the uneven development of capitalism in Europe, but drawing upon the Spanish experience specifically and as a necessary prelude to the analysis of the overaccumulation of capital in Spain and Europe that follows.

The restructuring of Spanish industry and the fragmentation of labour in the 1980s

After the death of Franco in 1975 and in the course of the transition toward civilian government, state managers sought to maintain social peace initially by means of rising real wages that outstripped both inflation and productivity, prompting levels of state and private borrowing to also increase (Encarnación, 2003: 82). By 1977, the first civilian government, headed by the Unión de Centro Democrático's Adolfo Suárez, was forced to broker drastic measures to prevent a full-blown crisis, including curtailing the money supply, reforming labour legislation and introducing wage controls. This occurred in the context of high interest rates across the classic countries and the monetary squeeze that constituted part of a global disinflation strategy – the first move having been made by the US

Federal Reserve and the so-called 'Volker shock' of 1979. As is well documented in IPE literatures, this marked an incipient process of economic and political restructuring ideologically justified by a new social realism and the championing of the 'free market'. At the same time, the process of European economic integration gathered momentum. From the perspective developed in this book, we argue that European national states found, in the process of integration and convergence toward a single market and then full monetary union, an anti-inflationary means of confining the demands of their own working classes within the limits of accumulation. As Bonefeld argued in 1998, 'EMU amounts ... to an institutional attempt of buttressing domestic policies of austerity with a supranational anchor'; and, further, that EMU ensures that the 'burden of adjustment is carried by labour and ... is so structured as to de-politicise the making of monetary policy from working class demands', while reinforcing its regional and national fragmentation (1998: PE67). In this period, states across the European South had to find some way to confront the problems of falling profitability, high inflation, de-industrialisation, rising unemployment, and public deficits (Hopkin, 2012: 38; Karamessini, 2008: 514) – problems to which EMU became the 'solution'.

The first majority PSOE (Partido Socialista Obrero Español) government, led by former unionist Felipe González and elected in 1982, continued the imposition of austerity upon the Spanish working class that began with tight monetary policy under Suárez. At the centrepiece of the PSOE government's agenda was the full accession of Spain to the EC. The opportunity to externalise pressures for its industrial restructuring programme ('*la reconversión industrial*') by citing the country's need to meet requirements for EC integration was not missed by the PSOE, who could also benefit from their image of being the agents of democratic consolidation and liberal progress after four decades of fascist rule. The central target of the PSOE's industrial reconversion programme rolled out in 1984 – sometimes referred to as a 'cleaning up' ('*saneamiento*') exercise – were those unprofitable sectors in which the INI still played a major holding role. Between 1982 and 1993, the number of workers employed by INI firms was reduced by 35 per cent, while a wave of privatisations resulted in the partial or full ownership of 46 firms being sold off between 1985 and 1989 (Rand Smith, 1998: 118). In the final estimate, restructuring in the four largest targeted sectors (integrated steel, speciality steel, shipbuilding, and home appliances) amounted to a reduction of the workforce from 118,000 in 1982 to 60,000 by 1990 (Rand Smith: 130).

Between 1977 and 1988, Spain's balance of payments steadily improved and inflation decreased (Boix, 1995: 35), but at the cost of high numbers of closures of credit-dependent industrial firms and, under the PSOE alone, a total loss of some 700,000 manufacturing jobs (Lieberman, 1995: 281–3). Thus, the burden of transition to a fully liberalised market economy was placed firmly on the Spanish workforce (Etxezarreta, 1991: 40). Between 1978 and 1982, a total of 1.35 million jobs were lost in Spain (Harrison and Corkill, 2004: 16). After the PSOE government's removal of restrictions on temporary contracts in 1984, fixed-term employment rose dramatically – reaching 30 per cent of total employment by 1991 (Jimeno and Toharia, 1994: 18). From 1979 to 1986, real wages experienced a sustained decline while business profits gained 10 percentage points of GDP (López and Rodríguez, 2010: 148). But crucially, levels of investment in industry remained relatively low – a problem exacerbated by a domestic banking crisis between 1977 and 1985 that restricted liquidity (and which culminated in the centralisation of 73 per cent of banking activity in the hands of 'the Big Seven' large financial groups by 1984; López and Rodríguez, 2010: 154).[3] As a foreboding antecedent of crises to come, unemployment had reached 22 per cent by 1984 and was accompanied by the emergence of a huge informal economy as workers strove to cope with layoffs associated with the *saneamiento* (Benton, 1992).[4] Case studies of particular sectors in this period show a marked increase in off-the-books work in a growing number of smaller firms, among industrial outworkers and by the self-employed (see Benton, 1992). Labour intensive industries in textiles, footwear, toys, and other light manufacturing sectors were particularly affected by the newly emergent subcontracting relations that transformed the spatial organisation of production in Spain and, with it, the structure of the Spanish labour market (see Santos Preciado, 1997).[5] The process of industrial restructuring had, in short, provided a fresh supply of low-wage labour to Spain's small capitals and on the basis of flexible work contracts (90 per cent of all annual contracts from the mid-1980s, according to Martínez Lucio and Blyton, 1995: 351), competing to supply to larger, foreign-owned capitals engaged in production in geographical proximity.

Profitability was restored in Spain after 1979 on the basis of the imposition of austerity and the fragmentation of labour. The rate of profit continued to rise throughout the 1980s, until the recession of 1992 (Nieto Ferrández, 2007: 200). The reduction in the size of the manufacturing workforce was compensated by an increase in labour productivity, which was associated with industrial restructuring and the reorganisation of production (see Jimeno and Toharia, 1994: 11) as well as the repression of real wages. According to Viñals et al. (1990: 161), labour costs in Spain by 1985 were about 43 per cent lower than in other industrialised countries, with the vast majority of new employment being on the basis of flexible contracts. At the same time, the growth of Spain's service sector and its recently territorially decentralised public sector in the form of the 17 Autonomous Communities – which drew many women into employment in education, health, and cultural sectors – began to grow disproportionately to manufacturing (Santos Preciado, 1997: 155). From this point, the markedly segmented character of the labour market served to reduce the membership base of the trade unions and to weaken their capacity to resist the downward pressures on wages and working conditions (Banyuls et al., 2009: 255).[6]

The collaborationist stance of the main trade unions toward the liberal-democratic state had begun to shift from the early 1980s. The CC.OO, linked to the Spanish Communist Party, refused to agree to the PSOE's 1984 proposals for labour reform. Only the PSOE-allied General Workers' Union (Unión General de Trabajadores, or UGT) sanctioned them, although by 1986 it too stood in direct opposition to the government, and by December 1988, it would join the CC.OO in a one-day general strike against further efforts by the PSOE to deregulate the labour market. Beyond the mid-1980s, successive governments in Spain would continue to frame the issue of a growing segmentation between core, older workers, and younger workers on temporary contracts in terms of the need to push flexibilisation further still – a discourse that persists to this day (see, for example, Boletín Oficial del Estado, 2012). As Martínez Lucio and Blyton (1995: 358) confirmed in the mid-1990s:

> if one takes a step further and refers to the unevenness of the Spanish training system and its own levels of investment, then one realises that the issues of quality employment, real skill development and supply side orientations are not on the agenda, whereas the issue of labour costs and the ability to dismiss are.

The first phase of European integration, overaccumulation, and the monetary crisis of 1992

In spite of the unions' resistance to the government's programme, the recovery was achieved under a PSOE government that in 1986 successfully secured Spain's accession to the EC, under the terms of the Single European Act (SEA) – a process that further enabled the transformation of Spain's economic structure. The prevailing image of the PSOE and its achievements by the late 1980s was neatly summarised by Share (1988: 418):

> While the Socialist program created unemployment and eroded workers' purchasing power, it did achieve success in reducing inflation, improving the balance of payments, and increasing investment (although budget deficits continue to plague the government). The Socialists have created a much improved climate for foreign and domestic capital, as reflected in the dramatic increase of [FDI] and the Spanish stock market boom

Under the terms of the SEA, the Spanish state pursued the full liberalisation of the domestic economy (Montes, 1991). And, for a while at least, it appeared to many commentators to be bearing fruit in terms of stable growth (see, for example, Viñals, et al.: 195–6).

After the re-election of the PSOE in 1986, the state continued with its efforts to restructure industry and labour markets, sustaining accumulation for the remainder of the decade (Román, 1997: 97). Between 1987 and 1990, the number of workers recruited on fixed term contracts increased by over 1.5 million, thereafter accounting for 30 per cent of the working population (Pérez-Amorós and Rojo, 1991: 361). By 1991, labour's share of national income in Spain was lower than that recorded in 1971, even though the rate of employment was 8 per cent higher than that in 1971 (Pérez-Amorós and Rojo, 1991: 369). In fact, although there was substantial employment growth during this period and total employment returned to the absolute level of 1979, it did not keep pace with labour force growth in the second half of the 1980s. Unemployment remained above 16 per cent at the peak of the boom in 1990 (Pérez, 1999: 662).

FDI also played a significant role in the post-1985 boom. Immediately following EC accession, Spain became the fourth most attractive country in the world for foreign investment, with the Bolsa de Madrid quickly becoming the most profitable stock market in Europe (Pérez, 1997: 154). The lifting of capital controls attracted a new influx of FDI, averaging 2 per cent of GDP between 1986 and 1992 (1.2 per cent above the OECD average) (López, 2006: 14). Longer-term FDI was attracted by the profitability of fixed capital investments because of relatively low labour costs,[7] extraordinarily undervalued industrial assets, and the largest domestic market among accession countries (38 million people). In industry, FDI led to some technological updating – mainly in strong and moderate demand sectors – with 17 per cent of gross fixed capital formation coming from abroad (Carreras and Tafunell, 2003: 13).[8] The terms of accession to the

EC allowed for staged tariff reductions during which time export restrictions for Spanish industrial products were progressively reduced while some import barriers continue to exist in some state-protected sectors. Coupled with further government privatisation incentives, Spain therefore became extremely attractive to TNCs (Transnational Corporations) looking for a cost-competitive export base for the European market (Gomez Uranga, 1991). Foreign TNCs assumed control of many high profile Spanish firms,[9] while American and Japanese TNCs incorporated Spanish firms into their European 'core-network strategies' – in which they created core facilities in Europe through FDI exposure and developed intra-firm trade networks among decentralised Spanish affiliates (Arestis and Paliginis, 1995: 279; Katseli, 2001: 106).[10] By 1991, foreign capitals controlled 97 per cent of Spain's information processing industry, 95 per cent of the country's automobile manufacturing industry, 90 per cent of its electronics industry, and 41 per cent of food processing firms (Lieberman, 1995: 338). Meanwhile, the PSOE government merged a variety of state-owned firms in strategic sectors to form a few large firms – its own 'national champions' – and ensured they were provided protection by various means (Etchemendy, 2004; Toral, 2008). The state's proactive role in the concentration and centralisation of capital in these sectors meant that firms such as Endesa, Repsol, Iberdrola, and Union Fenosa effectively monopolised key sectors of the economy and would be among the select number of firms that would develop competitive organisational and technological forms, allowing them to 'internationalise' (mainly into Latin America) from the 1990s (a process to which we return later).[11]

By 1988, however, it was evident that the deflationary policies undertaken by governments since 1977 had clear limitations. Inflation was back on the rise (up to 5.7 per cent from 4.4 per cent in 1987 [Boix, 1995: 35] and in the context of fiscal expansionism that saw social spending increase from 9.2 per cent of GDP in 1975 to 13.9 per cent in 1986, and to 15.3 per cent by 1991 [Encarnación, 2003: 100]). In short, the same 'juxtaposition' of policies of monetary expansionism, on the one hand, and the imposition of austerity upon social relations, on the other, that characterised state economic management across the classic capitalist countries after 1985 was in evidence in Spain (Bonefeld, 1996b: 51–2; López and Rodríguez, 2011: 8). In 1988, the CC.OO and the UGT opposed attempts by the government to moderate wage increases and to reform labour laws. The shift toward a 'conflictive rather than cooperative relationship' between the state and the unions therefore meant that the state would have to find alternative means of curbing inflation (Hamann, 2001: 160).

High interest rates were also central to Spain's entry into the Exchange Rate Mechanism (ERM) in June 1989 – a move that 'completed' the PSOE's 'deflationary strategy' (Boix, 1995: 12). The ERM provided the state with a potential means of confronting the problem of rising unit labour costs and popular demands for increases in public spending. By relying on the 'external exchange rate anchor of the ERM and allowing interest rates to rise to unprecedented levels', the PSOE government sought to compensate for a lack of an incomes policy as a means of restricting wage increases and to 'impose wage discipline in a fragmented bargaining structure' (Pérez, 2000: 448). In the context of the main trade unions intransigence towards collaboration with the state, the appreciation of the currency and the state's tightening of credit forced employers in exposed sectors to resist higher wage demands. However, this state policy became a key expression of contradictions in the accumulation process, seen most vividly in the disproportionate expansion of different branches of production. State protected sectors, such as utilities, and booming sectors such as construction and tourism became more profitable, and capital and credit flowed away from domestic industrial manufacturing sectors that were experiencing heightened competitive pressures due to European market integration.[12] The result was a surge in demand and prices across particular branches of production such as services, finance, and construction. As Lieberman (1995: 337) reports, foreign financed investment – 75 per cent of which was from other EC countries after 1986 – 'largely by-passed growth industries ... to favour the production of energy, construction, and, more particularly, banking and insurance'.

In other words, one of the principal features of the period of growth and EU integration in the late 1980s was the form taken by the uneven and disproportionate development of different branches of production in Spain, expressed in a rising external deficit. The limited development of the productive forces in manufacturing sectors meant that investment in services became attractive to the large domestic banks looking to make high profits during a period of expanding domestic consumption and in sectors that were protected from foreign competition by the state (Etchemendy, 2004). As we will see later in this chapter, this tendency was more pronounced in the period of the last Spanish boom, when the privatisation of former INI firms heightened competition in manufacturing, and access to cheap credit in the context of EMU convergence meant a select number of Spanish capitals were able to expand operations abroad – particularly in Latin American countries. We will also see how the disproportionate expansion of banking and utilities, and the residential construction sector in particular, went hand in hand with overaccumulation of capital – and increasing inflationary and current account pressures on the Spanish state – in the course of Chapters 4 and 5.

The result of the weak export performance of Spanish manufacturing, on the one hand, and the expansion of internal demand, on the other, was that the Spanish state's trade deficit deteriorated from 3.3 per cent of GDP in 1985 to 7.1 per cent of GDP by 1989 (Montes, 1991: 261) – by far the worst position of any OECD country at that time. Between 1986 and 1992, production costs rose faster than Spain's main trading partners, and the real exchange rate appreciated by 27 per cent (Katseli, 2001: 111).[13] As noted previously, the state maintained high interest rates so as to indirectly manage rising wage levels as well as to attract foreign investment to finance the growing external deficit. However, short-term speculative inflows of capital contributed to a sharp appreciation of the peseta and the cheapening of imports, thereby reinforcing a cycle of rising asset price inflation and rising levels of consumption.[14] The overvaluation of the peseta between 1985 and 1992 led to a 241 per cent increase in imports and a deteriorating current account deficit. The overvaluation was sustained temporarily by tourism revenues (which produced a surplus in services on the state's current account), inflows of FDI attracted by high interest rates on Spanish bonds, and the Bank of Spain's foreign exchange reserves (Etxezarreta, 2000). However, by 1992, speculation against the sustainability of the ERM in international money markets mounted pressure against the peseta. International investors withdrew capital, and the current account deficit – which had reached 2.5 billion pesetas (4 per cent of GDP) – could no longer be covered by any means (Lopéz and Rodríguez, 2010: 175). Unable to defend the overvaluation of the peseta or stem capital flight, the state was forced to undertake a three-step cumulative currency devaluation of 22 per cent between September 1992 and May 1993 (Powell, 2003: 154) – signalling the onset of the country's deepest recession in 30 years (Scobie et al., 1998: 5).[15]

The recession compromised the Spanish state's capacity to meet the nominal convergence criteria for EMU as set out by EC members in the Maastricht Treaty of 1992.[16] A further devaluation came in 1995. This was significant as it marked the last historical point at which the state could viably revert to currency devaluation to secure its balance of payments or to fund public deficits above 60 per cent of GDP (see Lucarelli, 2011). The PSOE rolled out its Convergence Plan in the period 1992 to 1996 in an effort to shore up the value of the peseta and to meet the Maastricht criteria. The main aspects of the Plan were control of public expenditure through tight fiscal policy, reduction of inflation and interest rates, further deregulation and flexibilisation of capital and labour market, control of nominal wage increases, and an accelerated privatization of public enterprises (Holman, 1996: 146). This represented the beginning of a second period of industrial devaluations which resulted in the loss of 500,000 jobs, and another hike in unemployment – peaking at 24.2 per cent in 1994 (Scobie et al., 1998: 2). Further labour reforms initiated in 1992 encouraged flexible employment contracts to expand in low productivity sectors of the economy, such that by 1994 only 2 per cent of all new labour contracts were permanent (Hamann, 2001: 167).

The 1992 crisis revealed the limits to accumulation on the basis of industrial restructuring, the imposition of austerity, and the expansion social consumption by means of debt.[17] The ensuing recession confirmed that industrial restructuring and the decomposition of the Spanish working class had succeeded only in consolidating Spanish manufacturing sectors' intermediate position within the NIDL.[18] While a few key industrial sectors made the jump to world market production after the 1970s – albeit at a pace of development dictated by the arrival of foreign capital, technology, and patents – they did so only to a limited extent, and on the basis of a parallel and related expansion in a number of small capitals competing to supply low-tech inputs and employing low-wage, casual labour. Meanwhile, between 1985 and 1991, investment in public companies increased dramatically in what amounted to state-guided concentration and centralisation of capital – especially in the banking, telecommunications, transport, and energy sectors. Newly privatised firms such as Endesa, Repsol, and Telefónica were protected from domestic and foreign competition by the state, allowing them to reap large profits from new productivity gains and cost reductions and to contribute some dividends to the state in the process (Arocena, 2004: 6).[19] Therefore, given the weakness of Spanish manufacturing and the state's policy of maintaining barriers to entry for other capitals into key sectors, the disproportionate development of some internationalised Spanish capitals relative to the mass of small capitals producing for the domestic market or in supply chains for world market capitals became a *formal* characteristic of the national process of accumulation.

The 'Spanish Miracle' redux?

The PP took office in Spain in 1996, after an electoral campaign in which they emphasised to a largely 'pro-Europe' electorate that the economic policies of the PSOE had jeopardised the fulfilment of the Maastricht criteria (Llamazares, 2005). Led by José María Aznar, the PP government pursued deflationary macroeconomic reform programme 'with an almost obsessive determination' (Powell, 2003: 161). Aznar himself was one of Europe's most vociferous defenders of the EU's Stability and Growth Pact (1997), which committed its members to strict fiscal discipline in line with low inflation targets. In Spain, tighter budgetary measures were introduced; sweeping structural reforms increased labour flexibility and held down wages; product markets were further liberalised; and the privatisation programme was accelerated. In 1997, the PP government negotiated an agreement with the unions to reduce statutory redundancy payments and social-security payments for employees on new contracts. A further law was prepared – without union agreement – in 2001, which was to extend reforms to new contracts. The PP government also attempted to reform the unemployment benefit system, provoking a general strike on 20 July 2002 that forced the proposals to be withdrawn. Such changes, together with the concentration of investment in sectors such as services and retail, compounded a plunge of 18.5 per cent in real wages between the 1992 recession and 2001 (Cámara Izquierdo, 2007: 556). The drive to increase fixed term contracts and labour flexibility served to exacerbate the low skill and productivity basis of the economy, as firms were reluctant to train new employees. Since the mid-1990s, exports as a share of GDP have practically stalled, and for the first time, productivity fell in tandem with broad employment creation (López, 2006: 5).

At the same time, the government also began transferring remaining INI-run firms to a new state holding company Sociedad Estatal de Participaciones Industriales (SEPI), originally founded in 1995 by the PSOE, where they were prepared for privatisation. Participation of the public enterprise sector went from 3 per cent of GDP in 1996 to just 1 per cent in 2002, and privatisations had raised US$38,401 million by 2001 – placing Spain fourth in the ranking of Europe's privatising states (Arocena, 2004: 339). In a bid to ensure that key companies would remain Spanish-owned in this process, large financial groups – such as Banco Bilbao Vizcaya Argentaria (BBVA), Banco Santander Central Hispano (BSCH), and La Caixa – were restructured; while the electricity utility company Endesa, the oil and gas group Repsol-YPF, and the hotel group Sol-Meliá were also systematically reorganised, with the state retaining a 'golden share' so as to prevent hostile takeovers prior to their sale (Salmon, 2002: 6). After privatisation, such firms went to have a considerable presence in the Spanish stock market.

The PP's commitment to fiscal discipline ensured that Spain was one of the countries that most comfortably qualified for participation in the group of countries forming the vanguard of EMU in 1999 (Martín, 2000: 243). At that moment, *The Financial Times'* Martin Wolf declared that 'Spain is one of the countries that has benefited most from the constraints imposed by the convergence process laid down in the Maastricht Treaty' (quoted in Harrison and Corkill, 2004: 22). Between 1996 and 2000, unemployment fell from 3.5 million to 2.3 million; at that time, Spain was the source of half the new jobs created in the EU (Harrison and Corkill, 2004: 154, 161). At the end of the 1990s, commentators began to speculate about a new *'milagro español'* (Salmon, 2002; López and Rodríguez, 2010: 179). After the PP's defeat in the 2004 general election, the new PSOE-led coalition government continued with a commitment to fiscal austerity – and understandably so given the PP's economic record.[20] By 2004, 1.8 million new jobs had been created since 2000 and unemployment had fallen to a record low of 8.1 per cent of the active workforce; indeed, some 60 per cent of all new jobs in Europe were created in Spain (Royo, 2009a). The period of sustained growth continued further for another three years. The Spanish economy grew at an average rate of 4 per cent per year until 2007 – a rate bettered only by Ireland within the EU. It is incredible today to recall that, as France and Germany were struggling to keep their fiscal deficits within original Stability and Growth Pact targets, the Spanish state enjoyed three consecutive years of surplus (from 2005 to 2007).

Behind the recovery, however, fundamental contradictions of the national accumulation process in Spain that were already evidenced in the 1992 crisis only intensified further still. Having outlined the general transformations associated with the 1980s and 1990s, the remainder of this chapter focuses on the uneven development of the forces of production in Spain – and in the context of uneven development within Europe more generally – that accelerated the process of overaccumulation, as analysed in Chapter 4.

The differentiation of Spanish capitals in the 1990s and 2000s

In Chapter 2 of this book, we argued that by the end of the 1960s, the limits to the development of the productive forces on the basis of expanding domestic consumption meant that the Spanish state was forced to negotiate with TNCs, like Ford, that were eager to use Spain as a low-wage export base for the geographically proximate European market. The heavy reliance of Spain's industrial capitals upon foreign investment and technology and the attractiveness of production in Spain based upon low-wage production meant that the development of Spanish industry proceeded on an 'intermediate' basis, in the context of the emergence of the NIDL.[21]

In this chapter, we have already seen how the PSOE governments of the 1980s sought to restructure industry in Spain in an attempt to restore profitability and on the basis of the deflationary imposition of austerity that destroyed surplus productive capacity and commodity capital, led to rounds of mass unemployment, and fragmented labour markets. By the 1990s, the period of restructuring imposed by the state had served to transform Spanish industry, but not in general on the basis of the development of the productive forces in step with normal capitals in sectors at the vanguard of production for the world market.

The reproduction of small industrial capitals in the new international division of labour

Since the 1990s, Spanish industrial production has continued to be concentrated in a mass of small capitals whose development is either restricted to the scale required for local markets or is dependent upon their ability to survive in competitive, geographically concentrated markets to supply mostly foreign-owned normal capitals with goods of low-technological content.[22] In terms of scale, between 1990 and 1996 only 25.2 per cent of the 33,203 new manufacturing plants established in Spain had more than 9 employees (Arauzo-Carod and Segarra-Blasco, 2005: 150–1). However, as we outlined previously, this reduced scale of operation with lower production costs and the ability to take advantage of informal labour to hold down wages also accounts for a relatively robust rate of survival; as 50.47 per cent of new manufacturing start-ups in 1994 were still in business by 2000 (Arauzo-Carod and Segarra-Blasco, 2005: 151). By 2000, 'Italy and Spain were the only two European countries in which more than 50 per cent of the total workforce was employed in production units with fewer than 50 employees' (Binda and Colli, 2011: 17).

In sectors that have been at the vanguard of the transformation of automation processes upon which the NIDL has been configured, Spanish capitals have in general failed to develop in step with world market norms. Research from the mid-1980s noted that Spanish industry was well behind the leading industrial countries in terms of the adoption of automated manufacturing processes – precisely because of the domi-nance of capitals operating on small scales of production (see, for exam-ple, Martínez Sánchez, 1994; Gómez, Salazar and Vargas, 2012).[23] By the mid-1990s, only 8 per cent of Spanish firms in the most technologically advanced manufacturing sectors in world market terms could compete with German firms on the basis of product quality (Martínez Zarzoso, 1999: 147). Take, for example, the machine-tool industry. By the mid-1990s, this sector accounted for only 2 per cent of Spanish industrial employment; compared with 8 per cent in Germany, where it was considered to be the 'crown jewel' of national industry (Köhler and Woodward, 1997). After the introduction of the SEA in 1986, the low productivity and almost shambolic organisation of production of Spanish firms in the sectors was exposed as being 'years behind northern European standards' (Köhler and Woodward, 1997: 67).[24] In Germany and France, for example:

> With the help of sophisticated computer systems and technical organisation planning, control and service functions became more and more accurate and production workers more and more confined to their immediate tasks. This was not achieved in Spain. [...]

> Hence in the 1980s, major parts of the Spanish machine-building industry were still in the 'early-Taylorist' stage with a relatively high degree of functional differentiation and bureaucratisation and a low level of technical organisation, and the Germans and the French became masters of functional rationalisation, while segments of Japanese industry were the vanguard of 'post-Taylorist' process-oriented, inter-functional, 'systemic' rationalisation. (Köhler and Woodward, 1997: 68)

The Spanish steel industry serves as another instructive case (see Montgomery and Sabaté, 2010). Once a key sector of 'national interest' – it accounted for 72.3 per cent of total INI investment in 1961 – the steel industry had been subjected to restructuring by the state between 1983 and 1986, but this had failed to address a secular problem of low productivity relative to international norms. A further process of restructuring from 1995 led to the privatisation and concentration of steel production in Spain, and a complete take-over by foreign capitals by 2006. This second restructuring process yielded productivity and profitability gains, but on the basis of a fourfold reduction in the size of the workforce and sectoral labour costs that are now among the lowest in Europe (Montgomery and Sabaté, 2010: 79).

Therefore, notwithstanding the arrival of FDI and the 'multinationalisation' (Holman, 1996: 149) of Spanish manufacturing firms from the 1980s, the development of the forces of production in branches oriented toward external markets has been of a limited character. The inflow of FDI in the 1980s had done little to encourage investment in productivity by the majority of Spanish firms; in general, only those few with already relatively advanced levels of productivity had been subjected to takeover and further investment in productivity by foreign capitals since the mid-1980s (Guadalupe, Kuzmina and Thomas, 2012).[25] By the mid-1990s, Spanish industry retained its 'intermediate' status in the world market. Inter- and intra-industrial trade continued to be characterised by the export of goods that were inferior in quality to those which were imported – a problem attributable to the pervasive use of relatively backward technologies (Martínez Zarzoso, 1999).[26] By 2005, Spain invested just 1.03 per cent of GDP in research and design (R&D) – half the average for the EU-15 (Mathieson, 2007: 22).

The development of the Spanish automobile Industry: From the 1980s to the present

The limited development of Spanish domestic industry is even further evidenced in its 'exceptional' industry (Banyuls et al., 2009: 251; see also Pérez et al., 2004) – the automobile industry. In Chapter 2, we explained how the arrival of the Ford Motor Company in the midst of the global crisis of the 1970s was negotiated under the terms of the 'Ford decrees'. These signalled Spain's insertion into the emergent NIDL, on the basis of providing a low-wage, disciplined workforce capable of manufacturing technologically backward small cars in short runs for the European market. The global crises of the 1970s impacted significantly upon the structure of the global car industry. Since then, production has been concentrated in a decreasing number of producers facing secular problems of overcapacity in European, Japanese, and US markets – even in periods of growth (Heneric et al., 2005: 38). As the NIDL developed on the basis of transformations in the production process associated with systemofacture, and in the face of heightening global competition,[27] Spain became an attractive export base for Ford's global competitors, precisely on the basis of offering relatively low-wage labour capable of adapting to labour processes of relatively low complexity (Rubenstein, 2001: 344). Following Ford, and the state's relaxation of the Spanish-made components quota to 60 per cent for all producers in 1979, General Motors established a plant near Zaragoza to produce the Opel Corsa (launched in 1983). This, together with the effects of the crises of the 1970s, was disastrous for SEAT, whose market share in Spain fell from 51 per cent in 1973 to 26 per cent by 1980 (Catalan, 2010: 222). At the height of recession in 1981, FIAT relinquished ownership of SEAT back to the INI and negotiations commenced with the German producer Volkswagen that culminated in the transfer of 51 per cent of the company in 1986. The impact of the takeover of Spanish automobile manufacturing by foreign capitals by the 1980s is made clear by Catalan (2010: 222):

> The policy of supporting a national champion was definitively over and the emerging national system of innovation was seriously jeopardised ... These changes led to Spain's consolidation as a world exporter of cars in the medium to low end of the market. Efficiency and competitiveness improved. However, decisions over the future of the industry would now be taken abroad and the bulk of R&D of the Spanish car industry would be answerable to foreign headquarters. In addition, the industry would experience a significant slowdown compared with the previous period.

In global terms, the automobile industry was at the vanguard of the adoption of automated manufacturing technologies and led the movement toward the NIDL from the 1960s until the 1980s (when machine tool and electronics industries became the principle drivers). Confronted with rising production costs and falling demand, the automobile industry's response to the crisis of the 1970s was to seek to lower costs by adopting 'leaner' production technologies and to reduce the minimum efficient scale of production through the introduction of automated production technologies – mainly industrial robots and computer-aided manufacturing (Grinberg, 2013: 181–2). This transformation entailed the vertical disintegration of production and the expansion of networks of labour-intensive auxiliary suppliers.[28] Unsurprisingly then, the takeover of Spanish automobile producers in the 1980s proceeded on the basis of the transformation of the technologies and organisation of production in line with recent revolutions in the labour process – a process mediated by the PSOE's further relaxation of the legal restraints on foreign capitals' restructuring of the labour process and the Spanish-made components quota (Ramos Barrado, 1986). Volkswagen acquired SEAT's Zona Franca production site in Barcelona in 1986, but by 1993, it moved production to a lower cost site in a new industrial zone near Pamplona, and later to another site near Barcelona in Martorell.[29] Nissan and Suzuki took over obsolete plants in Spain in the early 1980s, looking to produce for the EEC market without incurring tariffs. Nissan led the way in introducing 'lean', 'just in time' production techniques to its subsidiaries in Spain in the 1980s that led to the vertical disintegration of production and outsourcing to auxiliary capitals, as discussed next.

FASA-Renault and SEAT-Volkswagen introduced Flexible Manufacturing Systems and automated technologies in the same period and, along with General Motors, adopted outsourcing based on the 'just in time' model in the 1990s (Pallarès Barberà, 1997).[30] Volkswagen reported 'sustainable profitability' as a result of its SEAT Industrial Restructuring Programme, in which the size of the workforce was reduced from over 24,000 in 1992 to under 13,000 by 1996 (Álvarez Gil and González de la Fe, 1997: 22).

Since the 1980s, then, the structure of automobile production within Spain has also become markedly differentiated and, in a manner, consistent with the developments in Spanish industry and labour markets outlined earlier in this chapter. From the 1980s, there has been an expansion in the number of small capitals acting as auxiliary suppliers to foreign-owned capitals engaged in large-scale assembly for export. The former produce products of low technological complexity, while the latter involve more technologically complex, higher productivity labour processes (see Aláez Aller et al., 1999; Pallarès Barberà, 1997 and 1998; Truett and Truett, 2001). And, as Banyuls and Llorente (2010) point out, this has had definite repercussions in terms of the fragmentation of labour markets. In the latter, capitals are compensated for paying higher wages due to relatively high levels of labour productivity; while wages in the auxiliary sector have been relatively low. A greater proportion of workers in the assembly are unionised.[31]

Across Europe from the 1980s, there emerged a broader national and regional pattern of the uneven development of automobile production – a pattern into which the Spanish car industry's relatively backward position was further consolidated. A 'spatial hierarchy' in production emerged from the 1980s, with its productive and geographical centre in Southern Germany (Bordenave and Lung, 1996; see also Krempel and Plümper, 1999). There, producers have since specialised in the production of larger, high-end, technologically advanced cars using the most complex labour processes, with the highest levels of labour productivity and concentration of R&D development and adoption. For example, from its base in Wolfsburg, Volkswagen expanded across Europe to become the world's fourth largest producer and market leader in Europe by 2000 (Rubenstein, 2001: 343).[32] From the 1980s, Spain retained its backward position relative to the core producers within this hierarchy, as Catalan noted in the passage earlier. Ramos Barrado (1986) also concluded back in the 1980s that Spanish car production would specialise in the export of basic models, while the internal demand for superior models would have to be serviced by imports; and, further, that production would entail equipment and components of lower complexity than world market norms, while producers would have to import more complex components and technologies. And this is a characteristic of production in Spain that persisted through the 1990s.[33] Bordenave and Lung (1996) reported that the Spanish industry had 'inherent weaknesses': production was entirely controlled by foreign capitals; production was barely integrated, with a small supply sector; and it specialised in the production of small cars and lightweight industrial vehicles using low-wage labour (see also Lagendijk and van der Knapp, 1995; Alaez Aller et al., 1999). In profitability terms, by 2002 Spanish production accounted for 6.71 per cent of 'value added' in Europe – compared with 45.10 per cent in Germany and 16.68 per cent in France (Heneric et al., 2005: 7, Table 2).[34]

The global transformations in the technological and organisational forms of automobile production failed to counter secular problems in the industry. Economists identified 'structural overcapacity' as early as the 1990s (Bordenave and Lung, 1996) – a problem that persisted until the mid-2000s (Heneric et al., 2005: 38). This has made the Spain-based automobile industry particularly vulnerable to crisis. In 2008 alone, SEAT announced losses of €78 million (it registered a profit of €8 million in 2007) – a loss its management attributed to a fall in demand for its small cars (*La Vanguardia*, 2009). That same year, Volkswagen – its parent company – announced profits were up by 15.4 per cent. By 2012, SEAT registered a fourth year of annual losses – citing as principal cause the loss of demand, particularly in Southern Europe (*El País*, 2012a). *The New York Times*, however, ran a story that predicted an 'industrial bright spot' for crisis-ravaged Spain (Minder, 2012). Its reporter announced that Ford, Renault, and Volkswagen were all committed to expanding production in Spain by some 11 per cent, and for one reason: in the crisis, labour costs had been reduced to a level some 40 per cent less expensive than in Europe's other main car producing countries. Since 2008, the Spanish car industry shed 9 per cent of its workforce, and in the face of further possible job losses, workers have since accepted wage cuts.[35] In the words of business school professor cited in the story: 'When you look at car manufacturers and suppliers in Spain, a lot of the fat has been cut out since the start of the crisis'. Even Spain's 'exceptional' industry is not immune to the forms of 'internal devaluation' that we discuss in depth in Chapter 5.

The bases for the 'internationalisation' of some Spanish firms since the 1990s

The 15-year period following the 1992 recession in Spain witnessed the aggressive expansion of a select number of domestic banks and firms abroad. In 2005, and for the first time in Spain's history, the volume of outward FDI exceeded inward investment (Fernández, 2011: 151). In 2006, total outward FDI from Spain peaked at US$89.7 billion in 2006 – third only to the US and France (Chislett, 2008: 112). The bulk of Spanish direct investment abroad went into Latin America (see Santiso, 2007). The basis for the expansion of some firms after the mid-1990s lay in the state's proactive role in the centralisation and concentration of capital in sectors such as banking, energy, and telecommunications, as already outlined.

The so-called 'big five' (Endesa, Repsol, Telefónica, and the two major banks, BBVA and BSCH) were the main beneficiaries of state protection in the 1990s, and by 2004 shared more than 60 per cent of the net profits of the 35 companies that make up the Spanish stock market index (IBEX; Etchemendy, 2004: 648). By the mid-2000s, therefore, Spain's largest and most profitable capitals were concentrated not in the automobile sector, nor in manufacturing sectors in general, but in sectors such as banking, construction, utilities and public services, retailing, and hotels.[36] The particular form these capitals assume in relation to the production and circulation of surplus-value differentiates their valorisation from industrial capitals (Clarke, 1978: 57). As we have explained, the relatively backward development of the latter in Spain can be explained by their restrictive and low-technology intensive production for the domestic market, on the one hand, and on a scale required to compete in supply networks for foreign capitals, on the other (see Arocena, 2004). Spain's most profitable capitals, on the other hand, reached the degree of concentration required to compete as normal capitals at the scale of the world market – albeit in specific sectors largely based on direct investment abroad.

One significant result of the 'internationalisation' of certain Spanish capitals concerns the external debt that today weighs heavily upon the state.[37] As the accumulation cycle intensified in Spain during the last boom, the state used growing tax receipts – especially from construction and housing (see Chapter 4) – to support acquisitions abroad by Spanish firms under the terms of so-called 'goodwill payments'. As a continuation of the state strategy to support its 'national champions', Spanish companies were allowed to offset 30 per cent of the costs of any foreign company purchase against tax – the 'goodwill' thus representing the difference between the book value of assets and the actual price paid, a direct subsidy that allowed Spanish companies to outbid competing investors in foreign markets (Chislett, 2007: 4). With a competitive position in Latin American markets largely consolidated, the European and wider emerging markets became the next target for expanding Spanish capitals. Between 2005 and 2007, when the state boasted a current account surplus (generated from taxes collected during the height of the property boom), Spanish companies spent a total of €140 billion on domestic and overseas acquisitions (Royo, 2009b: 20–1).[38]

One other notable 'success story' that emerged from the last Spanish boom concerns the Spanish clothing industry and the enhanced international profile of high street fashion brands such as Mango and Zara. The latter, founded by the world's third-richest man (by 2013 estimates), Amancio Ortega Gaona, is part of the Industria de Diseño Textil (Inditex) group that has 17 manufacturing subsidiaries in La Coruña and Barcelona. It has been a pioneer of 'fast fashion – a "just in time" process of clothing production that does not compete on the basis of design but rather on its rapid response to emerging trends through an integrated information infrastructure, supply, marketing, and retail chains' (Walt, 2013). This made the 'Zara model' relatively unique when compared with many other normal capitals that do not own manufacturing facilities and instead network with suppliers mostly located in the Global South (see Tokatli, 2008: 22). Zara's initial success was based on two factors linked to the recession of the 1980s: namely, the lowest unit labour costs in Europe (it employed informal, female labour looking to supplement household income)[39] and an early move toward vertical integration in the context of many wholesale suppliers' entry into bankruptcy (Tokatli, 2008: 28). From the outset, therefore, Zara's business model combined low costs with sophisticated control over the production process, and as a result could quickly respond to consumer demand for cutting-edge fashions at a low cost. When its main competitors outsourced production, mainly to China, Zara was able to keep manufacturing in Spain and Portugal because its shorter lead times, smaller inventories, and speed of distribution compensated for around 15 per cent higher labour costs (Tokatli, 2008: 30). However, its global expansion in the 2000s, which included becoming a publically traded company, saw Zara outsource more production to countries such as India, Morocco, and Turkey, where the same skill levels could be sourced at lower costs. Zara now produces on this basis in more than 50 countries, making 55 per cent of its total sales abroad (Santiso, 2007: 11). Zara is, in short, a normal capital whose reproduction is now determined by its relation to the NIDL rather than prevailing material conditions in Spain.

Summary

The picture that emerges from our analysis of the differentiation reproduction of capitals in Spain since the 1990s shows that Spanish capitalism made some significant advances in terms of the development of the productive forces in key sectors. This process was marked by certain characteristics that attest to the necessarily uneven character of development within Spain and across Europe. Spain could boast globally competitive, 'internationalised' firms such as Telefónica and Zara, and banks such as BBVA and Banco Santander. At the same time, however, its domestic industries increasingly relied upon low-wage, low-productivity, informal labour producing either for local markets or in highly competitive and low-profit supplier networks. Even its 'successful' automobile industry developed disproportionately in terms of its own auxiliary and assembly branches, and in relation to the giants of global automobile manufacturing and R&D. We also acknowledge that the disproportionate development of the branches of production in Spain has been especially visible in the construction sector – which we have yet to discuss in any detail. We will devote a considerable portion of Chapter 4 to an analysis of this sector, and not simply to demonstrate with further evidence the process of uneven development. Rather, we also elaborate upon the dynamics of credit, debt, urban rents, and speculation in property markets that sustained social consumption in Spain until 2008 on a scale far beyond that which could be sustained by the production of surplus-value by Spanish capitals after two decades or so of the transformations outlined in the preceding sections of this chapter.

As Bellofiore, Garibaldo, and Halevi (2010: 132) explain, the transformations within, say, the automobile industries of Italy and Spain are incomprehensible unless one looks at the Europe-wide development of an industry that, by 2007 was in a state of 'endemic overproduction' – a state intensified since the integration of Eastern European and Chinese producers and labour markets within circuits of capital after the 1980s. The restructuring of the industry created new, disintegrated organisational and technological forms:

> productive *networks* or *filières*, based on the outsourcing of upstream production activities, made up of many small and medium enterprises, have been set up by the main automotive producers. Each chain is segmented in tiers having a different value added capacity, depending upon productivity. For instance in all the industries the producers of modules or complex components are stronger than companies producing simple parts. The overwhelming majority of these networks/chains are organized both in tiers and poles; the poles are the key players of each tier. At the bottom of this ladder we find the 'last', the companies just supplying an output of a certain

amount of simple manufacturing/processing activity or simple services; these units just struggle to survive. (Bellofiore, Garibaldo and
Halevi, 2010: 132–3)

Since the 1980s, they argue, European manufacturing has been characterised by productive overcapacity, a competitive struggle to produce
new product lines, the squeezing of wages, and the deterioration of
work conditions (Bellofiore, Garibaldo and Halevi, 2010: 133). We have
seen this much in Spain. However, we have also noted how the impact
of the current crisis has been markedly uneven across the Eurozone.
This, we can now claim, is a product of the historical and uneven
development of the productive forces across European national states
and regions that has been formalised by the process of European integration and EMU.

European Monetary Union and overaccumulation in Spain

Although the national form of capital accumulation in Spain was to a
large extent conditioned by its relatively 'backward' historical development and the turn toward protectionism and ISI as a result of the
collapse of the economy during the Civil War, by the 1990s the state
had managed a process of market integration and nominal monetary
convergence with the advanced, classical countries of Western Europe.
Spain was, as noted by Martin Wolf for example, a successful exemplar
of the benefits to European 'convergence'. Yet, as we have already seen
in this chapter, the development of Spanish capitalism proceeded from
the 1980s onward on the basis of deindustrialisation, the proliferation of small industrial capitals, the fragmentation of labour, and the
expansion of credit to fund social consumption but also the concentration and foreign expansion of certain Spanish capitals – a process
punctuated by a monetary crisis in 1992 and which necessitated three
successive devaluations of the national currency. With the meeting of
the Maastricht criteria and entry into EMU, however, the prospect of
managing future overaccumulation crises through national monetary
policy effectively disappeared.

As Bonefeld (2012b: 52) argues, the 'institutional structure of EMU
combines the supranational conduct of monetary policy with national
state responsibility for competitive labour markets'. The logic of subsidiarity at the heart of EMU is therefore one that seeks to guarantee
that member states cannot resort to expansionary – and therefore
inflationary – means of adjusting to competitive pressures; rather, the

only possible means of adjustment will be to lower labour costs and to enhance the profitability of their own territorially segmented labour markets (see Chapter 5). EMU guarantees, by legal means, the eurozone-wide subordination of social reproduction to the reproduction of capital and the social power of money:

> The convergence criteria and the Stability Pact subordinate countries with relatively high labour costs to those with low labour costs ... In addition, labour migration is expected to adjust the burden of unemployment on national budgets. In short, EMU inscribes in institutional form what capital and its national state(s) have sought in vain ... National governments see EMU as an anchor for deregulating welfare regimes, intensifying market discipline, and for redistributing wealth from labour to capital. (Bonefeld, 2002: 5)

Yet the equalisation (or 'equilibrium') logic at the heart of EMU convergence was always bound (to paraphrase Smith, 1984: 202), to be 'frustrated by the differentiation of geographical space' and the tensions between 'fixity and motion' that characterise capitalist development across space and time – crucially, in the territorialised differentiation of what Harvey terms 'physical and social infrastructures', consisting of working classes bearing different histories with respect to industrial development. As Hadjimichalis (2011: 259) contends as regards Southern European regions especially, little recognition was given by the architects of EMU to 'their pre-existing highly unequal regional production systems and specializations, to their structurally different regional labour markets and to their unequal accessibility to markets (economically, institutionally and spatially) vis-à-vis the "core" of the eurozone'. And with the prospect of European enlargement, the regions of Southern Europe in particular stood to lose competitiveness relative to well-educated, high productivity but low cost labour in Central and Eastern Europe (Hadjimichalis, 2004: 26).

EMU was therefore always going to exacerbate the tendency toward overaccumulation and crisis in Spain as its productive capitals struggled to cope with intensified competition. Behind the boom of the mid-1990s to 2008 – in which private sector wages grew annually at compound rates of around 2 to 5.5 per cent – productivity grew at a meagre average of only 0.2 per cent per year (it fell in 2004 and 2005), prompting repeated calls for further labour reforms and more flexibility in labour markets (*Economist*, 2010a). Spain failed to develop competitive strengths in information communication technology and market services (despite growth of the latter in employment share) – sectors that have been the major sources of growth in faster growing economies (Gomes da Silva and Teixeira, 2012; Mas and Quesada, 2005). Indeed from the mid-1990s there was a deceleration in the rate of technological investment in general, especially in the manufacturing sector (Estrada and López-Salido, 2004). The expansion of capital accumulation in Spain in this period was limited to particular sectors, as we have seen, and was fed by large inflows of money capital that supported the internationalisation of select Spanish companies, as well as unprecedented levels of growth in the Spanish construction sector (see Chapter 4). In construction alone, the ratio of debt to gross operating profit was more than 50 per cent higher in Spain than in a weighted average of eurozone economies (Roxburgh et al., 2012: 27). The role of cheap credit in the 'internationalisation' of some Spanish capitals was reflected in the rising level of corporate debt on the Spanish stock market in the mid-2000s (*Economist*, 2007: 77); while, outside of the activities of Spain's new 'national champions', the private sector as a whole became increasingly credit dependent (increasing by 192.8 per cent between 1996 and 2010 to reach 227.2 per cent of GDP, according to Eurostat, 2012b).[40] In fact from 2004, as Carballo-Cruz (2011: 318) confirms,

> the increase in the private sector's debt was five times higher than the eurozone average and credit growth rates to the private sector followed an upward trend until 2006, when the annual growth rate approached 30 per cent, remaining at levels higher than the nominal growth in GDP until the end of 2008.

The debt of non-financial corporations nearly doubled relative to GDP during the boom, from 74 per cent of GDP in 2000 to 137 per cent in 2008; by 2011, non-financial private sector debt would reach 134 per cent of GDP, a rate second only to Ireland (Roxburgh et al., 2012: 27).[41] At the time of writing this book, the average industrial company in Spain has a larger debt burden than anywhere else in Europe (Gordon, 2013).

Conclusion

The crisis that confronted the Spanish state in the 1980s necessitated a deflationary response that consisted of industrial restructuring, the imposition of austerity and the pursuit of integration into European-wide circuits of capital. As a result, Spain experienced two recoveries,

one in the late 1980s and another from the mid-1990s – each one culminating in crisis and a recession of greater depth than its predecessor.
This chapter has advanced our account of the limits to capital in Spain
by providing an historical examination of the 1980s onward, drawing
attention to the uneven development of production, the differentiation
of capitals, and the credit-dependency of Spanish manufacturing by
the mid-2000s. We have also introduced the question of uneven development within Europe more generally, and its formalisation through
EMU. Yet this only takes us part of the way toward a full understanding of the current crisis and the forms of revolt that have emerged as
a result. A fuller understanding requires that we pay closer attention
to the dynamics of fictitious capital formation and circulation within
the wider eurozone, also in addition to the specificities of overproduction within the built environment and overaccumulation in real estate
markets – since the two processes have been related in crucial ways during the last boom. And, beforehand, this requires a further detour into
the theorisation of the 'urban process' that has been beyond the remit
of this and preceding chapters. We therefore now turn to the limits to
urbanisation.

4
The Limits to Urbanisation

Writing in the British newspaper *The Guardian* in June 2012, an emeritus professor of international banking and finance at Barcelona's prestigious ESADE business school gave his own verdict on the roots of the crisis:

> Spain's banking crisis did not come out of the blue. In the 1990s the Spanish suffered a bout of collective madness. Interest rates fell from 14 per cent (with the peseta) to 4 per cent (with the euro) in a matter of weeks. In 1998 the centre-right government passed a law that significantly increased the amount of land for development. Developers got rich, selling the idea that everyone was going to win because property would always go up – never down – in value. German banks financed Spain's savings and commercial banks, which needed extra funds for high-risk mortgages. Greed made us rich for a while – but then it made us poor, and jeopardised our future.

He elaborates:

> All of these bubbles were like fires lit by greed: you could buy a flat on the Mediterranean coast (or in a city) for £100,000 and sell it the next day for £150,000; by the end of the month it was worth £250,000. And meanwhile, the flat, purchased off-plan, was still being built. The last buyer still believed that prices would never stop spiralling upward. All this began in 1998, and the bubble burst in 2007. Nine years of speculative madness. (Tornabell, 2012)

The crisis, in this reading, was a product of human frailty, gullibility, and greed.

Crisis, as we have explained and demonstrated thus far, is necessary to the capitalist form of social production. The periodicity of crisis can be understood as a result of the tendency toward overaccumulation. We have seen how successive crises and subsequent periods of devaluation managed by the Spanish state have transformed Spanish capitals, prefigured the uneven development of different branches of production within Spain, and fragmented labour markets. In Chapter 3, we argued that the development of industry in Spain – as a constitutive moment of the uneven development of the forces of production within Europe and at a global scale – could not have provided a basis for the sustained period of growth and the expansion of social consumption that transpired from the mid-1990s until 2008. In this chapter, we therefore turn to the *material* bases of the boom that preceded the present crisis.[1] Although we concede that Tornabell and others are correct to focus their attention upon the crucial role of construction and the real estate market as a sphere for speculative investment in the last Spanish boom (see, for instance, Bielsa and Duarte, 2011; IMF, 2009; OECD, 2010; Salmon, 2010), we develop a materialist account of the significance of urbanisation that is consistent with the value theoretical approach adopted and the historical account developed in preceding chapters (see also Burnham, 2011: 494–8). In order to most effectively trace the inner relation between the limits to capital accumulation in Spain and the role of construction and real estate markets in the overaccumulation of capital, we draw upon Marxian scholarship on the *urban process* in capitalism.[2]

Theorising the urban process in contemporary capitalism

Urbanisation, understood simply in terms of 'city formation and the production, appropriation, and concentration of an economic surplus' (Harvey, 1985b: 191), is by no means historically specific to capitalism. However, it is the case that in the course of the historical development of the productive forces, urban centres became crucial to the spatial organisation of capitalist production, and reproduction in specific ways. In short, urbanisation takes on a specifically capitalist meaning as soon as it is acknowledged that it takes on an active role in the processes of uneven geographical development and the overaccumulation and devaluation of capital. Today, then, urbanisation – and with it geographical locality and place – should be considered in relation to the necessity of crisis in capitalism, if only because, as Harvey (1982: 425) stresses, crises 'always fuse the particular and the individual (concrete labour) with the universal and the social (abstract labour). And the devaluation is *always* specific to a particular place and time' (see also Smith, 1984: 128–9).

This claim is fundamental to a processual understanding of urbanisation: how 'capital builds a geographical landscape in its own image at a certain point in time only to have to destroy it later in order to accommodate its own dynamic of endless capital accumulation, strong technological change, and fierce forms of class struggle' (Harvey, 2000: 177). In inter-relation with the territorially variegated picture that emerges in terms of the differentiated attributes of physical and built environments necessary to the production and circulation of commodities, there also emerges a territorialised network of social infrastructures pertaining to the reproduction of capital in particular locations – what Harvey (1982: 399) terms 'the human resource complex'. These fulfil myriad functions, from the institutional regulation of inter-capitalist competition, to the means for producing new scientific knowledge; and from health, education, and social services systems to means of surveillance and repression. The particular urban forms that emerge are therefore produced and transformed in the course of capitalist development, the competitive struggle between capitals and national states, and the coercive imperative to ensure that past and future speculative capital investments in physical and social infrastructures are validated by the surplus value that flows back to an assortment of place-bound developers, creditors, landlords, and state institutions once capital has successfully valorised. In order to bring these general insights to bear upon the specific material bases for the last cycle of overaccumulation and crisis in Spain, certain key categories and processes first need to be explained in brief: the process of *capital switching* into the *secondary circuit of capital*; the co-ordinating role of *urban ground-rent* in capitalism; and the notion of *urban entrepreneurialism*. These will subsequently feature in our analysis of overaccumulation and urbanisation that follows.

The secondary circuit of capital and the switching of overaccumulated capital

Put simply, the secondary circuit of capital is 'the circuit comprising the built environment for production (e.g. infrastructure) and for consumption (e.g. housing)' (Aalbers, 2008: 149). 'Capital switching' refers to the periodic tendency for large magnitudes of overaccumulated capital with origins in the primary circuit of capital (in which surplus-value is produced) to be 'switched' as fictitious capital into speculative investments in the built environment; implying that intensified periods of urbanisation tend to presage full-blown crises (Harvey, 1982: 264–6 and Chapter 13).[3] Christophers (2011: 1351) has recently pointed to two means of identifying possible capital switching in process. The first step involves comparing combined productive investment with the contemporaneous trend in investment in the built environment. The second means is to examine financial institutions' investments into infrastructural assets as compared to the securities issued by industrial capitals. We examine both of these processes within the EU and Spain later in this chapter, arguing that overaccumulated capital – much of it from the European 'core' – was indeed switched into Spanish mortgage-backed markets and construction. In order to fully understand why and how this was the case, it is also necessary to consider the relation of capital switching into the secondary circuit and the profitable opportunities to be found in the appropriation of different forms of urban ground-rent in specific contexts.

The appropriation of urban ground-rent and the mobilisation of property as a financial asset

In Chapter 2, we briefly discussed the process through which the Marxian theory of rent as an appropriation of surplus value has provided a material basis for the historical development of national forms of accumulation in certain parts of the world (or the lack thereof, especially in Latin America). At the urban scale, ground-rent – and with it the land market – also plays a significant 'co-ordinating role' in channelling the investment of money capital into physical and social infrastructures – acting, therefore, as a 'catalytic forcing agent that reorganises the spatial configuration of accumulation according to the underlying imperatives of accumulation' (Harvey, 1982: 372).[4] In other words, the Marxian theory of rent can cast light on how the urban process, introduced previously, plays an integral role in the overaccumulation of capital, discussed for the most part as an essentially global and national phenomenon in preceding chapters of this book (see Leitner and Sheppard, 1989).

The theory of urban rent is complex and has been debated in considerable depth, but for our purposes it is sufficient to draw attention to two particular forms of urban rent that can, both separately and together, explain how surplus value produced in different branches of production – and outside Spain – was appropriated through accelerated accumulation in the Spanish construction sector and real estate market.[5] The first form is *absolute rent*. It is argued that the highly labour-intensive character of the labour process in the construction sector can yield extraordinary profits – even given the relatively low productivity growth in that sector and especially where planning regulations and landed property rights act as barriers to the equalisation of the rate of profit relative to other branches of production (see Bruegel, 1975; Fine, 1979 and 2010; Lauria, 1984). This insight, we will suggest, can help shed light on the concrete development of the Spanish construction industry in recent years, into which flowed a mass of cheap immigrant labour – providing part of the basis for the high profitability that encouraged speculative investment by landowners, developers, and city councils seeking to appropriate profits from accelerated increments in land prices. The second form is *monopoly rent*. Urban monopoly rents can arise in two, often intersecting, scenarios: first, indirectly, when 'social actors control some special quality resource, commodity, or location, which in relation to a certain kind of activity, enables them to extract monopoly rents from those desiring to use it' (Harvey, 2001: 395); and second, directly, when land itself is traded, such as through real estate investment speculating upon future values, denoting that it is the uniqueness of the site which forms the basis for an independently determined monopoly price.[6] Here, it is worth noting that *rentier* capitalists can look to appropriate urban monopoly rents in several ways: for example, by allowing property of a certain kind to deteriorate in order to create scarcity and eventually raise rents; by lobbying the local council to limit the amount of land zoned for a particular use; or by looking to enhance the desirability of certain locations (Leitner and Sheppard, 1989: 69).

Urban rent theory, and its constitutive analytical categories, explains how *rentier* capitalists perform a role in the appropriation of surplus value and therefore mediate the relation between the circulation of capital and the urban process:

> *Landowners* receive *rent, developers* receive *increments in rent* on the basis of improvements, *builders* can earn *profit of enterprise, financiers* provide money capital in return for *interest* at the same time as they can capitalize on any form of revenue accruing from the use of the built environment into *fictitious capital* (property price), and the *state* can use *taxes* (present or anticipated) as backing for investments which capital cannot or will not undertake but which nonetheless expand the basis for the circulation of capital. (Harvey, 1982: 395)

Moreover, the often speculative basis for the appropriation of surplus value through urban rents also connects the overaccumulation of capital in general with urban land markets and finance capital, through the concept of fictitious capital (see Chapter 1). As Harvey explains, when land is treated as a pure financial asset:

> the rent figures in [the buyer's] accounts as the interest on the money laid out on land purchase, and is in principle no different from similar investment in government debt, stocks and shares of enterprises, consumer debt and so on. The money laid out is interest-bearing capital in every case. The land becomes a form of fictitious capital, and the land market functions simply as a particular branch – albeit with some special characteristics – of the circulation of interest-bearing capital. Under such conditions the land is treated as a pure financial asset which is bought and sold according to the rent it yields. Like all such forms of fictitious capital, what is traded is a claim upon future revenues, which means a claim upon future profits from the use of the land.... (Harvey, 1982: 347)

In such a manner, 'property comes to be treated by all types of owners less for the uses that can be made from it, and more for the money that can be extracted from it' (Christophers, 2010: 98). The mobilisation of urban property and land as pure financial assets in this way 'takes place under the auspices of rampant speculation, artificially induced scarcities', and therefore, 'loses any pretence of having anything to do with the efficient organization of production and distribution' (Harvey, 1973: 190). Rather, urbanisation becomes an active moment in the tendency toward overaccumulation and crisis.

The local state and urban entrepreneurialism

Lauria (1984: 20) has shown how 'the channelling of capital from the state increases the property values or the potential ground rent; [and] this provides incentives for private development'. Haila (1988: 92) further reminds us that 'rent-maximizing behaviour is not alien even to the state and city authorities'; by acting in the role of the landowner, the local state can also seek to capitalise on rising land prices by raising the 'calculated shadow price of their landed property.' Thus, local state policies can directly impact upon rent levels, while new tax revenues can be capitalised out of rising land values. Rent-maximising behaviour on the part of the local state has gained added significance in recent decades, now that property titles have increasingly assumed the form of financial assets – 'the fully developed capitalist form of the mobilisation of land' (Swyngedouw, 2010: 315). This full development can be understood in relation to the global crises of overaccumluation in the 1970s and the subsequent deflationary response by national states that was reproduced at the urban scale. In the classic capitalist countries, this marked the end of an era of 'demand-side' urban governance, and therefore of 'the Keynesian city' – ushering in a transformation of the urban process (Harvey, 1985b: 211–2). Under such conditions as those which presented themselves to myriad cities as an 'external coercive power' from the 1970s onward, 'urban governance has ... become much more oriented to the provision of a "good business climate" and to the construction of all sorts of lures to bring capital into town' (Harvey, 1989: 11). Intensified inter-urban competition has resulted in a shift in the practice and ideology of urban governance toward, what Harvey terms, 'urban entrepreneurialism'. This, he summarises, typically rests 'on a public-private partnership focusing on investment and economic development with the speculative construction of place ... as its immediate ... goal' (Harvey, 1989: 8). And, in terms of the strategies pursued by the local state, it can be reduced to four basic options, as summarised in Box 4.1

Box 4.1   Supply-side strategies for urban competitiveness

In the aftermath of the crises and of the 1970s, Harvey suggests that many European and North American cities were faced with the problem of how to adapt to a 'supply-side world'. Harvey (1985b: 213–18; 1989: 8–10) outlines four possible options open to local and regional state institutions and 'urban growth coalitions' experiencing the effects of heightened competitive pressures to attract capital investment, deindustrialisation, and urban decay (although some mix of these might be viable for a given city):

1. *Competition within the spatial division of labour*: A city can either (a) invest in physical and social infrastructure, or subsidise inwardly relocating capital (ideally bringing with it competitive technologies); or (b) can seek to raise the rate of exploitation of the workforce under its command. Both strategies entail speculative risk, and may well incite working class resistance.
2. *Competition within the spatial division of consumption*: A city can attempt to capture surplus revenues from tourism and luxury

consumption. This entails gentrification and rebranding the city as culturally innovative, exciting, and creative. Such a strategy risks sacrificing value production for the sake of derivative revenues, will accelerate deindustrialisation, and therefore risks resistance from the local (now precarious) working class and the local rich who then have to subsidise the strategy through taxation.

3. *Competition for command functions*: A city can invest in improved communications, transport infrastructure, office space, and certain kinds of education provision (e.g., business schools) – the hope being 'to subsidise the location of command and control functions in the hope that the monopoly powers that reside therein will permit the subsidy to be recaptured through the appropriation of surplus value' (Harvey, 1985b: 217).

4. *Competition for redistribution*: A city can hope to attract significant sources of public funds. The example Harvey uses is the competition in the USA for military and defence contracts, and the 'spillover' effect successful competition has upon physical and social infrastructures in a given location.

Equipped with a theoretical understanding of the switching of overaccumulated capital into the urban process, we can now turn to the matter of providing a materialist account of urbanisation in Spain from the mid-1990s to 2008 that is consistent with the approach adopted in preceding chapters. In so doing we will endorse the argument, summarised in Swyngedouw (2010: 315), that the 'crisis starting in 2007 undoubtedly arose out of the extraordinary speculative carousel of increasing rents while turning these promises into fictitious capital assets through complex derivative financial instruments'. And we will add further substantiation to our claim, first made toward the end of Chapter 3, that the process of European 'integration' was nominal rather than real.

Capital switching and the Spanish covered bonds market

Between 2001 and 2009, productivity growth measured in terms of GDP per employee in Spain remained at 0 per cent or was negative (Corsetti et al., 2011: 16; Estrada, Jimeno and Malo de Molina, 2009: 24). As we highlighted in Chapter 3 and will explain in further detail next, growth was concentrated in labour-intensive, low-productivity sectors such as construction (see also Juamotte and Sodsriwiboon,

2010: 6). In the late 1990s, speculative portfolio investments into Spain had accounted for 3 per cent of GDP, but by 2006 they had reached almost 15 per cent of GDP. Meanwhile, net FDI inflows decreased dramatically, making it difficult for non-financial capitals to access credit from abroad (Cabrero, Maza and Yaniz, 2007: 2–3). In other words, and with Christophers' first means of identifying capital switching in process in mind, we can claim with some confidence that foreign investors were attracted not by the competitive potential of productive capitals in general in Spain, but by high profits to be gained through speculative investment in the Spanish real estate market in particular (Yaniz Igal, 2006: 3).[7] This claim is further substantiated if we examine the expansion of financial capitals' investment in the built environment in the 2000s.

In the 2000s, asset backed securitisation became a significant feature of international financial markets. As Sassen (2009: 419) explains of this form of investment, 'the more mortgages can be sold the better because this allows financial services firms to package them into instruments that cross the money threshold necessary to make them attractive to investors. These are mechanisms that contribute to the high value of mortgages to GDP in a growing number of countries'. By 2007, the total outstanding balance of Spanish mortgage market securities stood at €353.735 billion – 75 per cent of which corresponded to *cédulas hipotecarias* (Mayayo, 2007: 3). *Cédulas*, for short, are mortgage-covered bonds issued by multiple financial institutions that are secured against a pool of dedicated collateral. This method of 'club-funding' permitted smaller financial institutions such as regional savings banks and credit cooperatives to access international markets, backed by a pooled mortgage base. The club-funding model also earned a triple-A credit rating, making it a cheaper method of securing investment. Foreign investors bought approximately 62 per cent of these bonds in the 2000s (Avesani, García Pascual, and Ribakova, 2007: 12), and Spanish *cédulas* became one of the largest asset classes in the European Bond market and a crucial source of finance for the expanding mortgage market. By 2007, 137 so-called 'jumbo' *cédulas* had been issued by Spanish financial capitals, to a total value of €248.2 billion, representing the largest national share of the European jumbo covered bond market at 30.7 per cent (Sánchez-Pedreño, Kennaird, and Arranz Pumar, 2009: 3).

The *cédulas* functioned as the principal means of attracting inflows of fictitious capital from outside Spain, and especially from EU countries that had generated large surpluses under the terms of EMU 'convergence' (see Chapter 3; also Aparicio, 2004; Bellofiore, Garibaldo and

Halevi, 2010: 137).[8] In a report to the European Council and Parliament published in 2012, the EU Commission (2012: 49) confirmed that:

> The most important bilateral financial relationship in terms of net flows, in the years preceding the crisis, linked Germany and Spain, the two countries with the largest surplus and deficit in nominal terms. Also in terms of gross intra-euro area flows, capital exports from Germany to Spain were among the strongest ... Financing via the short-term interbank market played an important role, but Spain stands out among the deficit countries by its large portfolio debt inflows, mostly accounted for by the purchases of Spanish covered bonds (*Cédulas*) issued to finance the expansion in the housing market.[9]

García (2010: 969) confirms of the period 1998 to 2006 that

> private foreign investment fuelled the economy, especially the real estate sector.[10] As the construction industry, and then the tourist industry, gained a larger share of the market (11–12 per cent and 11 per cent respectively), economic growth and urban growth became practically synonymous.

She further highlights how the housing boom was built on the expansion of debt: mortgage debt amounted to 74 per cent of total household debt in Spain in 2010, while the expansion of financial credit to real estate developers that was permissible due to the inflow of capital from international markets into commercial and savings banks amounted to a 12 per cent increase between 1997 and 2007 (García, 2010: 970).

The bases for accelerated urbanisation in Spain after 1998

The Spanish housing boom that began in the late 1990s was not without historical precedent. Spain has experienced three major housing and land price booms since the 1950s. The first (1969 to 1974) was fuelled by public subsidies aimed at coping with rapid urbanisation and popular demands for housing,[11] remittances from family members working abroad, and the internal demand created by a booming tourism industry (see Chapter 2). High inflation and negative real interest rates after 1970 encouraged families to invest savings in homeownership (García, 2010: 971), with the result that Spain became a country with a high proportion of homeownership by European standards. This first boom came to an end at the onset of the global crisis of 1974. The second (1987 to 1991) came after the Moncloa Pacts and with the implementation of the

1981 Mortgage Market Law (Ley del Mercado Hipotecario), which was designed to promote homeownership, again, as a response to popular demands for affordable housing. The Law permitted previously excluded banks and other specialised credit institutions to enter the market and to compete with public mortgage banks and savings banks (see Asociación Hipotecaria Española, 2006). The money capital available for new mortgages was expanded through the first issuance of *cédulas*, with over 100,000 new mortgages (worth 282,000 million pesetas) issued in two years.[12] Then, in 1985, the 'Boyer reform' enacted measures to stimulate private consumption and investment, promote employment, and boost the construction sector (López and Rodríguez, 2010: 278). This reform liberalised prices and credit and provided further tax relief, which further incentivised homeownership (reaching 78 per cent of all households in Spain by 1991; Cabré and Módenes, 2004: 222). Finally, entry into the EEC in 1986 consolidated what López and Rodríguez (2011: 8) have argued was a path of 'growth by means of a financial and property asset-price bubble that would have a positive knock-on effect on domestic consumption and demand without any significant support from industrial expansion'. Nominal house prices rose by an annual average of 15 per cent, reaching a cumulative average increase of around 50 per cent in just four years (Yaniz Igal, 2006: 2). This boom was cut short by the ERM crisis, when three consecutive devaluations of the peseta, coupled with high interest rates, punctured the asset bubble and plunged the economy into recession (see Chapter 3).

While house price rises were huge in the late 1980s, the rate of new property construction was low in comparison to the boom period preceding the onset of crisis in 2008. The construction of new properties in Spain in this last boom (1997 to 2007) reflected a wider global trend which saw the flow of huge amounts of fictitious capital into real estate markets, through new mechanisms of financial engineering linked to the securitisation of mortgage debt (Foster, 2008; Sassen, 2009). The period saw speculative investment in new Spanish property construction raised to new heights. Of the 25 per cent increase in credit growth in 2006 alone, 15 per cent was related to housing, construction, and property development (Fernández de Lis and García Herrero, 2008: 3). But what were the material bases for accelerated accumulation in construction and property markets?

Downward pressure on interest rates

Spain's entry into the EMU saw interest rates fall significantly: between 2000 and 2007, nominal interest rates ranged between 2.3 and 4.1 per cent and in real terms between 0.9 and minus 1.1 (Estrada, Jimeno and Malo de Molina, 2009: 48). Considering that housing income tax reductions in Spain lowered the cost of borrowing by 2 per cent, there was in effect a subsidy on credit that led to an estimated 15 to 20 per cent increase in borrowing for housing and real estate markets (OECD, 2005: 3). From the mid-1990s until the last years of the boom, mortgage rates fell from 15 to 4 per cent per cent while repayment periods were extended to as much as 50 years (Fernández-Durán, 2006). Between 2002 and 2005, the increase in house prices peaked (at 16.6 per cent) as low mortgage rates fostered demand (European Mortgage Federation, 2012: 3). By 2006, housing prices were overvalued by as much as 35 per cent (García, 2010: 970).

The aggressive expansion of the *cajas de ahorros* (savings banks) beyond their traditional regional territories also increased competitive pressures to lower interest rates.[13] The *cajas* aimed to maximise short-term profits by offering developers 100 per cent leveraged loans for construction costs, fixing the rate of interest to the low inter-bank market rate of 0.3 per cent. This stimulated residential construction and increased the mortgage client base of the *cajas*, intensifying competition between themselves and other commercial banks, and doubling their market share in terms of total assets from 20 per cent in the 1980s to 40 per cent in the 2000s – albeit on the basis of an increasing reliance on wholesale markets, rather than domestic deposits, for financing (46 per cent by 2010; IMF, 2011: 9–12). In this context, commercial banks reformed their commercial policy and lowered the criteria for granting mortgage loans to individuals – compensating for competitive pressures on profitability by increasing the volume of lending. A so-called 'bank war' maintained the downward pressure on interest rates and further expanded consumer access to mortgages with longer amortization periods and for 100 per cent or more of the market value of properties (Bernardos Domínguez, 2009: 30), as banks sought to sustain accumulation at low interest rates by increasing the scale of lending.[14]

Land reform and the maximisation of urban ground-rent

The increase in land prices in the 2000s was, in part, stimulated by the 1998 Land Act (Ley del Suelo), implemented under the Aznar government. In principle, the new law was designed to make land cheaper and therefore housing more affordable by reforming planning restrictions to urban development (Samaniego, 1997). By increasing the level of building density per hectare and removing the 10 per cent levy owed to public authorities, it was projected that the legislation would reduce transaction costs and maximise returns to developers. The Act was developed in line with neo-classical economic modelling that saw the reduction of land scarcity and increased competition as means of eradicating 'artificial' monopoly pricing in housing and property markets (see Roca Cladera and Burns, 2000: 547).[15] However rents are socially constitutive of economic relations on the land, and the Act favoured landowners and developers who were in a strong position to maximise their appropriation of ground-rent (Roca Cladera and Burns, 2000: 552).

The new planning legislation intensified competition between developers. Legally, land could be valued according to its future use, meaning that prices were set speculatively and landowners could generate fresh sources of ground-rent. It has been estimated that in the six years since the Act was implemented, the average price of land in Spain increased by over 200 per cent (Martínez Hinojal, 2004). Many real estate developers aggressively expanded their asset base, buying up enough new land to develop 5 to 10 years of new housing stock (Smyth and Urban, 2013). The rapid commercialisation of new developments and the growing trend to sell off-plan generated a high turnover and fed further speculation in land and housing markets. Rising land prices then led to increasing house prices (Naredo, Carpintero and Marcos, 2007: 80). A study commissioned by BBVA (Uriel et al., 2009), and which examined housing stock and its territorial distribution in Spain from 1990 to 2007, found that house prices grew at an annual average of 8.4 per cent whereas average GDP for the same period grew at 4 per cent; that urbanised surface area grew 2 per cent per year whereas population growth was only 0.9 per cent; that the total market value of housing went from just under €1 billion in 1990 to over €5 billion by 2007; and that the market value of land grew by 20.7 per cent between 2000 and 2007.[16] In this, the opportunities for maximising the appropriation of ground-rent by landowners and developers were clear: between 1996 and 2004, the average return on the cost price of land in new housing construction grew from 7.7 per cent to 22.7 per cent; while, on average, developers netted 26 per cent of the final price of housing in 2004, compared with only 8.8 per cent in 1996 (Mayals and Iglesias Fernández, 2008: 51).

Contrary to the government's expectations, then, Spain had the highest level of new builds in all of Europe, suggesting abundant supply, but consistently increasing prices. An increasing supply was fuelled by inflated demand induced by the speculative real estate and housing bubble, a knock-on effect of which was the widespread conversion of industrial and agricultural land into residential land for the highest possible yield (Nogueira, 2005). This is consistent with Marxian theories of urban ground-rent: Edel (1992: 72) notes that, if real interest rates are low because inflation undercuts nominally high rates, the result may be either speculative construction (creating oversupply) or the speculative withholding of undeveloped land so as to generate monopoly rents (see also Harvey, 1982: 367–8). And this explains how the overproduction of housing stock deepened as the appropriation of rents through accelerated urbanisation gripped the Spanish economy.

The 'dotcom crisis' and the profitability of the Spanish housing market

A further crucial boon to investment in Spain's built environment came from the bursting of the so-called 'dotcom bubble' in 2000 (see Chapter 1). In the ensuing period, commercial property became further 'embedded in worldwide capital markets and [came to be] evaluated by these markets as a financial asset', a fact vividly demonstrated when investors wary of stocks and interest rates being slashed to historic lows quickly moved into investment in commercial real estate (Rutland, 2010: 1173). And in the wake of the crash, huge sums of money were diverted into international housing markets – to the extent that, as Foster (2008: 3) claims, a 'speculative bubble in the home mortgage market miraculously compensated for the bursting of the stock market bubble'.[17] Spain's residential construction and civil engineering industrial sectors were at this time attractive spheres for international investors taking refuge from the crash (Muñoz, 2001; González Pérez, 2010: 1577). Real increases in house prices, for example, had increased by 124 per cent since 1980, compared with European average of 19 per cent; and in 2001 alone the increase was some 11.4 per cent (*Economist*, 2002).

Immigration and tourism

Another basis for the expansion of residential construction in Spain, even in the context of declining productivity and competitiveness across other sectors, were the huge numbers of immigrant workers that arrived from the late 1990s. Spain was Europe's leading recipient of inward migration between 2000 and 2007, registering over 4.8 million immigrants in total and bringing the total foreign population in 2008 to 5.3 million (Domínguez-Mujica, Guerra-Talavera, and Parreño-Castellano, 2012: 2). As noted earlier, it has been suggested that the highly labour-intensive character of the labour process in construction is a source of absolute rent (for example, Fine, 2010: 106). At the height of the boom, immigrant labour accounted for approximately 30 per cent of direct employment by the construction sector – many in low-skilled jobs on temporary contracts (and disproportionately so compared with Spanish nationals; Meardi, Martín and Lozano Riera, 2012: 6, 10).[18] Wages for immigrants in construction were around 20 per cent lower than for nationals (Estrada, Jimeno and Malo de Molina, 2009: 29), lowering production costs and raising profitability even though it is a low productivity sector.

Inward migration was also significant in boosting demand for housing in the 2000s (Girard-Vasseur and Quignon, 2006: 4), as was the booming tourism sector. Unlike immigration, however, tourism continued to make a positive contribution to the state's current account and to provide compensation for structural trade imbalances that were exacerbated by the disproportionate expansion of non-tradable sectors in Spain.[19] In 2006, this sector alone accounted for 11 per cent of GDP and 11 per cent of direct employment (Suárez, 2010: 4; García, 2010: 969). The tourism sector similarly makes extensive use of cheap and unskilled labour – it is a significant source of real estate and infrastructure development demand, is a major consumer of non-traded goods and services, and also provides an important source of foreign exchange (Sastre-Jiménez, 2002; Cortés-Jiménez et al., 2009; Balaguer and Cantavella-Jordá, 2004). Residential tourism came in the form of the purchase of second homes by other EU countries' citizens (mainly British and German), especially in Mediterranean coastal areas (García, 2010: 973). This saw annual net foreign investment in housing range between 0.5 and 1 per cent of GDP between 1999 and 2007 (Fernández de Lis and García Herrero, 2008: 14). Tourism has therefore been a critical element of accelerated urbanisation.

Summary

Prior to 2008, overaccumulation related to the secondary circuit of capital deepened as *cajas* and commercial banks competed to finance developers' production in construction and the ability of individuals to buy property with cheap credit and lengthy mortgage amortisation periods. As we will see with reference to specific cities, developers, office-building firms, financial institutions, and local governments played a significant *rentier* role in increasing land prices and intensifying speculation. The Spanish construction sector became a magnet for investment from 1998, sending house and land prices soaring and further fuelling national and international speculation (González Pérez, 2010: 1577). Demand for second homes as investment vehicles rose rapidly, while increased aggregate demand created by new employment, including from newly arriving immigrant labour, compounded that of first time buyers.

The boom was unquestionably built on the expansion of credit, and, for many families in Spain, expanded consumption depended upon cashing in the equity from rising house prices (López, 2007: 219). The ratio of resident household debt to GDP in Spain grew from under 55 per cent in 2000 to over 90 per cent in 2010,[20] while estimated net household debt as a percentage of disposable income grew from 85.97 per cent in 2000 to 144.32 per cent in 2006 – almost 40 per cent greater than the eurozone average (OECD, 2008: 25, Figure 1.3). As is widely acknowledged, the disproportionate expansion of the construction sector relative to other sectors during the boom raised the price of non-tradable goods and reduced the competitiveness of exports, fuelling inflation and exacerbating the need to fund social consumption through the further expansion of credit. Overproduction in the construction sector was endemic: between 2001 and 2011, there was a 24 per cent increase in the housing stock (to more than 26 million homes), relative to just a 5.8 per cent increase in the population (to approximately 47 million inhabitants; Stücklin, 2013; see also García, 2010). Speculative leveraging in construction and the increase in household indebtedness that was by the state's admission 'significantly more than that of other peers' (Ministerio de Economía y Hacienda, 2011), therefore, fuelled the process of the overaccumulation of capital in Spain.[21]

The local state and urban entrepreneurialism in Spain

In the years following the transition to democracy in Spain, industrial restructuring and social austerity accompanied political decentralisation to the 17 Autonomous Communities. This coincided with the turn to urban entrepreneurialism across much of Europe and North America, as identified by Harvey. And, as Prytherch and Huntoon (2005: 42) suggest, 'no place better embodies this complex intersection of global restructuring and local politics as the Spanish regional city'. With the transformations outlined in Chapter 3, the 1980s saw the spatial diffusion of industrial activity toward the outskirts of major cities, leading to devaluations and decay in urban centres. Deindustrialisation therefore became an urban management issue, putting regeneration issues firmly on the agenda for many Spanish city councils from the 1990s. The mobilisation of land and real estate as financial assets, and as a means of appropriating urban monopoly rents, became a common local development strategy from the late 1990s – implicating the local state in Spain in the crisis-ridden processes of urbanisation and overaccumulation. In the circumstances outlined in the previous section, regional governments, city councils and local development agencies assumed an increasingly proactive *rentier* role as the construction boom took off. While Spain's 8,111 municipal councils have limited powers to raise taxes, they do control the granting of building permits and the re-sale of up to 10 per cent of public land, and, by 2005, almost 50 per cent of local authority revenues came from property-related income streams (Salmon, 2010: 47). In 2006 alone, Spanish municipal councils issued 911,000 building permits – more than those of Germany and the UK combined (Chislett, 2008: 21). The opportunity to appropriate revenues from accelerated urbanisation became an attractive possibility even in localities that were relatively isolated from metropolitan or tourist areas (López and Rodríguez, 2010: 333).[22]

Harvey stresses that specific cities may have pursued a mix of entrepreneurial strategies (Box 4.1), depending on their own material and historically developed attributes and capacities. The spatial concentration of Spain's internationally competitive telecommunications equipment (77 per cent) and defence electronics industries (59 per cent) in the capital city of Madrid, for example, can be explained by the national state's control of these industries until the 1980s (Rama, Ferguson and Melero, 2003: 76). The concentration and centralisation of capital in 'internationalised' firms in the 1990s, in which the national state took a proactive role (see Chapter 3), resulted in the majority of normal capitals of Spanish origin having their headquarters in Madrid by the mid-2000s – as well as the expansion of its stock exchange, the Bolsa de Madrid.[23] In addition, the capital attracted more than 50 per cent of all inward FDI in Spain between 2000 and 2005 (Rodríguez López, 2007a: 65). But the regional government also pursued an entrepreneurial *rentier* strategy from the late 1990s, undertaking large-scale urban redevelopment[24] – and investing directly, or facilitating private sector investment – in new infrastructures and a spate of new luxury hotels (Rodríguez López, 2007a: 86–8).[25] Other Spanish cities have pursued their own entrepreneurial strategies, albeit with a necessarily greater focus on capturing revenues from tourism and luxury consumption, given their relative weakness in terms of the competitiveness of their industrial and service economies. For instance, the regional government of the Basque Country ploughed investment into Bilbao in the late 1990s, setting the precedent for commissioning world famous architects to build 'iconic' buildings with the Frank Gehry-designed Guggenheim Museum (González Ceballos, 2005; Prytherch and Huntoon, 2005). This gave rise to the notion of a 'Guggenheim effect' in which such iconic developments were said to boost tourism economies. Another example is that of Palma, the largest city in the Balearics, where the city council reformed its General Urban Plan in 1998 and embarked upon a series of high-cost public-private initiatives to build so-called 'mega-projects' (Vives Miró, 2011).[26] This pattern was replicated across Spain's major regional urban centres. But the extent to which the local state came to play a significance *rentier* role during the boom is perhaps no more evident than in the cities of Barcelona and Valencia.

The Barcelona case

Barcelona, the capital city of the Autonomous Community of Catalonia, has been at the vanguard of entrepreneurial urbanism since its hosting of the 1992 Olympics (McNeill, 1999), and to the extent that the so-called 'Barcelona model' of urban transformation became an international reference point by the late 1990s (Garcia-Ramon and Albet, 2000).[27] Well over a decade ago, Harvey (2001: 405–7) had already criticised the entrepreneurial transformation of the city precisely for its 'amassing of symbolic capital and its accumulating of marks of distinction' in an attempt to generate monopoly rents as high revenues from consumption (most conspicuously from tourism) flowed through the city; the upshot being to overinflate property prices, to implicate Barcelona in the serial and homogenising replication of place (see Boyer, 1988) and to incite local opposition to gentrification and the destruction of sites of collective symbolic memory (see also Pascual-Molinas and Ribera-Fumaz, 2009). Urban redevelopment efforts since the late 1990s have concentrated on the district of Poblenou – a nineteenth-century manufacturing centre, commonly known as the 'Catalan Manchester' – which had suffered the effects of deindustrialisation and urban decay since the 1980s.[28] In 2000, Barcelona city council designated Poblenou a 'new knowledge district', re-branded it '22@Barcelona', and set about an ambitious project of urban regeneration – then, the largest of its kind in Europe (see Charnock and Ribera-Fumaz, 2011).[29]

Elsewhere, we highlight how the local state in Barcelona played a significant role in the speculative development of the 22@ project (Charnock, Purcell and Ribera-Fumaz, 2013). At its basis is a financing model that is dependent upon the generation and capture of revenues by the municipal company 22@bcn Inc., major real estate developers and private investment fund managers – a model that has been termed 'Value Capture Financing' (VCF; see Huxley, 2009). As we argue, VCF is precisely the kind of supply-side regeneration financing mechanism characteristic of entrepreneurial urban governance, in which the local state minimizes the debt it takes on for large-scale redevelopment while incentivising the private sector to make the bulk of the investment, enabling it to lay a claim a portion of anticipated future rents in return for facilitated access to public land. In the Barcelona case, the city council claimed between 10 and 30 per cent of planned developments, or the equivalent in monetary terms, and charged a levy of €80 per m^2 of land developed (a charge updated annually). In addition, the city council acted as a brokering agent between local institutions and financial capital, facilitating the switching of fictitious capital into the built environment.

As we detail elsewhere, in 2001 alone Barcelona received €800 million of investment in real estate – 70 per cent of which was of foreign origin at a time when international pension funds in particular targeted the office real estate market as a profitable opportunity for financial investment (*Europapress*, 2002). By 2006, investment in the Barcelona real estate market topped a record €1.627 billion (*El País*, 2006). In short, the city council along with real estate developers and finance capitals were able to manipulate the value of single large developments as direct sources of monopoly rents – fuelling the process of overproduction in the process.[30] However, demand for office space plummeted after the onset of the crisis in 2008, putting competitive pressures on rent levels. By 2011, 14.2 per cent of total office space was vacant, up from 10 per cent in 2010 and 7.7 per cent in 2009 (*El País*, 2011a). That year also saw a fall of 46 per cent on the yield of properties, as compared to the level reached in 2007 (*el Periódico*, 2011). Since the crisis began, the problems faced by two of the most prominent developers involved with 22@ have revealed the scale of debt leveraging by major Spanish construction firms during the boom. The promoter Habitat had acquired the real estate division of Ferrovial, the world's fourth largest infrastructure company, in 2006, and on the basis of leveraging €1.6 billion through a *cédula* involving the Barcelona-based savings bank La Caixa, the Institut Català de Finances (Catalan Finance Institute, or ICF), and the commercial banks Sabadell and Santander (*El País*, 2006). In 2008, Habitat failed to refinance its debt of €2.8 billion. In 2010, the Catalan construction firm Grupo Sacresa announced that it too was unable to meet repayments on its debt of €1.8 billion (*Cinco Días*, 2010). These insolvencies exposed the degree to which public institutions had assisted in the debt leveraging common to such capitals. The ICF, a public credit institution of the regional government, was exposed to the tune of €181.3 million by the Habitat and Sacresa crises alone – the equivalent of half of the total non-performing loans on its balance sheet when it was down-graded by Standard and Poor's in May 2012.[31]

The Valencia case

The Autonomous Community of Valencia was another pioneering entrepreneurial region, this time in terms of the liberalisation of planning regulations that facilitated speculative urbanisation (González Pérez, 2010: 1592). Its own Law for the Regulation of Urban Land, a forerunner of the Ley del Suelo, was passed in 1994. The reform separated legal property rights from development rights and, in so doing, removed the barrier of private ownership to the flow of capital on to the land but not the social basis of rents. In brief, it allowed public and private real estate and land development agencies to develop new infrastructure on lands under the terms of the 'public interest'. Landowners were reclassified as 'urbanising agents' (*agentes urbanizadores*) and, in return for co-financing production costs, were granted new concessions to develop land (Burriel de Orueta, 2008; Muñoz Gielen and Korthals Altes, 2007). Central to these developments were Integrated Action Plans (Planes de Actuación Integrada, or PAIs), which granted real estate companies greater flexibility to modify and adapt urban plans during a project to facilitate expansion in the city and around the urban fringe (Prytherch and Boira Maiques, 2009). There was an explosive growth of PAIs from the 1990s. Despite claims that they would increase real estate supply and thus reduce prices, development rights were granted to large real estate companies that were able to fix prices under monopoly conditions (Miranda Montero, 2007). Burriel de Orueta (2009) examined urban development in 100 municipalities in the Valencian region between 2004 and 2008 and reports chronic oversupply, exacerbated by speculative re-zoning. By 2006, 25 residential units per 1000 inhabitants were being produced – a rate five units higher than the national average and some 13 times greater than the rate in Germany (Prytherch and Boira Maiques, 2009: 113). In the province of Castellón, the rate was 65 per 1000 inhabitants.

The declining scale of industrial and agricultural production around the city of Valencia from the 1980s meant that residential tourism and the hosting of 'mega events' shaped urban development from the 1990s (Calatayud Giner, 2011).[32] The rent-seeking landed bourgeoisie realised that new rents could be appropriated through urban development – for example, through investment in the high speed AVE rail network – and also on the fringes of the city (Calatayud, Millán, and Cruz Romeo, 2002/3). The Ciutat de les Arts i de les Ciéncies, a science and entertainment complex, took centre stage in the Valencian regional government's entrepreneurial strategy for the city, into which they invested over a billion euros of financing (Prytherch, 2006: 203). Opened in 2000, and designed by the Valencian architect Santiago Calatrava, it epitomised the local state's ambition to compete with Barcelona, Bilbao, and Madrid through the high-cost development of iconic architecture and as a means of attracting tourism and further investment (Moix, 2010: 46; Prytherch and Huntoon, 2005: 47).[33] After this project came a string of high profile, speculative ventures spearheaded by the regional government: in the city of Valencia, a new port area including a harbour for super-yachts (which had to be financially rescued by the national state in March 2013) and an Opera House modelled on that of Sydney;[34] a new airport in Castellón;[35] and the Ciudad de la Luz film studio in Alicante. Many of these developments were facilitated by the local state using a version of VCF – or what has been termed 'Public Value Capturing' in the Valencian case (Muñoz Gielen and Tasan-Kok, 2010). Additionally, the regional government spent an estimated US$730 million on a street circuit as part of a seven-year deal to host Formula One racing (a deal which was not renewed in 2013); and, in 2007, it hosted the Americas Cup – the world's premier competitive sailing event (see del Romero Renau and Trudelle, 2011). To secure the latter, and in competition with Lisbon, Marseilles, and Naples, the regional government offered the Cup's organiser some €90 million, prime land to build a luxury hotel and new residential units, and a concession to develop the aforementioned port area (Miranda Montero, 2007: 721).[36]

The highly speculative character of local state investment in entrepreneurial ventures in Valencia is acutely visible in the current crisis. At the close of 2012, the Community's debt stood at over €20 billion – 19.9 per cent of regional GDP, second only to Catalonia (with debt worth 20.7 per cent of regional GDP).[37] On 20 July of that year, the regional government became the first in Spain to request assistance from the newly created Regional Liquidity Fund – in effect, a bailout worth €4.5 billion (*BBC News*, 2012).

Conclusion

The incredible expansion of fictitious capital and debt relating to the Spanish construction industry and real estate market was a result of the immanent tendency towards overproduction in capitalism – a tendency that was mediated by the particular material circumstances within

Spain that made these such profitable spheres for investment from 1997 and until the crisis of 2008. The *rentier* practices of landlords, capitalists, and local states in Spain – that were experiencing heightened competitive pressures on their own revenues and abilities to manage the urban effects of deindustrialisation and social fragmentation after the 1980s – only fuelled the process of overaccumulation that saw levels of speculative urbanisation and indebtedness raised to new heights in a country that was no stranger to housing booms and real estate bubbles. It is no wonder, then, that in the course of the devastating crisis that erupted in 2008, issues of fundamental importance to the reproduction of capitalists and workers alike have been focused politically upon the national state as guarantor of property rights and of the social power of money. It is to the political crisis of the state, therefore, to which we now turn.

5
The Limits to the State

The European South is mired in a profound crisis of overaccumulation – a reality that, sadly, demonstrates the veracity of the analysis provided in the preceding four chapters of this book. Thus far, we have located the development of capitalism in Spain within the crisis-ridden development of global capitalism, by providing an account of the material bases for successive cycles of overaccumulation and crisis since the Civil War. We now turn to the fallout from the last cycle of overaccumulation, expressed not only in the destructive devaluations of surplus capital but also in social and political crises. We return, in other words, to the forms of revolt that have been so conspicuous in Spain – and indeed across the European South – since 2008 (see Introduction).

In Chapter 1 of this book, we theorised the state in capitalism in processual, relation terms. The approach adopted in this book holds that 'the development of the capitalist state is processed in immediate form through social conflict and in mediated form through monetary constraints' (Bonefeld, 1993: 60). The immediate, *political* form of the state, in other words, is determined 'most particularly by the struggles of the working class which arise as the working class confronts the subordination of social production to capital as a barrier to its own physical and social reproduction' (Clarke, 1992: 136, also Clarke, 1990); whereas the mediated form of the national state is determined by its subordination to world money and the limits established by the global overaccumulation of capital. The state must constantly manage the contradiction between the need to secure the conditions for the expanded reproduction of capital, on the one hand, and the demands of capitalists and the working class to secure their own continued reproduction, on the other. But, and especially under EMU, states are committed to doing so without compromising the social power of money. In the current crisis, states in the European South are bound under the terms of convergence and of the Stability Pact to pursue a deflationary response to the crisis and to place the burden of readjustment squarely upon labour.[1] It has long been the case that should the working class refuse to acquiesce to their subordination to the social power of money – expressed through policies of state austerity, labour market reforms, and so on – what first appears as a crisis of money can threaten a *political crisis of the state* itself. Under EMU and in the current crisis, then, the contradictory constitution of the state has been revealed with stark clarity.

In this final chapter, we provide an account of the unfolding of the crisis of overaccumulation in Spain and the ensuing political crisis of the state. We first illustrate the depth of the crisis. We provide an account of the failure of successive governments to end recession and establish a stable basis for the reproduction of expanded accumulation since 2008 through the imposition of austerity and a policy of 'internal devaluation'. We then examine popular revolt against crisis management undertaken by the state, highlighting how these struggles have often targeted the form of the national state itself. Our examination is by no means exhaustive of all forms of political mobilisation that have emerged in Spain since 2008 (in 2012 alone, there were an estimated 36,000 different demonstrations across the country – almost 120 per day, according to *Europapress*, 2013). We simply focus on a couple of the most visible manifestations of struggle over the reproduction of the working class and against the state – namely, the broad-based 15-M movement commonly known as the *indignados* (the angry ones) and the anti-evictions movement centred around the Plataforma de Afectados por la Hipoteca (PAH). Finally, we examine the resurgence of nationalism in the crisis – focusing on the threat posed by the Catalan independence movement to the form of the Spanish national state.

The depth of the crisis in Spain

The onset of the global recession in 2007 exposed the contradictions of Spain's ten-year period of economic growth, built as it was upon the expansion of fictitious circuits of capital and debt. When the government could no longer finance a growing current account deficit (which went from a surplus of 1.9 per cent of GDP in 2007 to a deficit of 11.1 per cent by 2009) and banks could no longer raise sufficient quantities of cheap money to offer new mortgages, the so-called 'Spanish miracle' came to a sharp halt. The crisis intensified in Spain when German and French banks, in particular, began redirecting funds to their own national liabilities, exposing the Spanish banking system (García, 2010: 967).[2] The state was forced to provide public funds to the support the overexposed financial sector, thus transforming a so-called 'financial crisis' resulting from the expansion of private indebtedness and speculative investment in property markets (see Chapters 3 and 4) into a 'sovereign debt crisis' (see Burnham, 2011).

Within a year after the recession that began in the US reached Europe, all the signs were that Spain was implicated in a global downturn. The research department of the bank BBVA summed up the situation as follows:

> This downturn in the outlook for the world economy has meant an intensification of the adjustment process of the Spanish economy ... In this context, the deterioration observed in employment indicators during the last months of 2008 and the beginning of 2009 is especially worrying, with very negative effects on consumer and business confidence. The destruction of jobs has not just continued in the construction sector, but has also spread to other sectors of the economy which have been affected by the fall in international trade and by the climate of uncertainty. This general worsening of employment prospects, and its effect on families' disposable incomes has intensified the deleveraging process of the private sector, which has increased its savings out of precaution. The desire by households and corporations to reduce their debt levels has led to a significant drop in the demand for credit, leading to negative growth for the first time in many years. All these downward biases will lead to a 2.8 per cent decline in the Spanish economy in 2009. (BBVA, 2009: 2)

In the four to five years that have passed since this snapshot of an economy slipping into recession was published, the real depth of the crisis has been manifest in the levels of corporate and personal debt (see Chapter 3), the reported exposure of national and foreign banks to over-accumulation in construction and real estate markets, and the level of overproduction in the housing market in particular (see Chapter 4). It is estimated, for example, that 28,000 firms filed for bankruptcy between 2008 and 2013 – the bankruptcy rate reaching a record high for Spain early in the latter year (Cobos and Kane, 2013). And, in June 2013, it was reported by the National Institute of Statistics (INE) that, on average, house prices had fallen by 36 per cent since late 2007 – with the regional average in Catalonia reaching 45 per cent (to almost 50 per cent on second hand houses), and 43 per cent in the Community of Madrid (Pellicer Mateu, 2013).

The crisis has had a devastating impact on the Spanish economy and on the ability of the working class to guarantee the means of its reproduction (see Table 5.1). The impact on housing provision has been particularly severe – unsurprisingly so, perhaps, given that mortgage debt had been key to expanded consumption during the boom. In 2011 alone, there were an estimated 58,241 evictions in Spain due to home mortgage defaults (*el Economista*, 2012: 15); in 2012, the total fell to 39,167 – of which 15,227 were executed by court order.[3] In all, between 2008 and 2012, there were 172,000 evictions, with a further 178,000 still under judicial consideration (de Barrón, 2012). But the dramatic rise in unemployment is perhaps the starkest indicator of the depth and human cost of the crisis. By April 2013, unemployment in

Table 5.1   Economic indicators of the crisis in Spain (2007, 2010, and 2012)

	2007	2010	2012
GDP (2002 base = 100 per cent)[†]	105	99	97
Population (millions; 2001 = 40.5) [††]	45.2	47.0	46.7
Total unemployment (1000s) [††]	1,833	4,632	6,202*
Unemployment rate (percentage) [††]	8.26	20.06	27.2*
Public surplus/deficit (percentage of GDP) [†]	1.9	−9.7	−10.6
Public debt (percentage of GDP) [†]	36.3	61.5	84.2
Private debt (percentage of GDP) [†††]	311.13	336.34	323.23
Non-financial Institutions	131.5	142.5	130.7
Households	83.2	86.0	79.8
Financial Institutions**	96.43	107.84	112.73
Foreign private debt (percentage of GDP) [†††]	136.57	135.96	136.127
Gross capital formation (€millions) [†]	323,216	233,515	200,491
Cumulative fall (percentage)		−27.75	−37.97
Domestic demand (€millions) [†††***]	1,123,949	1,071,882	1,038,825
Cumulative fall (percentage)		−4.63	−7.57
Household savings/gross disposable income[†]	9.0	11.8	7.6
Employee remuneration as percentage of GDP[†††]	47.9	48.9	45.8
Gross operating surplus as percentage of GDP[†††]	41.9	42.1	46.1

Sources: [†] Eurostat (http://ec.europa.eu/eurostat); [††] INE (http://www.ine.es); [†††] Banco de España (http://www.bde.es/bde/es/areas/estadis/). All accessed 26 June 2013. * Data from first trimester 2013; ** Includes the sum of loans and securities on financial institutions' liabilities sheets; *** Data at June 2013 prices.

Spain reached a record high: over 6.2 million people, or more than 27 per cent of the population of working age (rising to 57 per cent for under-25s; INE, 2013: 5). As the crisis has developed, the profile of job destruction has broadened. The first jobs to go were those of younger workers on temporary employment contracts in or around the construction and services sectors – many of them immigrant labourers (Meardi, Martín and Lozano Riera, 2012: 12–13; Seminari d'economia Crítica TAIFA, 2010: 58–61).[4] More recently, however, higher-qualified workers with fixed-term contracts in hitherto 'protected' public sectors added to the rise. And even in the tourism sector, where numbers of tourists have continued to rise since 2008, the number of jobs in the sector has declined annually (Delgado, 2013).

The impact of the destruction of jobs across Spain brings into question the reproduction of the working class. Between 2011 and 2012, the average wealth of Spanish households declined by 18.4 per cent (*El País*, 2012b) and the real purchasing power of salaries fell by a further 2 per cent from 2012 to 2013 (Tremlett, 2013). By April 2013, 1.9 million households were un-waged (INE, 2013: 7) and 300,000 households depended upon grandparents' pension income (PCE, 2013). At the same time, around 3.2 million unemployed workers were receiving no unemployment benefit and 30 per cent of the active labour force had salaries below €1,000 a month (Gómez, 2013). In late 2012, 21.1 per cent of the population were reported to be at risk of poverty (INE, 2012a), with Oxfam warning that this could rise to as much as 38 per cent of the population in the coming decade (Intermón Oxfam, 2012).

From a 'financial' to a 'sovereign debt crisis': Austerity and the imposition of 'internal devaluation'

On 11 July 2012, the President of Spain, Mariano Rajoy, announced a three-point hike in value added tax (VAT) – to 21 per cent. His defence of this measure was reminiscent of that given by the Greek Prime Minister George Papandreou when revealing a three-year austerity package in May 2010 (see Introduction): 'The Spanish people cannot choose whether to make sacrifices or not. We do not have this liberty' (Rajoy quoted in Cué, 2012). In Chapter 3 of this book, we argued that the logic of subsidiarity at the heart of EMU is one that seeks to guarantee that member states cannot resort to inflationary means of adjusting to competitive pressures. Eurozone states cannot, of course, undertake monetary devaluations – as has been the Spanish state's historical response to successive crises (Seminari d'economia Crítica TAIFA, 2010: 64). The only possible means of 'adjustment' is to lower labour costs and to enhance the profitability of their own territorially segmented labour markets. By design, EMU assigns the working classes of Europe to a 'role as a readily adjustable, competitive factor of production', resting upon the solidarity of member states 'against working class aspirations for jobs, wages, and conditions – a solidarity for market freedom, founded on European market enabling law and money' (Bonefeld, 2012b: 55). This much has been demonstrated in the course of the crisis that has unfolded since 2007, and, in which, eurozone member states have sought to impose austerity upon their respective working classes, in the common aims of engineering fiscal consolidation and securing price stability.

The beginning of austerity in Spain can be pinpointed to May 2010 (Estefanía, 2013) – some 33 months or so after the so-called 'sub-prime crisis' in the US that initiated a series of coordinated measures by North American and European states to alleviate a 'credit crunch' through the lowering of interest rates, expansion of the money supply, and introduction of emergency fiscal stimulus packages. In March 2008, the PSOE was elected to a second term in government (led by José Luis Rodríguez Zapatero), which spent much of its first months in office denying that the Spanish economy was vulnerable to what increasingly appeared to be a crisis of global scope. The prevailing but naïve argument at that time was that strong banking regulations had prevented Spanish banks from risky 'sub-prime' lending and that its bank system was therefore more robust to the threat of 'contagion' (Fernández-Villaverde and Ohanian, 2010; Lopéz and Rodríguez, 2010: 404).[5] When the PSOE announced a programme of 24 economic reforms in August 2008, including lowering taxes, it maintained that Spain's position was still strong. The mood began to change over subsequent months, however. By mid-2009, Spain was officially in recession, unemployment was on the rise, and the extent of Spanish banks' exposure to speculative urbanisation was becoming apparent.[6] Among other measures gathered together under the expansionist Spanish Plan for Economic Stimulus and Employment (the so-called 'Plan E'), the Zapatero government moved to create a fund worth €50 billion to shore up the financial system and to guarantee a further €200 billion of debt emission over two years (Royo, 2009b: 30).[7]

This was followed, in June 2009, by the launch of the Fund for the Orderly Restructuring of Banks (Fondo de Reestructuración Ordenada Bancaria, or FROB), to which the Bank of Spain allocated €9 billion, with a view to leveraging up to a further €99 billion in international markets (Seminari d'economia Crítica TAIFA, 2010: 68).[8] These measures meant that by June 2009 the Spanish state had directed 2 per cent of GDP to shore up the exposed financial sector – the highest level of public investment of this kind among OECD countries (double that of Ireland, four times more than in the US, and six times that of the UK; Lopéz and Rodríguez, 2010: 401). Spain's public deficit as percentage of GDP plummeted from a 1.92 per cent surplus in 2007 to an 11.2 per cent deficit in just two years (Estefanía, 2013), thereby transforming what first appeared as a 'financial crisis' into a 'sovereign debt crisis'. In early 2010, the Zapatero government duly began preparing its austerity plans and, in May, announced public spending cuts amounting to €15 billion over two years (*Economist*, 2010b).

Spanish elections were brought forward by the Zapatero government to November 2011 in a bid to secure a mandate to implement the programme of cuts, as well as reforms to the pensions system (although Zapatero himself did not run for office). In the preceding months, and in return for its buying of Spanish government bonds in secondary financial markets, the ECB stepped up pressure on the Spanish government to press on with structural reforms – placing emphasis on the need for labour market reforms, the removal of inflation-linked wage rises, further cuts, and reforms to energy and housing rental markets (Gómez, 2011). Furthermore, and in agreement with the main opposition party (the PP), the government reformed Article 135 of the Constitution to limit the Spanish national state's and Autonomous Communities' 'structural deficit' – setting the maximum target to 0.4 per cent of GDP by 2020 (Aizpeolea, 2011).[9]

Shortly after the election of Rajoy's PP government to office in the 2011 elections, a further spate of public spending cuts were announced along with a hike in taxes. In adherence to ECB recommendations, the aim was to reduce the state's fiscal burden by €150 billion or 15 per cent of annual GDP by the end of 2014 – with €8.9 billion worth of public spending cuts in the first trimester of 2012 alone (Benoit, 2012; Cué, 2011). Meanwhile, the crisis in Spain's banking sector intensified. In May 2012, the state was forced to part-nationalise Bankia – Spain's fourth largest bank, which was exposed to the tune of €30 billion to abandoned construction projects and repossessions – in a €4.5 billion bailout (Tremlett, 2012b). A month later, the government approached the EU for a €100 billion rescue package for its banking system. Strict conditionalities were laid down by the EU, and in July, the Rajoy government announced a further combination of cuts and tax increases worth €65 billion – including the aforementioned hike in VAT. The Asset Management Company for Assets Arising from Bank Restructuring (known as Sareb or 'the bad bank' – '*el banco malo*') was also established as part of the agreement with the EU for bailout funds (FROB, 2012). Banks such as Bankia, Banco de Valencia, and CatalunyaCaixa were forced to transfer their 'toxic' real estate assets to Sareb at reduced prices. By March 2013, Sareb's portfolio consisted of 200,000 assets worth an estimated €50.45 billion, including 76,000 empty homes; 6,300 rented homes; 14,900 plots of land; and 84,300 loans (Buck, 2013a) – a portfolio it is charged with divesting over a 15-year period.

In between the announcement of the late 2011 and July 2012 austerity plans, the Spanish state passed the country's most comprehensive labour market reforms since the 1970s. These included a series of measures designed to restore competitiveness by means of so-called 'internal devaluation' – namely, in this case, by increasing flexibilisation (the ease of hiring and firing), reducing severance pay, and allowing individual firms to set wage levels independently of industry-wide collective agreements (see Dolado, 2012).[10] By 2013, and as a consequence of these reforms, Spain was the only large eurozone country where unit labour costs were lower than they were in 2009 (Gordon, 2013), with the rate of year-on-year labour cost reductions set at 1 per cent (Banco de España, 2013). Whereas a real exchange rate devaluation would see a fall in the value of debt denominated in the national currency, and also provide a boon to the competitiveness of capitals with export capacity, internal devaluation transfers the burden of 'adjustment' to crisis directly onto the back of the working class.

Unsurprisingly, then, Spain has witnessed an increase in industrial unrest and strike action. According to the Spanish Ministry of Employment, there was a 2.6 per cent increase in the number of days lost to strikes in between 2011 and 2012 (to a total of 1.3 million).[11] The year 2012 saw the CC.OO and the UGT call two general strikes across Spain – the first in May and a second in November, coordinated to coincide with Europe-wide strikes and demonstrations.[12] In July 2012, coalminers from the Asturias and Leon regions attracted global media attention by walking up to 250 miles to Madrid in order to protest against public spending and subsidy cuts in the mining sector (*Guardian*, 2012b). The miners' protests were but one short-lived yet emblematic manifestation of a widespread rejection of austerity, and of mass protest movements that have targeted the national and local state, but also the EU. However, the most vivid expression of mass revolt came on 15 May 2011, with the dramatic events associated with the move-ment of the *indignados*: the 'historical beginning of a new wave of social and political conflict' (Espinosa Pino, 2013: 228).

Indignation: A generalised condition

The *indignados* movement in Spain was born out of the action of ¡Democracia Real YA! (Real Democracy Now! or DRY), an Internet-based social movement created by activists opposed to a 2011 law on intellectual property rights.[13] Through a new social media network and small local platforms, demonstrations were planned to take place in 57 cities across Spain on 15 May 2011. The protests attracted many other social movements and sympathetic citizens. According to police data, some 130,000 people demonstrated across Spain on 15 May – including 15,000 in Barcelona and 20,000 in Madrid (Anduiza, Martín, and Mateos, 2012: 2). Hundreds of protestors took the initiative to occupy and set up encampments in major urban squares, such as Madrid's Puerta del Sol and Barcelona's Plaça de Catalunya, attracting the attention of the world's media. Days later, an estimated 60,000 defied a ban on protests in the run up to regional and municipal elections and to join the '15-M' movement in protest marches in a number of cities against austerity cuts, a high unemployment rate (with youth unemployment then at 41 per cent), and the predictable dominance of the main Spanish politi-cal parties in the elections (Tremlett, 2011). Subsequently, on 19 June, the 15-M movement was central in the mobilisation of more than 250,000 people (75,000 in Barcelona and 38,000 in Madrid) in protest against the 'euro-Plus Pact' (Anduiza, Martín and Mateos, 2012: 2) – a series of crisis management measures that committed all 17 members of the eurozone to meeting 'specific deficit, revenue and expenditure targets' and to several areas of 'structural reform' such as labour markets (aimed at lowering unit labour costs and standardising so-called 'flexi-curity' in all signatory countries) and pension reforms (including raising the standard age of retirement; European Council, 2011).[14] Then, on 15 October 2011, an estimated half a million people joined protests in Madrid to coincide with a 'global day of action'. This culminated in the occupation of the vacant Hotel Madrid close to Puerta del Sol and, what Abellán, Sequera, and Janoschka (2012) see as a moment in which the movement broadened its 'repertoire of civil disobedience toward ques-tions of urban politics and property rights' – highlighting the extent to which the mortgage debt crisis was becoming a focal political issue (a matter to which we return in the discussions to follow).[15]

The movements involved in the 2011 protests made it clear that they understood what the crisis meant for them, and most sought to attribute blame to what they saw as a corrupt and self-aggrandising alliance political elite (*'la clase política'*) that was at the beck and call of bankers. While the active 15-M movement was largely composed of university-age young people, a June 2011 survey estimated that almost 80 per cent of Spaniards thought the criticisms expressed by the movement were justified (cited in Calvo, Gómez-Pastrana, and Mena, 2011: 5). The slogan of the organisation Juventud SIN Futuro (Youth Without a Future) certainly encapsulated the mood among young *indignados*, warning that they foresaw a future 'WITHOUT A HOUSE, WITHOUT WORK, WITHOUT A PENSION', but therefore, 'WITHOUT FEAR'.[16] For its part, DRY proclaimed:

> We are the unemployed, the poorly remunerated, the subcontracted, the precarious, the young ... we want change and a dignified future. We are fed up with antisocial reforms, those that leave us unemployed, those with which the bankers that have provoked the crisis raise our mortgages or take our homes, those laws that they impose upon us that limit our liberty for the benefit of the powerful. We accuse the political economic and economic powers for our precarious situation and we demand a change of direction.[17]

At the very least, the *indignados* movement expressed widespread popular rejection of traditional parties and political elites at the national and local scale in Spain (Hughes, 2011: 413). For some, the 'anti-political' character of the movement (Castañeda, 2012: 310) – and the refusal to vote in the 2011 elections by many *indignados* – was in itself a significant political statement; while, for others, it raised questions about the political potency of the movement (see Espinosa Pino, 2013: 231).[18] For Taibo (2013), it is possible to distinguish between two divergent positions within the *indignados* movement. On the one hand, there is a *'ciudadanista'* ('citizenist') position that seeks to advance a reformist agenda and to deal with what it identifies as immediate political barriers to dealing with the crisis (see also Espinosa Pino, 2013: 239).[19] On the other hand, there is also a distinctively 'anti-system' position that is more willing to question capitalism and to experiment with novel forms of autonomous forms of self-organisation – as illustrated in the use of public assemblies and the various occupations of vacant properties (Castañeda, 2012). And, while the popular media has largely reported that the movement has lost momentum since 2012,[20] other commentators have noted the extent to which the movement has led to a proliferation of initiatives that reflect the 're-politicisation of society' (Sánchez, 2012) – from campaigns against police impunity and precarious forms of employment to the establishment of new Internet-based political parties, neighbourhood cooperatives, and social centres (Iñaki Oliden, Requena Aguilar, and Luis Sánchez, 2013). For Ainger (2013), on-going protests and forms of collective action against austerity that have emerged in the months and years immediately following 15 May 2011 represent the transformation of indignation toward a 'generalised condition'.[21] The *indignados* created a space in which the 'culture of transition' in Spain could be publicly debated (Martínez, ed., 2012), and serious questions could be asked about previously sacrosanct institutions: namely, about the form of the national state and the supposed benefits of European integration. And without this opening, it is hardly conceivable that we might have witnessed the rise and popular backing of mobilisations that have since challenged the subordination of the reproduction of the working class to money and law, such as the PAH (Plataforma de Afectados por la Hipoteca).

The 'stop *desahucios*' campaign and the struggle against money and law

The action of the PAH, in particular, represents perhaps the starkest manifestation of how the crisis of overaccumulation and of speculative urbanisation, as discussed in Chapter 4, has led to a crisis of the reproduction of the working class in Spain – and with it the new forms of political action that are challenging property rights, law, and money. Under Spanish law, a homeowner remains liable for mortgage loan even after foreclosure and eviction. In short, Spanish banks can seize land and properties as assets in the event of a mortgage payment default, but the homeowner retains the debt. In addition, banks also have the right to collect a percentage of a working debtor's income at source. Many evicted individuals and families therefore remain indebted to the very financial institutions that channelled fictitious capital into the real estate market (see Chapter 4). In 2012, the number of homeless people in Spain rose to 22,938 – approximately 2,776 were due to evictions (INE, 2012b: 4) – in a country with a vacant housing stock of 5.6 million units (García Lamarca, 2013).

The PAH was formed in Barcelona on 22 February 2009 with the aim of increasing public awareness of the growing number of evictions and of the aforementioned 'juridical anomaly' (Colau and Alemany, 2012: 31) but gained prominence as a significant component of the 15-M movement in 2011. By 2012, there were more than 70 active *plataformas* across Spain (Colau and Alemany, 2012: 100). In November 2010, PAH activists physically prevented an eviction order from being executed in Tarragona, Catalonia, by blocking the entrance to the foreclosed property with a 'human shield'. As of June 2013, the PAH had successfully prevented a total of 720 evictions in this manner throughout Spain,[22] often encountering 'heavy-handed' policing in the process.[23] The PAH has expanded its repertoire of action over time to include the re-housing of recently evicted and homeless families in vacant properties owned by savings banks, under the banner of *'Obra Social PAH'* ('PAH's Social Work').[24] Once evicted and homeless families have been installed, the PAH has then sought to negotiate affordable rental agreements with the savings bank in question. Meanwhile, in 2013 the PAH stepped up its strategy of occupying bank premises as a means of protest and disruption.[25]

Since its inception, the PAH has demanded reforms that challenge the legal status quo that allows banks to profit from 'what, in the words of David Harvey, constitutes a clear example of accumulation by dispossession' (Colau and Alemany, 2012: 144, our translation).[26] For example, they have demanded that homeowners unable to pay their mortgages be allowed to 'walk away', free of debt, and that homeowners be allowed to cede ownership to mortgage providers in return for rental payments worth no more than 30 per cent of their monthly income (*El País*, 2011b). The PAH has been very critical of the formation of Sareb – the 'bad bank' – condemning its divestment mission as a state-orchestrated 'socialisation of the losses' incurred by the banking system in the crisis (Colau and Alemany, 2012: 71). And in 2012, the PAH collected over 1.4 million signatures in support of a Popular Legislative Initiative (Iniciativa Legislativa Populara), as permitted under the Spanish Constitution. The proposals contained in the Initiative included the introduction of *'dación en pago'* – the ability for homeowners to use assets in lieu of mortgage payments; a moratorium on all mortgage-related evictions; and that the state seizes empty homes owned by the banks involved in the FROB and transforms them into low-rent social housing.[27]

The PAH's activities represent a concrete and symbolic challenge to property rights and to the rule of law in Spain. Whatever the outcome of the PAH's campaigns, it has confronted the state as the guarantor of the subordination of social reproduction to the power of money in the current crisis.

The Catalan question and the challenge to the Estado de las Autonomías

In 2012, the Autonomous Community of Catalonia was home to over 7.5 million people and 16.2 per cent of the Spanish labour market. The region accounted for 19.8 per cent of national GDP and 2.2 per cent of that of the eurozone. Its GDP per capita was 18.8 per cent above the EU average and 22 per cent higher than the country as a whole.[28] But the region had been hit badly by the crisis. In 2012, the unemployment rate was 22.7 per cent, with youth unemployment at 50.7 per cent; while unit labour costs had decreased by 3.3 per cent in 2010 and 2.9 per cent in 2011 (a faster rate than the national average and 14.5 times faster than the EU average in 2011). The debt of the Generalitat de Catalunya (the regional government) stood at 25.9 per cent of GDP – some €50.95 billion by the end of 2012 – meaning that in order to meet the 0.7 per cent structural deficit target set by the national government in 2013, the Generalitat would have to introduce further spending cuts worth €4.4 billion (Catalan News Agency, 2013). Yet, under a decentralised welfare state (see Gallego and Subirats, 2012) and the fiscal regime of the Estado de las Autonomías (State of the Autonomies) that redistributes regional tax income,[29] it was estimated in 2012 that Catalonia continued to transfer outward up to €17.5 billion annually (around 8–9 per cent of GDP) to pay for services and investments in other regions (Catalan News Agency, 2013). The crisis has therefore prompted 'significant reappraisals of the structure of the welfare state in Spain' (Gallego and Subirats, 2012: 287) in the form of a resurgent 'administrative nationalism' (CV, 2012b), and especially so in Catalonia.[30]

As the crisis unfolded since 2008, popular discontent in Catalonia with 'fiscal asymmetry' (Ruiz Almendral, 2004) has mounted, to the extent that many of its inhabitants support a secessionist challenge to the current form of the Estado de las Autonomías. Already, between 2009 and 2011, more than half of the region's 947 municipalities had held non-official referenda on Catalan independence (Muñoz and Guinjoan, 2012: 45), galvanising supporters of secession across the region. Then, according to police data, as many as 1.5 million people marched through Barcelona on 11 September, the national day of Catalonia, in support of independence (Baquero and Márquez Daniel, 2012). This was easily the largest demonstration in the city since the transition to democracy in the late 1970s.[31] Two weeks later, the regional president and leader of the nationalist Convergència i Unió (CiU) coalition, Artur Mas, dissolved the Catalan Parliament and brought regional elections forward to that November. Mas claimed that the region's debt crisis would be insurmountable without first offering the Catalan people the opportunity to give the Generalitat a mandate to pursue independence from Spain (*El País*, 2012c). The CiU failed to win an outright majority, but parties committed to holding a referendum on independence in 2014 dominated the new Parliament. According to Santamaría (2012: 11), support for independence came mainly from a squeezed Catalan 'middle class' that had been re-politicised since the onset of crisis and the 15-M movement, while the 'high bourgeoisie' and 'working class' remained distrustful of the secessionist project. An October 2012 poll estimated that 74 per cent of Catalans were in favour of a referendum on independence (cited in Rodon, 2012: 145), while a July 2011 survey found that 45.9 per cent of respondents favoured secession from Spain (cited in Serrano, 2013a: 3).

The independence movement in Catalonia represents a fundamental challenge to the form of the Spanish national state as established in the 1978 Constitution and subsequently reconfigured along 'recentralised' lines after accession to the EEC and, later, EMU (see Bullain, 2013). There has been much debate, within and outside the region, regarding the economic feasibility of an independent Catalan national state (in support, see Antràs and Ventura, 2012; Becker and Posner, 2012; Galí, 2013; and Serrano, 2013b). Most secessionists advocate an independent Catalonia *within the framework of EMU* (Galí, 2013). In the event of secession, this would entail a formal application to be admitted to EMU – a lengthy and complex process that would bring 'significant transition costs', even assuming that trade between Spain and Catalonia were unaffected, according to a report by JP Morgan Chase Bank (2012: 3; also see de Carreras, 2012). The Bank's researchers estimate that independence within the EU would actually only yield a 3 per cent improvement in the new state's fiscal position, at best (and it is worth recalling that, in 2012 and 2013, the Generalitat required two bailouts from the Spanish state together totalling €14.5 billion – see Buck, 2013b).

Few commentaries on Catalan independence acknowledge that secession is no defence against immediate pressures to impose state austerity and internal devaluation, given that any government committed to EMU convergence and accession would have to refuse the possibility of monetary devaluation as a strategy to alleviate the effects of the crisis. In the interregnum between secession and formal re-entry into EMU, a new Catalan state would have to pursue a monetary policy based on a version of 'dollarisation' – the continued use of the euro or pegging of a new Catalan currency to it (in effect, '*eurización*'). In such a scenario, the new state would make itself vulnerable to overvaluation, monetary instability, and inflation (Polo, 2013). In short, secession within the EMU would provide no easy exit route out of present or future crises of overaccumulation. Significantly, the JP Morgan Chase Bank report also concludes that, should the Generalitat secure a greater degree of autonomy for the Catalan state even within the Estado de Autonomías, there would be serious implications for not only the Spanish national state but also the wider eurozone:

> Should Catalonia be able to renegotiate the terms of its relationship with the centre in a way which limits fiscal transfers this would have an impact on the Spanish central government's fiscal path. It would also set a further precedent, which would have an impact on Madrid's ability to control the other 16 regions, the wealthier of which may also be encouraged to request greater fiscal freedoms. This would pile further pressure on the sovereign if, as is likely, it is the transferring regions would choose to renegotiate the terms of their relationship with the centre. More broadly, this opens a larger political question for the euro area as a whole; namely, that if Catalonia is unprepared to subsidise Spain's poorer regions, why should Germany or other countries of the European north? (JP Morgan Chase Bank, 2012: 4)

Conclusion

A national economy that is reproduced through the expanded consumption of imports over the production of exports, has stagnant or deteriorating productivity, but which grows at an annual average rate of 4.4 per cent for almost ten years can do so only on the basis of debt (see Chapter 3).[32] The cycle of growth in Spain prior to 2008 rested upon huge inflows of fictitious capital – speculative investment that was switched into the then particularly profitable construction sector and real estate market in Spain (see Chapter 4). Once profitability was brought into question, such investments were revealed for what they truly are: speculative claims on the future production of surplus value. Investment ceased, money capital was withdrawn from circulation, and crisis ensued. As we write this book, more than five years after the onset of severe recession in Spain, the crisis endures. Fears abound regarding the future of EMU amid high unemployment and social unrest across the eurozone, and not just in the South (see, for example, Elliott, 2013).

Bonefeld (2012a: 446) writes that 'the struggle against austerity is a struggle for the basic provision of human needs: housing, food, heating, clothing, and also for the time of affection and love. It is a struggle for existence'. As such, the struggle can take a variety of forms. The *indignados*, the PAH, and Catalan secessionism all express responses to the fallout from the crisis and the struggle against imposed devaluations aimed at re-confining capital accumulation within the limits of profitability. In a crisis, such forms of revolt inevitably confront the state acting in its immediate role as guarantor of the subordination of social production and reproduction to capital and the social power of money. That these mobilisations often lack a cohesive, all-encompassing political agenda or manifesto, or appear ideologically contradictory, is to be expected. This is especially the case given the explosive character of revolt – when, as if from nowhere, indignant masses take to the streets and threaten a political crisis of the state. On 15 May 2011, we witnessed such an explosion in Spain. For some, the air has now cleared to reveal only a residue of small, inchoate, and disparate movements with relatively little momentum (Etxezarreta and Ribera-Fumaz, 2012). Yet it is also clear that the events of 15 May 2011 represented a mass political awakening in a society that, since the end of fascist rule, had placed a good deal of blind faith in the benign promise of liberal democratic governance and European integration.[33]

Conclusion

Marx's theory of crisis has not lost any of its veracity. The necessity of crisis is, and will always be, an integral feature of the capitalist form of social reproduction.

In this form of social reproduction, the production and circulation of capital is the general fundamental process which gives unity to privately performed social labour. Capital, as we saw in Chapter 1, is self-valorising value: 'it can only be grasped as a movement, and not as a static thing' (Marx, 1978: 185). The substance of value is human labour, but, in value producing society, this social content appears in and through the fetishised relationship between things. The unity of social labour therefore assumes the form of an impersonal and indirect relation between independent and private producers whom themselves are differentiated by capital into social classes.

In capitalism, therefore, social production and reproduction are subordinated to the anonymous rule of money – the most developed, independent form of value, and that which confronts direct producers in the form of capital. The reproduction of capital requires that an increasing magnitude of surplus value be pumped out of living labour. The production of (relative) surplus value is therefore the immanent content that determines the transformations associated with the development of the forces of production; a process which is mediated by the competitive relations between different capitals, which, in turn, results in the uneven material development of the forces of production on a world scale, and its spatial corollary in uneven geographical development.

The production of relative surplus value and the reproduction of capital is an inherently global process, albeit one that is politically mediated by national states. That the accumulation process is one that is predicated upon antagonistic class relations means that the state must take an active role in processing these relations. As Clarke (1988: 18–19) elsewhere summarises:

> The class character of the state, embodied in its liberal form, requires it to secure the reproduction of capital. The national form of the state requires it to express, politically and ideologically, the national interest, against all particular interests. The reproduction of the state requires it to resolve this contradiction. The contradiction appears to the state in the form of the social and political aspirations of the working class, to which it has to respond within the limits of its form, confining the working class within the form of the wage and the constitutional form of the state. The admission of the working class to the constitution on a national basis increases the pressure on the state to secure the sustained accumulation of domestic productive capital. However this constraint introduces a further contradiction, between the national form of state and the global character of capital accumulation.

The preceding chapters of this book have presented an account of the development of capitalism in Spain, drawing upon these more general and abstract insights into the contradictions of the value form, capital accumulation, and the state. Our intention has not been to provide an historical account for its own sake, but to demonstrate how past crises of accumulation and the state in Spain have prefigured the bases for subsequent cycles of overaccumulation and crisis. The current crisis that began in 2008 and in which most of the world's advanced economies are still mired cannot simply be put down to contingent or exogenous shocks to an otherwise efficiently functioning market system. To attribute blame for the crisis by explaining it in terms of human frailty, poor regulatory design, institutional failure, the influence of particular ideas, the avarice of bankers, and political elites, or certain national-cultural traits is one-sided at best; dogmatic and racist at worst. Make no mistake; this crisis is a crisis of the value relation, of the global overaccumluation of capital and of the state as the political concentration of a capitalistically constituted society. To substantiate this assertion, we have provided a materialist account of the Spanish state's successive and crisis-ridden attempts to confine social production and the reproduction of the working class within the limits of capital by subordinating these to the rule of money and law by various means; always in the midst of the production of uneven geographical development and the differentiated accumulation capacities of particular states and regions across Europe and on a world scale. Let us recap.

The limits to capital in Spain

Chapters 2 and 3 of this book examined the development of the national form of capitalist production in Spain – focusing upon the period immediately following the Civil War. In the 1940s, capital accumulation in Spain was barely sustainable. Agriculture and industry were backward in world market terms, and much of what remained of the war weary Spanish population was reduced to surviving at subsistence levels. Politically isolated and with limited means of securing foreign aid and revenue in international markets, the fascist state had to take a proactive role in centralising and concentrating capital and thereby in securing a more viable means of social reproduction and its own survival. The state established the INI, which oversaw the establishment of new industrial capitals producing solely for the domestic market, and under the protection associated with ISI. By the 1950s, the drive toward industrialisation was having a transformative effect on Spanish society. There were, however, limits to sustained accumulation on the basis of ISI. Whereas in Latin American countries, where the capture of an extraordinary magnitude of ground-rent has periodically sustained accumulation through ISI (and still does to this day in countries such as Argentina), growth in Spain in the 1950s was sustained largely on the basis of wage repression – the payment of labour-power below its value. Yet even this failed to deliver profits to Spanish capitals and therefore denied the state its own means of reproduction.

In 1959, the Spanish state was confronted with severe balance of payment problems and a credit crisis that expressed the limits to ISI. Yet, and fortunately for the fascist state, developments in Western Europe provided means of recovery and of averting a more assertive crisis of ISI. First, the take-off of the mass tourism industry permitted the state to capture an extraordinary flow of revenue. Second, a marked rise in the emigration of Spanish workers to Western European labour markets led to a high volume of remittances – a portion of which was captured by the state. These two sources of external revenue underpinned rising domestic demand and sustained the expanded reproduction of capital in Spain for most of the 1960s. By the close of the decade, however, the state was confronted with rising inflation and further pressures on its balance of payments. The state was therefore forced to relax restrictions on foreign capitals' involvement in production and to permit the inflow of FDI into key sectors of production – mainly in the form of patents and technologies that were already obsolete outside of Spain's protected domestic market.

By 1974, tourism and remittance revenues fell sharply as Europe descended into recession, exposing the fragility of production restricted to the scale of the domestic market. The Spanish state's response was both repressive and inflationary as it struggled to confine the aspirations of an increasingly militant working class. In the years immediately following the 1974 crisis, the world market stagnated and fell into deeper recession. National states throughout the world were confronted with the need to re-confine production and social reproduction within the limits of the market. By 1978, the fascist form of state gave way to a liberal democratic form that was able to secure the cooperation of the main trade unions as it confronted further recession. After the election of the PSOE in 1982, the state pursued an aggressive deflationary strategy – assisted at first by trade unions' acceptance of wage restraint – and embarked upon a programme of state austerity and 'industrial reconversion' which resulted in mass unemployment and the widescale destruction of obsolete capital. This period marked the acceleration of a process that had begun with the relaxation of protectionism in some sectors and most emblematically with the establishment of the Ford Motor Company's manufacturing plant in Valencia in the mid-1970s: namely, Spain's full insertion into the NIDL. From the late 1960s, organisation and technological transformations in the system of machinofacture – toward what some have termed 'systemofacture' – together with developments in transport and communications systems meant that capital could relocate production around the world in order to benefit from cheaper production costs. By the 1980s, Spain had become a profitable source of cheap and readily exploitable labour that could be quickly adapted to new work processes, and which offered geographical proximity to what would soon be a single European market.

The recovery that came in the late 1980s was marked by contradictions that have been fundamental in the subsequent course of accumulation and crisis in Spain. Industrial reconversion and the arrival of foreign capitals into Spain encouraged the fragmentation of the working class: a sizable proportion of which was forced to find work in low-wage, 'flexible' production by an increasing mass of small industrial capitals; while relatively higher wage production in large assembly plants remained a domain for the manufacture of export commodities of low to intermediate technological content by world market standards. On this basis, rates of profit and employment recovered post-1985, but at the expense of rising inflation and growing tensions between the state and the unions. The state sought to curb inflation and to moderate wage increases through entry into the ERM in 1989. The strategy only encouraged capital to flow speculatively into more profitable 'non-tradable' sectors that were heavily dependent upon rising domestic demand, thereby bypassing other manufacturing sectors and accelerating a process of overaccumulation that resulted in monetary crisis by 1992 and the onset of the deepest recession in Spain since the early 1960s.

In 1999, Spain qualified for EMU convergence under the terms of the Maastricht Treaty. By then, the economy was in recovery and *en route* to a growth boom that lasted until 2008. During this period, certain 'national champions' that emerged as a result of the liberal democratic state's own proactive role in the concentration and centralisation of capital in the late 1980s were in a strong competitive position to secure a stable basis for their valorisation in foreign markets – particularly in Latin America – and to 'internationalise'. A select number of Spanish capitals became a globally competitive force in banking, telecommunications, and energy production sectors. Yet, behind the boom, fundamental weaknesses in social production remained within Spain – a result of the uneven development of the productive forces as the more dynamic and internationally competitive normal capitals left behind a domestic manufacturing sector that still exhibited the traits of the late 1980s: low productivity and a dependency upon foreign capital that set limits to the organisation and technological development of the productive forces in all but a few sectors. Entry into EMU therefore consolidated Spain's differentiated and relatively 'backward' position within the NIDL and further compounded the production of uneven development both within the national economy as well as relative to other regions and countries within Europe.

In Chapter 4, we necessarily broadened the focus of our analysis to consider the national process of accumulation during the last Spanish boom in its proper global context. Of crucial importance to understanding how expanded accumulation and rising levels of social consumption could be sustained on a scale well beyond the production of surplus-value by Spanish capitals was the confluence of material bases that made investment in Spanish construction and real estate markets particularly profitable spheres for the recycling of fictitious capital of largely foreign origin. Surplus capital from Germany, in particular, flowed into Spain via the latter's highly competitive covered bond market to be subsequently channelled by regional savings banks into the mortgage market. A huge volume of interest-bearing capital from the 'core' flowed into speculative overproduction in the Spanish construction sector, incentivised by low interest rates, reforms to planning laws that removed barriers to the flow of speculative capital into new urbanisation projects, the availability of low cost, largely immigrant labour power in the labour-intensive construction industry, and rising demand for infrastructure, hotels and second homes associated with mass tourism. Meanwhile, local development agencies and city councils across Spain embarked upon supply-side, 'entrepreneurial' strategies associated with inter-urban competition within the spatial division of consumption. Local state initiatives to incentivise private sector participation in urban development projects in cities such as Barcelona and Valencia were highly speculative and premised upon future anticipated returns from the rapid construction of infrastructure, housing, and office real estate.

The massive speculation in housing and urban development fuelled the expansion of social consumption in Spain prior to 2008, but it also accelerated the overaccumulation of capital. The collapse of leading investment banks in the US marked the onset of a global recession, in which the future profitability of past investments in housing and urban development could not be guaranteed. After 2008, the construction industry all but collapsed prompting a sharp increase in unemployment, depressing consumption and ushering in the devaluation of residential real estate by a third over within five years. As covered in our Introduction, the fallout for Spain's banking sectors has been significant, necessitating a state-led 'recapitalisation' funded by a €100 billion bail-out package from the EU in 2012. In return for bailout funds, the Spanish state has rolled out successive austerity programmes in a desperate bid to assure its creditors that it will meet the EU's 'structural deficit' target by 2014.

In 2013, unemployment reached its highest rate since records began in the 1970s, and average household disposable income had dropped by 10 per cent since 2008 (Tremlett, 2013). In these five years, the threat to the reproduction of the working class led to a series of high profile national and regional struggles over issues such as public sector cuts, proposals to reform labour market legislation, forced property evictions and political corruption. The movement of the 15 May 2011 (the *indignados*) marked the repoliticisation of Spanish society and, with it, the end of a 'culture of transition'. The people of Spain began to question and to challenge the liberal-democratic state and the purpose of EMU. As we write, the PAH, specifically, continues to challenge the state of money and law by means of physically preventing evictions executed under court order, initiating popular reforms to legislation regulating mortgage foreclosures, and illegally installing evicted families in vacant properties owned by Spanish savings banks. The Catalan independence movement represents a different, nationalist, response to crisis and austerity. All of these express the on-going struggle against state austerity and the subordination of social reproduction to the accumulation of capital and the rule of money.

European Monetary Union and the limits to capital in the European South

A central theme that has emerged in our analysis of crisis and revolt in Spain concerns the class character of European integration. EMU especially, is 'conceived as a disciplinary mechanism that encourages "competition" on the basis of disinflation and increased labour productivity' – an offensive device 'that seeks to make the European working class work harder in the face of deteriorating conditions' (Bonefeld, 1998: PE-55). Our analysis of the development of capitalism in Spain before and after 2008 substantiates this claim. But it is equally as valid with reference to other countries across the European South.

Behind the rhetoric of 'convergence', 'integration' and 'union', EMU has exacerbated the uneven development of capitalism within Europe. Because some Southern European countries entered EMU with higher nominal exchange rates, the absolute reduction in trade costs due to open market access disproportionately benefitted the Northern member states (Hadjimichalis, 2011: 261). After EMU, the ECB's commitment to maintaining low price inflation also served to hamper export competitiveness in countries with relatively lower industrial productivity levels. This was expressed in growing trade and current account deficits across the European South.

In the years prior to EMU, a persistent current account deficit would threaten the quality of money circulating in a national economy, leading to speculative pressures from international markets and to periodic devaluations by central banks confronting balance of payments crises. The 1992 ERM crisis was a vivid example of this in Europe (see Chapter 3). However, in the euro system national central banks 'had no need to accumulate stocks of foreign currencies to maintain their membership of the euro area and so the issue of current account imbalances largely disappeared from macroeconomic discussions' (Whelan, 2012: 5). Meanwhile, between 2000 and 2007, unit labour costs increased sharply across the European South, and at a much faster rate than in 'core' EU member states (Cambridge Econometrics, 2011: 10), compounding losses in competitiveness. For many mainstream analysts, the current crisis has revealed the negligence of Southern states in controlling labour costs and reforming obstructive labour market legislation and institutions. However, the relatively high cost of production in the South was an expression of the inability of backward capitals in these national economies 'to increase productivity at levels bridging productivity discrepancy between them and their German or other core European rivals' (Vlachou, 2012: 187). In this scenario, economic growth and the expansion of social consumption across the European South was possible only through the expansion of corporate and household debt.[1] The cycle of post-EMU growth rested upon the accelerated inflow of fictitious capital into the European South, encouraged by low interest rates, expanding social consumption on the basis of debt, and the profitability of key non-tradable sectors in countries like Spain.[2]

As a result of EMU, then, the higher productivity eurozone 'core' generated huge trade surpluses (EU Commission, 2012). The eurozone as a whole has maintained a current account balance with the rest of the world since EMU. However, significant variations in the current accounts of eurozone member states have seen Austria, Belgium, Finland, the Netherlands, and especially, Germany run significant surpluses; while Greece, Ireland, Portugal, and Spain ran deficits from the mid-2000s (Uxó, Paúl, and Febrero, 2010 and 2012; Whelan, 2012). In 2007, on the eve of the crisis, the Greek state reported a current account deficit of 13.6 per cent, in Ireland 4.9 per cent, in Portugal 11.1, and in Spain 9.5, whereas the German state registered a surplus of 7.5 per cent of GDP (Eurostat, 2012b).

Today, the European South is undoubtedly bearing the brunt of a crisis of European 'integration' and of the fallout from a pronounced cycle of the global overaccumulation of capital. In this context, some would like to see current account 'imbalances' redressed by means of the 'surplus' countries taking a proactive role in stimulating domestic demand by ending wage moderation and relaxing their commitment to price stability (for example, Uxó, Paúl, and Febrero, 2010: 590). Others have tabled a more radical solution and advocate withdrawal from the eurozone so that national currencies might be reintroduced and monetary devaluations undertaken.[3] Yet the ability to depreciate 'national' money does not guarantee any national state an exit from the uneven development of the productive forces within and across national economies, from cycles of the global overaccumulation of capital, and therefore from the necessity of crisis.[4] And with respect to the European South, it will not guarantee a fundamental restructuring of the economy away from a longstanding dependency upon inflows of foreign capital in the form of tourism or debt, or toward high productivity and globally competitive manufacturing.[5]

State austerity in the European South – and resistance to it – looks set to continue for some time yet. Clarke (1990: 195) assures us that

> the form of the state is such that if the political class struggle goes beyond the boundaries set by the expanded reproduction of capital, the result will not be the supersession of the capitalist mode of production but its breakdown, and with it the breakdown of the material reproduction of society.

This is the very real problem that faces much of the European South today as the state's efforts to impose austerity as a means of securing 'fiscal consolidation' confronts the struggle of the working class to resist 'internal devaluation' and to guarantee the means of its own reproduction. The transformation to a world society whose reproduction is no longer subordinated to the accumulation of capital remains an urgent necessity, and one that can only be born out of the fully conscious struggle of the international working class. The European South will therefore be a crucial laboratory for anti-capitalist politics and critical imaginaries.

Notes

Introduction

1. Spain's rate of annual growth was bettered only by Ireland in this period, with both countries reflecting a wider trend within the EU: 'for a decade, 1995–2005, the countries of Europe's "South" (Spain, France, Greece, Ireland, Italy, Portugal) had growth rates almost one per cent higher than the countries of the "North" (Germany, Austria, Belgium, Finland, the Netherlands)' (Husson, 2012: 331).
2. By late 2010, the OECD (2010) had already reported youth unemployment in Spain (then at 40.7 per cent) to be 22.2 per cent above the OECD average.
3. The rate of unemployment in the eurozone as a whole in June 2013 was 12.2 per cent, with youth unemployment then at 24.4 per cent (Elliott, 2013; Allen, 2013).
4. As the German Chancellor, Angela Merkel, told the Bundestag during a debate on the Greek bailout: 'This is about nothing less than the future of Europe and the future of Germany in Europe' (quoted in *Deutsche Welle*, 2010).
5. By 2007, Irish banks' liabilities were the equivalent of 75 per cent of GDP (*World Policy Journal*, 2011). Much of these were connected to speculative investment in the construction sector.
6. By June 2012, unemployment had more than doubled in Ireland from its pre-crisis level, to reach 14.8 per cent – the third highest rate in the EU after Spain and Greece at that time (Halpin, 2012).
7. Matsaganis (2012: 413) estimated that by the end of 2012 income losses in Greece had pushed 30 per cent of the population below the pre-crisis poverty line in terms of purchasing power.
8. The fifth eurozone bailout would come in March 2013, when the Troika agreed a €10 billion bank recapitalization package with Cyprus (worth some 57.1 per cent of GDP).
9. Italy's national debt stood at 130 per cent of GDP in early 2013; unemployment stood at 11 per cent, with youth unemployment at 36 per cent (*Economist*, 2013a).
10. Both sets of accusations have sometimes been tinged with casual racism and prejudice – from the widespread use of objectionable acronyms as a shorthand for these countries, to the stereotyping comments made on 17 May 2011 by the German Chancellor to a meeting of the Christian Democratic Union party: 'It is also important that people in countries like Greece, Spain and Portugal are not able to retire earlier than in Germany – that everyone exerts themselves equally … We can't have a common currency where some get lots of vacation time and others very little' (quoted in *Spiegel Online*, 2011). The speech was widely criticised, not least for being factually spurious (for example, Böil and Böcking, 2011).

11. See, for example, a speech made by Lorenzo Bini Smaghi (2009), then on the Executive Board of the ECB and now a Harvard University Professor of Economics: '... it's human nature to drive fast, over the limit. So accidents are inevitable. You can only try to make them less serious by fitting stronger brakes in cars, or by giving them airbags or by improving the roads. This analogy is frequently used to explain the financial crisis and to suggest that since we can't really avoid new crises, we should rather try to reduce their impact and enhance our defences by having tougher regulations and more effective supervisory mechanisms ... We know what the solution to this problem is – more regulation ... It took the high inflation of the 1970s to convince the political authorities that monetary policy should be implemented by independent central banks. It would be better not to 'waste' another crisis to come to the same conclusion for financial stability'.

12. On the confinement of human social practice to the mere execution of 'objective' economic laws in capitalism – including 'adjustments' undertaken under the 'necessity' of austerity in times of crisis – see Bonefeld (2000; 2012a).

13. Here, we are paraphrasing a passage from Marx's *Theories of Surplus Value* (1861–3):

> In the crises of the world market, the contradictions and antagonisms of bourgeois production are strikingly revealed. Instead of investigating the nature of the conflicting elements which erupt in the catastrophe, the apologists content themselves with denying the catastrophe itself and insisting, in the face of its regular and periodic recurrence, that if production were carried on according to the textbooks, crises would never occur. Thus the apologetics consist in the falsification of the simplest economic relations, and particularly in clinging to the concept of unity in the face of contradiction (http://www.marxists.org/archive/marx/works/1863/theories-surplus-value/ch17.htm, date accessed 3 July 2013).

14. This is certainly the case within the US academy – to the extent that Cammack (2007; 2011) has argued that most American IPE 'cannot identify, let alone address, the questions posed by the issue of global economic interdependence today' (2011: 166; see also Burnham, 1994).

1   The Limits to Capital

1. Marx discusses the natural limits to the production of absolute surplus value and the historical establishment of a normal working day in England in chapter 10 of *Capital*, Volume One (1976).

2. 'When the various instruments of labour are produced as commodities, exchanged as commodities, productively consumed within a work process given over to surplus value production and, at the end of their useful life, replaced by new commodities, they become, in Marx's lexicon, *fixed capital*' (Harvey, 1982: 205). Fixed capital therefore takes the material form of plant, equipment, and the physical infrastructures of surplus value production.

3. Harvey (1982: 187) clarifies his own concept: '[T]he credit system provides the mechanism to reduce different turnover times to a common basis, and ... this "common basis" is the rate of interest ... [T]he market processes surrounding money itself (in particular, that part of the money market called the capital market) reduce diverse concrete production processes with their specific and often highly idiosyncratic time requirements to a standard socially necessary turnover time'.

4. Marx (1981) argues that the appropriation of surplus value is also the basis for the accumulation of ground-rent, as discussed in further detail in Chapters 2 and 4.

5. See Clarke (1988: 107–10) and Harvey (1982: 300–5) for representations of the accumulation cycle through its successive phases (stagnation, recovery, credit-based expansion, speculative fever, and the crash).

6. In the preceding account, we have followed Clarke (1990/1, 1994) and Heinrich (2012, 2013) in downplaying the significance attached to the 'tendency for the rate of profit to fall' in some readings of Marx's theory of crisis in capitalism. Several heterodox analyses of the development of capitalism in Spain do rely heavily upon tracing trends in the rate of profit (for example, Cámara Izquierdo, 2007; Román, 1971 and 2002). These will be drawn upon in Chapter 2 but only insofar as they allow us to make empirical observations about successive cycles of accumulation from the 1950s onwards. Similarly, although we discuss the contradiction between the reduced scale of production in Spain, on the one hand, and the expanding scale of social consumption, on the other, in Chapters 3 and 4, we see this as a necessary expression of the limited development of the forces of production in Spain within the new international division of labour and the uneven development of European integration.

7. Bonefeld (1992: 105) adds that 'the term "mediation" is of vital importance here since it connotes the mode of existence of a dynamic relation of antagonism which allows antagonistic relations to exist side by side'.

8. This insight is not explicitly conceptualised by Marx, but is developed as an extension of Marx's writings in, for example, Bonefeld (2000).

9. This is because the national state is a differentiated, particular form of the general social relation in capitalism. This insight also explains why in this book we discuss global economic transformations in terms of the difference-in-unity of the (new) international division of labour, rather than in terms of the 'internationalisation' of production which tends to confuse the result of transformations within the global system of surplus-value production with the 'conscious' strategies of transnational corporations (TNCS). Both the national state and TNCs *mediate* the underlying material unity of the global process of capital accumulation in their competitive relations with other national states and capitals (see Starosta, 2010a).

10. Inflation brings the possibility of centralising and socialising devaluation so that the process of overaccumulation can be attenuated and its impact spread across society (see Harvey, 1982: 307–11). However, Harvey points out that inflation also tends to refocus the class struggle in terms of the real wage and against the state's management of monetary and fiscal policy. Ultimately, Harvey explains how inflation can only ever stave off a crisis of overaccumulation while making its likely impact more destructive – an

argument supported by Bonefeld (1996a: 199–200). Clarke (1988: 144–5) similarly explains that, while 'inflationism' has proven attractive to opportunistic politicians historically, inflation 'threatens to provoke domestic industrial and political conflict as it erodes wages and devalues *rentier* capital, and to provoke speculation against the currency. The limits of the ability of the state to resolve the crisis by such expansionary means appear in the form of the political conflicts unleashed by escalating inflation, on the one hand, and the financial pressures of a deteriorating external position, on the other'. This more general observation will have resonance in the particular experience of Spain, as discussed in Chapters 2 and 3.

11. On the global turn to monetarism from the late 1970s, and the failure of such a deflationary strategy to restore accumulation on a less periodically destructive basis, see Bonefeld (1996b) and Clarke (2001).

12. Marx (1981: 257) defines the 'price of production' of a commodity as 'its cost price plus the percentage profit added to it in accordance with the general rate of profit, its cost price plus the average profit'. In value theory, prices of production therefore act as 'centres of gravity regulating the movement of (actual) market prices' (Guerrero, 2003: 77–8). For a discussion of the relation between value, market values formed in competition, prices of production, and the formation of an equalised rate of profit within and between sectors of production, see Fine (1979: 242–5).

13. In accordance with the Marxian notion of capital-as-process, and of the concentration of capitals, Iñigo Carrera (2008) uses the Spanish word '*monto*' ('amount' or 'discrete magnitude') for 'size'. As Starosta (2010b: 445) clarifies, 'at first sight, some small capitals can be impressively "big". The point is that they nonetheless do not reach the specific magnitude needed to be turned into normal capitals'.

14. The Marxian theory of value therefore exposes one of conventional economic theory's most enduring myths concerning the 'entrepreneur': the latter 'idealises firms in ways that never existed and fetishises the small-scale enterprise, which lacks any degree of monopolistic market power, as the ideal agent for achieving competitive equilibrium. Hence has arisen an unjustified association between small scale of organisation and competitiveness' (Harvey, 1982: 144).

15. Iñigo Carrera (2008: 59) coins the term 'classical' to refer to those countries in which capital accumulation has historically taken 'a concrete form that most immediately reflects the unity of its essential determinations' (our translation), and in which the production process has in general been undertaken by industrial capitals of average, or normal, concentration. We discuss the contrasting form of capital accumulation in late industrialising countries in Chapter 2.

16. For Marx, the 'real subsumption of labour to capital' (Marx, 1976: 1034) that is the content of the development of large-scale industry and the system of machinofacture contrasts with that of simple manufacturing insofar as the rhythm of the labour process is thenceforth dictated by the machine rather than by the worker (with all the implications for alienation, de-skilling, and class struggle that brings) (see Marx, 1976: Chapter 15). This aspect of the critique of political economy is of fundamental

importance to the approach developed in Iñigo Carrera (2008) – see Chapter 2 of this book.

17. 'Keynesianism' refers to the ideology that accompanied forms of state management oriented towards expanding domestic markets, maintaining full employment, and raising wages, welfare benefits and public spending – all of which denoted a crisis-ridden strategy of expansionism as a means of containing working class demands within the limits of capital accumulation (see Clarke, 1988).

18. Iñigo Carrera (2008, chapter 2) gives a general overview of the content of this reconfiguration of the international division of labour since the 1970s. He outlines an increased differentiation of national processes of capital accumulation on the basis of a threefold fragmentation of the global labour force into concentrations of (a) workers of advanced productive subjectivity involved in scientific and technological development, (b) workers of degraded productive subjectivity involved in direct production in automated and computer-integrated machinofacture or manual assembly, and (c) an expanding pool of consolidated surplus labour that cannot be absorbed in production. This process, he argues, is the real content of the NIDL as determined by the valorisation of global capital as a whole – that which is missing from descriptive literatures on the emergence of global commodity and value chains (for example, Alcorta, 1999; Cattaneo, Gereffi, and Staritz, 2010; Kaplinsky, 1989; Schaeffer and Mack, 1997).

19. Both of these developments have been conspicuously characteristic of manufacturing in Spain since the period of industrial restructuring in the 1980s (see Chapter 3).

20. For data on the rate of profit in the US, see Duménil and Lévy (2011: 58) and Iñigo Carrera (2008: 223). See Duménil and Lévy (2004: 24) for comparative data on the US and Europe as far as 2000.

21. Iñigo Carrera (2008: 223–8) uses data on the US to show that the 1982 crisis did not result in a destruction of capital of a sufficient magnitude to restore the material unity between social production and consumption.

22. Bonefeld (1996b) cites the example of the UK, where, according to Keagan (1989: 53), personal financial liabilities rose from 45 per cent of gross income to 81.3 per cent by 1987.

23. The US endured a sluggish recovery from 1991, while in the UK the recession lasted until 1993 (at that time, the longest since the 1930s).

24. Walker (2006: 119) reports that the stock value of the region's 500 largest public corporations almost tripled to US$3.5 trillion in 1999 alone, while the NASDAQ itself doubled.

25. The trend towards increased indebtedness actually accelerated during this last cycle, because of the low level of interest rates prevailing in the world markets since 2000 (see Grinberg, 2007).

26. See the comparative international data in Iñigo Carrera (2008: 84–5, 92–3).

27. At this point, we would distance our argument from those which locate the roots of the current crisis in the process of so-called 'financialisation' (see, for example, Lapavitsas, 2009a and 2009b). In our analysis, the quantitative expansion of fictitious capital in recent decades has been an expression of the general tendency towards overproduction, not its cause (see also Fine, 2010).

2 The Limits to Import Substitution Industrialisation

1. In Marx, the transformation of surplus value into ground-rent assumes two forms: differential ground-rent (DRI and DRII) and absolute ground-rent (AR). DR derives from the individual private monopolies over land in the same sector with differentially favorable natural conditions (Marx, 1981: 779–87). Lands that raise productivity – as a result of either differential fertility/location (DRI) or of greater applications of capital to lands of the same quality (DRII) – and which thereby lower individual production costs below prevailing market norms, are extremely attractive to capital. Competition to access these lands can be capitalized by landowners into higher rental prices, allowing the landlord to capture extraordinary profits in the form of DR. AR is based upon Marx's argument that because of the relatively higher content of living labour embodied in them, the value of agricultural products can be higher than their price. And, because of the institution of private property, this difference is not equalized across sectors of the economy. Therefore, even on marginal lands for which there is solvent demand, a rent must be paid. This can take the social form of monopoly power and allows commercial prices to be set further above prevailing market norms to include a rent that must be paid by the capitalist to access a privately owned non-reproducible natural resource – a 'monopoly rent'. AR will be discussed again, together with monopoly rent, in Chapter 4 of this book.
2. This represents an interesting historical example of what is now a key element of state development strategies in the Americas (see Phillips, 2009).
3. A full Marxian theorisation of the relation between rents and industry during this transitional period for Spain, and indeed for what was to become the capitalist world market, is beyond the scope of this chapter. If we were to attempt this, we might start with some of the pointers provided by Harvey (1985b: 103–8).
4. As an interesting point of international comparison, even the share of Spanish exports of industrial goods and commercial goods to Latin America before the break-up of the Hapsburg Empire in 1808 contrasted sharply with those of the British economy toward its colonies between 1688 and 1815 (O'Brien and Prados de la Escosura, 1998: 44).
5. Rosés (2003: 996) reports that, by 1910, 'Catalonia and the Basque Country accounted for over 61 per cent of total employment in metallurgy, engineering, chemicals, and textiles'.
6. Gomez-Mendoza (1988) provides a useful overview of the development of the Spanish shipbuilding industry from 1850 to 1935, which illustrates several of these more general limitations.
7. Tortella (2000: 67) suggests that 'by opting for tariff protection, the Spanish politicians, whether consciously or not, made a choice in favour of social stability, and against economic and social change'.
8. Even internationally competitive strengths in certain regional industries, such as in iron and steel production in the Basque Country, had diminished significantly by the mid-twentieth century (Carreras and Tafunell, 1994: 38).
9. According to Guerrero (2009: 5), cumulative GDP growth at factor cost between 1939 and 1975 (the year of Franco's death) was just over 5.22 per cent, while in the 33 years since then the rate has been much lower: just

under 3.15 per cent annually. The post-Franco growth rate was even lower than the autarkic stage (3.77 per cent between 1938 and 1958).

10. The Spanish Institute for Foreign Currency controlled the deposits and trade in all currencies. This separated the Bank of Spain from exchange rate policy – creating a dual internal and external system of monetary control – and granted the state absolute control over imports (Prados de la Escosura, Rosés and Sanz Villarroya, 2010).

11. Carreras and Tafunell (1994: 23) report that of the twenty leading Spanish firms by assets in the 1960s, eleven private firms registered a mean profitability of 5.1 per cent; the two public telephone and petroleum monopolies made 5 per cent profits; and the remainder of public firms 1.9 per cent. RENFE, the national rail firm, operated at a loss.

12. At this time, over 80 per cent of Spanish firms employed fewer than five workers (Wright, 1977: 40).

13. Rationing and additional compensatory payments for workers in larger industrial firms did not appear to have had any significant impact on workers' consumption during the 1940s and 1950s (Molinas and Ysás, 2003).

14. Remittances to Spain from Argentina alone amounted to US$26.5 million between 1946 and 1950, constituting over 55 per cent of total remittance flows (Martínez Ruiz, 2001: 234).

15. As Pack (2006: 91) explains, Spain and other Southern European tourism economies benefitted from the liberalisation of Western European border controls after 1958 and the deregulation of charter air travel across Europe.

16. Balaguer and Cantavalla-Jordá (2002: 878) estimate that tourism receipts amounted to 62.1 per cent of the balance of trade from 1965 to 1969, 86.4 per cent from 1970 to 1974, and 75.2 per cent from 1975 to 1979.

17. Pack (2006: Chapter 4) also provides a telling account of how open disputes between the INI – which wanted to establish new industrial firms in southern, coastal regions of Spain – and landed *rentier* interests in those localities that stood to reap significant returns from speculative tourism developments (hotel construction and such) resulted in the drawing up of zonal planning legislation in 1963.

18. Of key importance here was the 1960 Law of Horizontal Property (Ley de Propiedad Horizontal), with which the state regulated the buying and selling of apartments, and which has encouraged the social tendency toward home ownership in Spain (to which we return in Chapter 4).

19. As Karemessini (2008: 521) explains of Italy, Greece, Portugal, and Spain: 'Mass emigration prevented mass unemployment in these countries by exporting labour surpluses created by industrialisation and the modernisation of agriculture. Emigration policy may thus be viewed as a functional equivalent of employment policy until the mid-1970s'. This phenomenon has returned to the European South in the current crisis (see Conclusion).

20. Tourism-related service sectors already accounted for the remainder of output (O'Brien, 1975: 529).

21. While it was able to export some capital-intensive goods to Latin America, Pakistan and the Philippines – on the basis of the cheap technology imports – facilitated under ISI (Donges, 1972).

22. See Medina Albaladejo (2010) on the Spanish canned fruit and vegetable industry. See Román (1971: 82–4) and Montgomery and Sabate (2010) on

the Spanish steel industry. These serve as illustrative historical examples of other sectors that shared several key characteristics with the automobile manufacturing industry in this period (high levels of state support, initial export competitiveness based upon production below world market process of production, the impact of FDI, enduring low productivity, and so on).

23. Pallarès-Barberà (1998: 349) reports an 18 per cent average annual growth in car registration in Spain between 1954–69.

24. Álvarez Gil and González de la Fe (1997) explain how the takeover of SEAT in 1986 marked the end of the period in which foreign firms' presence in Spain was mainly on the basis of producing obsolete models of car for the domestic market.

25. According to Encarnación (2003: 89): 'Wage earners in Spain were receiving per capita about 12 percent more of the national income in 1975 than they had in 1962. The total flows of revenues into the nation's social security system more than doubled as a share of GDP from 4.2 to 9.3 per cent. The share of the budget devoted to education between 1953 and 1973 more than doubled from 8.2 to 17.7 per cent of government spending'.

26. For a detailed, descriptive account of the transition see Tusell (2007: Chapter 4).

27. Of additional significance, of course, is the fact that the 1978 Constitution granted limited self-governance to the 17 Autonomous Communities of Spain (see Colomer, 1998; Schrijver, 2006: Chapter 4).

3 The Limits to European Integration

1. In 1998, Bonefeld argued forcefully that: 'The attempt at creating a zone of monetary stability in Europe and the worldwide crisis of capitalist accumulation belong together ... [EMU] moreover seeks to ... reinforce and exploit its regional and national fragmentation' (p. PE55). That uneven development has since been reinforced by the process of European 'integration' has been noted by the philosopher Slavoj Žižek (2013):

> What we can see emerging on the horizon is the contours of a divided Europe: its southern part will increasingly be reduced to a zone with a cheaper labour force, outside the safety network of the welfare state, a domain appropriate for outsourcing and tourism. In short, the gap between the developed world and those lagging behind will now exist in Europe itself.

2. We do acknowledge that, in a superficial sense, our argument chimes with that of many other mainstream economics commentaries that have attributed the current crisis in Spain to various 'imbalances' in the economy. There is, after all, a widespread acknowledgement that the growth in wages and unit labour costs in Spain after 1999 – which exceeded the eurozone average – was not on the basis of industrial productivity and competitiveness, but on the basis of increased productivity in financial intermediation and non-tradable sectors; the expansion of domestic demand based on rising asset price inflation; and enduring labour market 'rigidities' (see, for example, EU

Commission, 2012: 25). However, our overriding aim is to substantiate the claim that such 'imbalances' are not the product of policy failure (to reduce labour costs), contingency, or human frailty. Rather, over the course of this chapter and Chapter 4, the explanation for the necessity of the current crisis will be shown to lie in the uneven development of the productive forces in Spain – as well as geographically across different national states within the EU – and the associated tendency toward the overaccumulation of capital.

3. These were Banco de Bilbao, Banco Central, Banco Español de Crédito (Banesto), Banco Hispano-Americano, Banco Popular, Banco Santander, and Banco de Vizcaya.

4. Jimeno and Toharia (1994: 23) argue that 'the foremost cause of employment loss in the 1975–85 period was the inefficiency and weakness of Spanish firms, whose viability was based on the existence of cheap labour and lack of competition'. In this period only the service sector continued creating jobs, but at a lower rate than before (Viñals et al., 1990: 167).

5. Benton (1992) reports how a loophole in Spanish business law actually facilitated this transformation as factory owners filed *en masse* for bankruptcy, allowing them to wipe out social security and debt obligations to employees. Many started up again as small firms and in some cases ex-factory owners assisted former employees to buy old machinery and to set up small subcontracting shops.

6. Boix (1995: 38) confirms that only 16 per cent of the Spanish workforce was in a trade union by 1989, with most membership concentrated in medium to large firms with skilled workers on permanent contracts. Some of the literature suggests that by the late 1980s there existed a form of 'voter trade unionism', rather than 'member trade unionism', in which many workers preferred to vote in confederate elections rather than join a union. See Rigby and Lawlor (1994) for a report on how low membership impacted negatively upon the main unions' organisational and financial capacities between 1986 and 1994.

7. As was the case in the textiles sector – see the discussion of Zara specifically, next.

8. Holman (1996: 159) confirms of the period 1985 to 1989 that:

> The volume of manufacturing investment in Spain increased by 79 per cent, while the growth of industrial production amounted to 17 per cent. During the same period, however, 35 per cent of manufacturing investment was accounted for by foreign-owned companies and tended to be centred on high-demand growth sectors (computers, electronics, pharmaceuticals). Between 1996 and 1989, 88 per cent of the investment in these sectors originated from foreign capital. Finally, foreign-owned companies accounted for only 11 per cent of investment in low demand sectors.

9. Some of the major acquisitions were the SKF Española ball-bearing plant by SKF Sweden (already a minority share-holder) in 1985; Purolator (a filter manufacturer) to the West German company AG in early 1986; Secoinsa (electronics) to Fujitsu; MTM to Alsthoum-France; Enfersa to the Kuwaiti

Investment Office; and Ensa (the truck-maker) to FIAT (see Wright and Pagoulatos, 2001: 244). Foreign acquisitions also extended to the more traditional sectors of the Spanish economy such as food, drinks, and textiles (López and Rodríguez, 2010: 164).

10. These concrete developments can, in our view, be theorised on the basis of small capitals acting as suppliers to 'fragmented' normal capitals (which are today, by definition, world market capitals); a relation in which the latter can benefit from a flow of extra surplus value by sourcing inputs below their normal price of production while selling their own commodities at their full price of production (see Starosta, 2010b).

11. In their analysis of the development of capitalism in Portugal, Rodrigues and Reis (2012: 197) explain how Portuguese firms that benefitted from a close relationship with the state have used the 'profits generated at the national level and their access to international financial markets to reduce their dependence upon the progressively exhausted internal market, thus becoming progressively transnational in orientation.'

12. Along with this came the secular problem of dual inflation and the state's inability to control rising wages in certain sectors. Between 1985 and 1992, for example, the consumer price index for (non-tradable) services exceeded the price index for tradable goods by almost 60 per cent, compared with a divergence in Germany of only 10 per cent (Peréz, 2000: 450).

13. Between 1987 and 1992, Spanish per unit labour costs rose by 38.8 per cent (a 6.7 per cent annual rate), compared with an average of only 12.8 per cent (2.4 per cent annual rise) in Belgium, France, Denmark, Germany, Luxemburg, and the Netherlands (Lieberman, 1995: 343).

14. A further feature of this period was the second Spanish property boom, which we discuss in Chapter 4.

15. Other states struggled to defend exchange rates in a Europe-wide monetary crisis of 1992 – notably Italy and the UK, which were forced out of the EMS. In 1993, the permitted EMS fluctuation band was increased as France faced a similar problem.

16. The Treaty demanded a public sector deficit of no more than 3 per cent, public debt no more than 60 per cent of GDP, interest rates no more than 2 points above the lowest three comparable rates in the EC, and inflation no more than 1.5 points above the three lowest rates in the EC. At the time of signing the Treaty, Spain met only one of the objectives by having a 45.6 per cent debt to GDP ratio. Inflation was at 4.1 per cent, interest rates were the highest in the EC at 13 per cent, the exchange rate was 6 points wide of the ERM band, and the peseta was seriously overvalued (Salmon, 1995: 14).

17. As Román's (1997: 78) data confirms,

> the recovery of accumulation in the second half of the 1980s was short-lived and by 1993 the rate of accumulation had fallen to levels comparable with the late 1970s. While the mass of gross profits including interest costs recovered in the mid-1908s, profits in excess of such costs crested in the early 1970s and turned into losses after the mid-1970s ... the recovery of profits for non-financial firms (profits minus interest opportunity costs) in the second half of the 1980s was not only reversed

in the early 1990s but the level of such profits in 1993 (measured in 1980 pesetas) was much lower than in the mid-1950s.

18. Martín-Marcos and Jaumandreu (2004) find that accession to the EEC in 1986 facilitated a high rate of firm turnover (liquidations and start-ups), and that this explains approximately 80 per cent of the gains made in manufacturing productivity as far as 1990. They conclude that this process of 'creative destruction' was exhausted by the mid-1990s, which explains the subsequent decline in productivity. See also Medina Albaladejo (2010) for an account of how EEC accession precipitated a crisis in the previously price competitive canned fruit and vegetable industry, as it was exposed, after 1986, to competition from technologically advanced foreign capitals.

19. Lest our account be identified with various 'fractions of capital' approaches to state–capital relations, it is worth underlining here that the protection afforded by the state to these 'national champions' served to establish barriers to the entry of competitive capitals to these sectors – entry that might otherwise have prevented these Spanish capitals from becoming normal, world market capitals (see Clarke, 1978).

20. The defeat of the PP in the general election of 2004 was widely attributed to the Aznar government's support of the 2003 invasion of Iraq, and importantly the handling of the 11 March 2004 train bombings in Madrid – when, in the face of mounting evidence to the contrary, Aznar's government attributed the attacks to ETA.

21. The findings of Amin and Tomaney (1995: 205) show that Ireland, Portugal, and Spain all became investment sites for international companies looking to locate lower-quality plants (using older technology, limited R&D, and strictly limited autonomy) in less industrially developed European regions.

22. For example, Martínez-Sánchez (1992) examines industrial development in the Aragon region to highlight how, by the 1990s, only 2.2 per cent of manufacturing therein could be considered hi-tech; that 89.3 per cent of this industry was concentrated around the city of Zaragoza; that 92 per cent of such firms employed fewer than 50 workers; and that they were producing for the domestic market and largely for adjoining regions. He reports that over 60 per cent of all investment in high-tech industries in Spain was concentrated in Barcelona, Madrid, Valencia, and Vizcaya by this time.

23. On the slow uptake of robotisation in Spanish industry compared with other OECD countries, see the data in Edquist and Jacobsson (1987) and Martínez Sánchez, Pérez Pérez, and Alonso Nuez (2000). The latter piece confirms that while Spanish industry gained ground in terms of the adoption of industrial robots, the majority of these had to be imported (compared with Germany, for example, where domestic production could meet demand by the 1990s). Martínez Sánchez, Pérez Pérez and Alonso Nuez (2000) explain that, while the domestic production of industrial robots in Germany and Italy was sufficient to meet domestic demand between 1990 and 1998, Spain had to import the majority of robots due to the lack of a national robotics industry. Gomez Villascuerna and Vargas Montoya (2008) report that, by 2002, computer numerically controlled machines had been widely adopted by Spanish firms of more than 200 employees – much less so by smaller firms; only 37 per cent of industry in Spain used computer-aided design (CAD), while

only 28 per cent used robots. Albors and Hervás (2007) and Castany (2010) examine the adoption of 'continuous improvement' management strategies in Spain, as associated with 'Flexible Manufacturing Systems' (FMS) developed first in Japanese world market industries in the 1980s. Both analyses suggest that Spain lags well behind the EU average in terms of the implementation of 'lifelong training' that is integral to FMS, due to the inability of small firms to provide training and the unwillingness on the part of such firms to invest in training for a largely temporary workforce.

24. Köhler and Woodward (1997: 79) cite a 1993 report on the competitiveness of the Spanish mechanical engineering industry that found 'the low turnover rate of fixed and circulating capital in Spain compared with Germany indicates major deficiencies in production planning'.

25. Guadalupe, Kuzmina, and Thomas (2012) cite the examples of SEAT, which was acquired by Volkswagen in 1986; Guinness acquired Cruzcampo in 1991; Cemex acquired the two main cement companies Compañia Valenciana de Cementos and Sanson in 1992; and Allied Domecq acquired Bodegas y Bebidas in 2001. With the large scale of operation of the new MNC, lower costs, and larger market access, these firms were subject to process and product innovation, the purchase of new machines, and the introduction of new methods of organising production. These strategies raised productivity and increased wages (by 6 per cent), an increase based on the wage bill rather than number of employees suggesting an upgrading of the skill level of the workforce following foreign acquisition. This much is consistent with the transformations associated with the NIDL, outlined in Chapter 1.

26. For example, only 8 per cent of Spanish firms engaged in production in high-profitability sectors using sophisticated technologies could compete with similar firms producing in Germany on the basis of product quality (Martínez Zarzoso, 1999: 155).

27. The number of producers in these markets has fallen from 36 in 1970, to 31 in the 1980s, to 22 in the 1990s, and to 14 by 2003 (Heneric et al., 2005: 34).

28. This process has been termed 'centralisation without concentration' (Bellofiore, Garibaldo and Halevi, 2010: 7).

29. The state refused Volkswagen a new greenfield site in 1986 for fear of reprisals over large job losses at SEAT's Zona Franca factory in Barcelona (García Ruiz, 2001: 149). Zona Franca had been a significant locus for workers' struggles against the Franco regime in the 1960s and 70s. Yet by the late 1990s, productive capacity there was limited only to the pressing of metal body panels, and the bulk of production had been relocated to the new Martorell plant, outside the city of Barcelona.

30. Martínez Sánchez, Pérez Pérez, and Alonso Nuez (2000) report that 61.4 per cent of all industrial robots installed in Spain by 1998 were in the car industry, and that between 1990 and 1998 64 per cent of all new robots were installed in the sector.

31. In 1992, 40 per cent of workers employed in assembly were unionised, compared with only 15 per cent in the components sector (Pallarès Barberà, 1998: 350). By the mid-2000s, 57 per cent of assembly workers were unionised – a relatively high rate for Spain, especially when compared with the components sector (Banyuls and Llorente, 2010: 44). And there is a geographical dimension to patterns of auxiliary-assembly networks as well. By 1992,

40 per cent of components suppliers were concentrated around Barcelona, and 20 per cent around Madrid (Pallarès Barberà, 1997: 67; see also Lagendijk and van der Knapp, 1995). Martínez Sánchez, Pérez Pérez, and Alonso Nuez (2000) confirm that of the 39 flexible manufacturing systems installed in Spain by 1999 (a relatively low figure compared with other advanced industrial countries), almost half were installed in Barcelona and Madrid.

32. By 2000, the European market was dominated by just four large-volume German and French producers: Volkswagen, Daimler-Chrysler, Peugeot-Citroen, and Renault (Rubenstein, 2001: 343).

33. Aláez Aller et al. (1999) reported that Spanish-based producers were, by then, net importers of systems and components, adding that such components which make up 70 to 80 per cent of 'value-added' in the production of the final automobile). By 2007, the Spanish automobile industry imported 63.5 per cent of components (compared to only 15.4 per cent in 1968) (Ortiz-Villajos, 2010: 161).

34. According to Heneric et al. (2005: 161), 'value-added' per employee in the automobile industry by the mid-2000s was highest in Germany, Luxemburg and the UK; it was lowest in Italy, Portugal and Spain.

35. Since the arrival of Ford, wage bargaining at its Almusafes plant in Valencia has been conducted at plant level and with a single union – the UGT. This made the plant one of Ford's most flexible and profitable since the 1970s (Piccione and Cerezo, 2012) and explains how recent negotiations with Spanish workers have succeeded in lowering wages across the sector (Minder, 2012).

36. The annual average profit in the automobile and transport equipment sector between 2000 and 2007 was 0.7 per cent, compared with 19.7 per cent in post and telecommunications, 14.7 in electricity, gas and water supply, and 8.9 in hotels and restaurants (BBVA Research, 2011: 6). Chislett (2008) reported at the peak of the last boom that

> Spain has nine companies in Fortune's Global 500 ranking of the world's largest corporations based on 2006 revenues (a decade earlier it had none), one less than Italy but well below France's 38 and Germany's 37. Three of these companies – Repsol YPF, Endesa and Telefónica – are among the world's top 100 non-financial [TNCs] ... Grupo Santander and BBVA were ranked among the top financial TNCs (16th and 34th, respectively), and Mapfre was the world's fourth-largest reinsurance group ... Santander, BBVA, Telefónica, Endesa and Repsol YPF are also among the largest companies in the Euro Stoxx 50 by market capitalisation.

37. For a discussion of how the Greek state's debt crisis was a result of its role in the reproduction of Greek capitals in the context of European 'integration', see Vlachou (2012: 181–2).

38. As a result Spanish capitals can boast ownership of many formerly British companies: for example, in 2004, BSCH bought the Abbey National bank; in 2005, Telefónica bought the telecommunications, Internet, and financial services provider O$_2$; and in 2006, Ferrovial took over the British Airports Authority (see Mathieson, 2007: 21). In 2007, a subsidiary of the Spanish

property company Metrovacesa bought the Canary Wharf headquarters of the banking group HSBC in the biggest ever single-property deal in the UK (*Economist*, 2007: 77). Another notable global venture was BBVA's €1 billion investment in China's banking system in 2006 (see Santiso, 2007: 12).

39. 'Spanish and Portuguese suppliers employed seamstresses who received something less than half the average industrial wage, "maybe $500 a month", according to a *Forbes Magazine* estimate, if they were "lucky"; and nobody knew whether or not these suppliers paid the social security premiums and taxes to the state' (Tokatli, 2008: 32).

40. In the same period Greece's private sector debt increased by 227.7 per cent, Portugal's by 184 per cent, Italy's by 82.3 per cent, and Ireland's by 110 per cent (Eurostat, 2012b – Ireland's time series from 2001).

41. For example:

> In the tourism and hospitality sector, [the ratio of debt to gross operating profit] is more than twice as high in Spain as in other European countries. Spanish corporations hold 20 per cent more debt relative to national output than French and UK companies, twice as much as US companies, and three times as much as firms in Germany. (Roxburgh et al., 2012: 27)

4 The Limits to Urbanisation

1. Jerez Darias and Martín Martín (2011) set out the bases of a similar project, albeit in a somewhat rudimentary form.

2. For a parallel account of overaccumulation and the property boom in Ireland, see Kitchin et al. (2012) and the account given in Ó Riain (2012).

3. Space limitations prohibit a full discussion of the debates surrounding the theory of capital switching and its concrete empirical verification. Key insights into these debates are to be found in Ball (1985), Beauregard (1994), Charney (2001), Clark (1987), Edel (1992), Feagin (1987), Fine (1979), Haila (1988 and 1991), Harvey (1974), and King (1989). See, also, the contributions to a 2009 special issue on mortgage markets and the crisis in the *International Journal of Urban and Regional Research*; in particular, those by Fox Gotham and Wainwright. We acknowledge that the heterogeneity and complexity of land and real estate markets means that they can be spheres of capital accumulation with certain institutional and local specificities (as argues Ball, 1985). We also recognise the intractability of a 'comprehensive and watertight empirical substantiation of switching' (as does Christophers, 2011: 1351). Nonetheless, we maintain that a general theory (as defended by Kerr, 1996) helps to explain how speculative investment in Spanish construction and real estate markets was central to the mediation of deeper contradictions of EU integration.

4. Harvey (1982: 369) clarifies:

> Not only is the appropriation of rent socially necessary, but landowners must necessarily take an active role in the pursuit of enhanced rents. There

is nothing inconsistent in such behaviour, provided, of course, that the land is treated simply as a financial asset, a form of fictitious capital open to all investors. The freer interest-bearing capital is to roam the land looking for titles to future ground-rents to appropriate, the better it can fulfil its co-ordinating role.

5. See Chapter 2 for definitions of the categories of ground-rent developed by Marx.

6. In the former locational scenario, 'it would be centrality (for the commercial capitalist) relative to, say, the transport and communications network or proximity (for the hotel chain) to some highly concentrated activity (such as a financial center). The commercial capitalist and the hotelier are willing to pay a premium for the land because of accessibility' (Harvey, 2001: 396). In the latter scenario, the scarcity of certain buildings or land permits landlords and developers to engage in monopoly pricing and speculative investments.

7. The rate of investment expenditure in construction during the 2000s closely paralleled the accumulation of state debt (Alcidi and Gros, 2012: 3, Fig. 3). The growth of credit consistently exceeded that of deposits by more than 5 per cent points during most of the boom period (Fernández de Lis and García Herrero, 2008).

8. In addition to the terms of EMU convergence that were more advantageous to German manufacturing rather than its Southern European counterparts, a range of critical scholarship on the bases of the German export surplus places much emphasis upon real wage repression since the 1990s (see Bellofiore, Garibaldo and Halevi, 2010: 134–5; Hadjimichalis, 2011: 270; Lapavitsas et al., 2010: 26; Weeks, 2013).

9. The same report highlights the broader geographical structure of financial, trade, and service flows within Europe. From 2004 to 2006 financial flows from surplus to deficit countries amounted to around €75 billion annually (EU Commission, 2012: 48–9; see also Vlachou, 2012 for a discussion of this in relation to Greece). All Southern European countries recorded growing trade deficits in the period, but compensated for this to some extent with a surplus in services due to tourism.

10. Germany's Landesbanken (regional savings banks) are especially exposed after investing heavily in *cédulas* in the early 2000s. In September 2012, German banks' total exposure to Spanish banks stood at US$49 billion according to the Bank for International Settlements (Stevens and Henning, 2012).

11. Under Franco, 60 per cent of annual housing construction was designated Vivienda de Protección Oficial and subject to strict price controls by the state. This rate remained constant until 1986 but has subsequently declined to 16.9 per cent in 1991 and 10.4 in 2007 (Idoate et al., 2008: 73).

12. These were 15 per cent tax deductible and exempted from transfer tax, and quickly gained a reputation as a haven for so-called 'black money' (Navarro, 1984).

13. Deregulation in the 1980s meant that the *cajas* could carry out universal banking activities and open branches outside of their original home region.

14. This form of banking sector behaviour was also apparent in the Irish case (see Kitchin et al., 2012: 1315).

15. The policy therefore rested on two main assumptions: first, 'that the existence of "boundaries" must necessarily involve the restriction of the supply, and therefore the inefficient use of land as a resource', and second, 'that, on the urban fringe, the price of fully liberalised land should equal the alternative agricultural cost, with "expectant" or "absolute" rents disappearing' (Roca Cladera and Burns, 2000: 554). The misconception regarding the ability of policy to eradicate rents derives from neo-classical urban land use theory's notion that rent is simply 'the return to a scarce factor of production and that land is in essence no different from labour and capital'. As such, removing institutional barriers to the market also removes the basis of rent (Harvey, 1973: 177).

16. This contrasts with a European average of 10 to 15 per cent (cited in Kitchin, et al., 2012: 1308).

17. Shortly after the dotcom crisis, *The Economist* (2002) similarly noted the relationship between the crash and the expansion of housing markets:

    If there is one single factor that has saved the world economy from a deep recession it is the housing market.

    Despite the sharp fall in share prices and a worldwide plunge in industrial production, business investment and profits, consumer spending has held up relatively well in America, Britain and several other economies, supported by low interest rates and the wealth-boosting effects of rising house prices. Over the 12 months to February average house prices in America rose by 9 per cent, and those in Britain by 15 per cent. Adjusting for inflation, this is the biggest real increase on record in America and the biggest in Britain since 1988.

18. In 2004, for example, total direct employment in construction grew by 37.84 per cent, compared with growth of 23.14 per cent for the economy as a whole (Bielsa and Duarte, 2011: 331). Muñoz de Bustillo and Ignacio Antón (2010) find that in Spain – but also Greece and Ireland, two other historically 'sending' countries that became recipient countries in the 2000s – new immigrants tended to be employed in low-wage sectors such as construction, hotels and restaurants. It is noteworthy that, as with many other industrial sectors (see Chapter 3), the Spanish construction sector is largely composed of small capitals. By January 2009, 86 per cent of these firms employed five or fewer salaried workers (Salmon, 2010: 47)

19. Meanwhile, remittances from new immigrants to their home countries also contributed to the current account deficit and low level of national savings (Suárez, 2010: 4).

20. IMF data from 2011, at http://research.stlouisfed.org/fred2/series/HDTGPDESA163N, date accessed 14 May 2013.

21. Alcidi and Gros (2012: 3) estimate that: 'If construction were to continue at the still relatively high rate of today, the process of absorption of the bubble would take more than 30 years'.

22. In this, endemic corruption was significant. Insider land deals became a way for many within local state institutions to appropriate funds (see, for example, Jiménez, 2009). For a materialist insight into why political corruption is inherent to capitalist accumulation, see Iñigo Carrera (2006: 204).

23. By 2007, Madrid was the principal home to 61.2 per cent of Spanish firms with more than 5,000 employees (57 of 93); 50.8 per cent of those with more than 1,000 employees; and 41.2 per cent of those with more than 500 (Rodríguez López, 2007a: 53). It should be noted, however, that Madrid occupies what might be termed an 'intermediate' position within the European urban-regional hierarchy insofar as it rarely included in the *banane bleue* that is said to resemble a discontinuous corridor of urbanisation across Europe, and in which is contained the highest concentrations of people, money and industry (see Chapter 2; also Rodríguez López, 2007a: 82–4).

24. See, for example, Díaz Orueta (2007), who details the transformation of the Lavapiés neighbourhood in central Madrid after 1997.

25. Employment in construction in the Community of Madrid grew by 83.5 per cent between 1995 and 2004, compared with 6.4 per cent in industry. Employment in agriculture declined by 26.9 per cent in the same period (Rodríguez López, 2007b: 100, Table 7).

26. This included the Palau de Congressos, a new convention centre and luxury tourism complex. Its construction was suspended in 2010 after the private developer Grupo Barceló withdrew from the project, leaving the regional government with €34 million in outstanding costs for unfinished work (Efe, 2013).

27. Notably, the city was the first to be awarded the Royal Institute of British Architects' Gold Medal in 1999.

28. Manufacturing as a share of total economic activity in Barcelona declined from 23.1 per cent in 1991 to 11.2 per cent in 2006 (OECD, 2009: 20).

29. As Charnock and Ribera-Fumaz (2011) explain, the stated aim of Barcelona city council was to transform the physical and social infrastructures of Poblenou in line with received wisdom concerning the determinants of urban competitiveness within the so-called 'knowledge-based economy' – as reflected in the reform of the city's planning regulations to allow land formerly designated for industrial use, under the classification '22a', to be developed for '@ activities' (new information and communications technologies industries, R&D, publishing, multimedia, and database management). Under the new regulations, developers could build higher than the three floors previously permitted and were allowed to mix commercial and residential developments. The redevelopment aspect of the project was on a considerable scale, involving a total investment in infrastructure of €180 million.

30. For an account of three such specific examples in Barcelona, see Charnock, Purcell, and Ribera-Fumaz (2013).

31. The Catalan regional government itself was downgraded to 'junk' status by the credit rating agency in August 2012.

32. Between 1994 and 2001 in Valencia, the share of total employment in industry fell from 28.5 per cent to 23.9 per cent; the share in agriculture also fell from 8 per cent to 4.4 per cent; service employment grew from 55.9 per cent to 59.4 per cent; and the share in construction grew from 7.7 per cent to 12.4 per cent (Banyuls et al., 2002: 91).

33. Moix (2010: 71) estimates that the final cost of El Palau de les Arts, one part of the complex, was some €500 million – approximately 310 per cent more than the original planned cost. L'Oceanogràfic, the complex's open-air

aquarium, came in at a cost 336 per cent greater than the designers' original projection.

34. The Opera House cost €400 million to construct, and costs €40 million annually to operate (Mason, 2012).
35. Built at a cost of €150 million, the new airport at Castellón was yet to open in 2012 – eighteen months after completion (see Tremlett, 2012a).
36. According to del Romero Renau and Trudelle (2011: 7) the cost of housing in the port and neighbouring suburbs rose by an average of €300 per m² in the run-up to the Americas Cup event, and remained inflated until 2008.
37. Data from *El País*, at http://ep00.epimg.net/economia/imagenes/2012/05/22/ actualidad/1337711094_209173_1337711355_sumario_grande.png, date accessed 4 June 2013.

5 The Limits to the State

1. This much is an immanent necessity in capitalism:

    > Fundamentally, the attempt to regain control over the money supply involves the imposition of the global limits of capital upon the working class so as to integrate the category of abstract labour with value form through the guarantee of credit. This guarantee secures the formal exchange equality of commodities on the world market. The guarantee of global credit-relations rests upon the ability of the (multiplicity of) state(s) to impose the money power of capital upon social relations. (Bonefeld, 1993: 61)

2. 'Capital flight' from Spain towards EU 'core' countries amounted to €296 billion between June 2011 and June 2012 (López Garrido, 2012: 16).
3. Data from *El País* at http://politica.elpais.com/politica/2013/05/26/actualidad/ 1369594520_731419.html, date accessed 24 June 2013.
4. In April 2013, the unemployment rate for foreign nationals was 39.21 per cent (INE, 2013: 5).
5. From 2000, the Bank of Spain forced banks to make provisions for latent portfolio losses, created a reserve capital buffer, limited the payment of dividends, and prevented off balance sheet activity and investment in vehicles linked to 'toxic' assets. Instead of mortgage loans being sold off balance sheets to Structured Investment Vehicles – as was the case in securitisation strategies pursued by US banks – Spanish banks had to retain at least half their balance as collateral for covered bonds (see Chapter 4). Upon the outbreak of the crisis in the US in 2007, the then Finance Minister of Spain, Pedro Solbes, stated that '[he did] not see the construction sector affected in a specific way. It is business as usual, with a slight downshift that allows the sector to adjust to reality' (quoted in Bergareche, 2011: 55).
6. Close investment relationships between developers and regional savings banks led to the latter being especially exposed in the highly speculative construction and real estate booms (see Chapter 4). The *cajas* accounted for half of the Spanish financial sector's assets in 2009 (Royo, 2013: 8).

7. 'Plan E' centred upon four main axes:

(i) the support of small and medium-sized enterprises through financial incentives; (ii) employment promotion through hiring benefits and social security rebates for hiring on permanent contracts of unemployed workers with family obligations; (iii) support of the financial system; and (iv) further structural reforms in services, transportation, energy and telecommunications, as well as reform of the pension system (Wölfl and Mora-Sanguinetti, 2011: 10).

8. The state's measures kick started a process of concentration of capital that put underway merger processes in 27 of Spain's 45 *cajas* by 2010 (Royo, 2013: 11).

9. For a critical interrogation of the concept of the 'structural deficit', see Radice (2013). As of March 2012, 25 EU member states, including Spain, are committed to maintaining a maximum cap on the structural deficit as signatories to a Fiscal Compact incorporated into the Treaty on Stability, Coordination, and Governance.

10. See Chapter 3 on the fate of the Spanish automobile industry in the crisis as a result of these reforms.

11. Data at http://noticiasbancarias.com/economia-y-finanzas/02/04/2013/mas-de-un-millon-de-jornadas-perdidas-por-huelgas-en-2012/35114.html, date accessed 14 June 2013.

12. The reader should note, however, that radical commentators remain critical of collaborationist industrial relations in Spain and the 'banalisation' of the general strike on the part of weak trade unions (see CV, 2012a).

13. The Sustainable Economy Law, or 'Ley Sinde', dictates that content in breach of copyright law can be removed from the Internet and remains unpopular with many 'free culture' and new social media networks.

14. Spain's Parliament passed a bill to increase the standard retirement age to 67 years on 27 June 2011.

15. As in Greece, protests in those early months sometimes took a violent turn, despite the pacifist intensions of the vast majority of the movements involved. In Barcelona, for instance, the Catalan police were widely criticised for the disproportionate use of force in evicting camping protestors from Plaça de Catalunya on 27 May, while a small number of *indignados* were also denounced by the wider movements for attacks against members of the Catalan regional parliament on 15 June (see Hughes, 2011: 411–12). In Madrid, on 27 July, the police forcibly removed a group of *indignados* that had ascended on the Spanish Parliament to deliver a list of demands.

16. 'SIN CASA, SIN CURRO, SIN PENSION, SIN MIEDO' (see http://www.juventudsinfuturo.net/).

17. At http://www.democraciarealya.es/quienes-somos/, date accessed 19 July 2011, our translation.

18. One Spanish journalist writing for *The Guardian* surmised that:

For all its far-reaching rhetoric, [the movement] addresses solely the left. It ultimately represents the frustration of those who see that it doesn't matter which way you vote, the economic policies are dictated by the markets; hence the critique of 'the system' and the demands of account-ability and transparency. Most of the protesters seem to be the people who voted Socialist in 2008 only to prevent a win for the People's Party. They don't want their vote to be taken for granted yet again ... They may not change Spanish politics forever, but they have succeeded in something difficult enough: in putting all politicians to shame at least for a few days. (Murado, 2011)

The Economist (2011) similarly played down the radical credentials and efficacy of the 15-M movement, likening its public assemblies to Monty Python sketches, labelling its selling point 'well-mannered rage', and concluding that the broad support for the movement can be put down to 'common complaints, [but] not solutions'.

19. A June 2011 survey estimated that 62 per cent of 15-M participants interviewed considered themselves 'reformist' rather than 'anti-capitalist' (cited in Calvo, Gómez-Pastrana and Mena, 2011: 14). One radical commentator explains that:

the experience of political conflict of the people who unleashed the May 15 mobilisation is predominantly intellectual, academic, ethical, and ideological, [that is] an experience specific to those generations who lived with the illusion of economic expansion ... and who are puzzled by its collapse. These generations had benefited from a certain accumulation of family resources and from public spending (a social peace subsidised with scholarships, employment and training schemes, NGOs, etc.), which ran parallel to the consolidation of the democracy elaborated at the time of Franco's death, and whose social and political experience is not based on confrontation. This would explain why the May 15 movement, at least initially, did not call for a break with the 'system', but rather for its cleansing. (CV, 2012b)

In 2013, a network of *indignados* launched Partido X – a leaderless, Internet-based 'party of the future' with four principal demands: greater transparency in public administration, 'wikigovernment' modelled on the Icelandic experience, the right to vote continuously in popular legislative initiatives, and the right to vote for laws in binding referenda. Partido X is therefore committed to revolutionising the political process, but not necessarily its content (see Luis Sánchez, 2013).

20. On the second anniversary of 15-M in 2012, *El País* reported that a mere 50 'militants' convened at Puerta del Sol in Madrid. The previous Saturday 150 people turned out in what was described as a 'playful and minority act' of music and arts (Tejedor, 2013).

21. The *mareas ciudadanas* (citizens' tides), for example, were collectives of over 350 organisations demanding plebiscites on austerity and privatisation measures in 2013.

22. According to the PAH's website: http://afectadosporlahipoteca.com, date accessed 28 June 2013.

23. In 2012, fire fighters' unions in Catalonia and La Coruña and the Assembly of Locksmiths in Pamplona agreed not to help execute eviction orders in solidarity with the PAH's 'stop *desahucios*' campaign (García Lamarca, 2013).

24. Spanish savings banks are committed by law to undertake charitable 'social work' (*la obra social*). The *Obra Social PAH* campaign has added to a long

tradition of squatters' movements in Spain (see Martínez, 2007), as well as to an increase in the incidence of squatting and occupations since the outbreak of the crisis by movements such as Madrid-based okupatambién (Smyth, 2013).

25. For example, on 21 June 2013 500 PAH activists occupied the headquarters of BBVA in Sabadell, Catalonia (Vallespín, 2013).

26. Harvey's (2003) notion of 'accumulation by dispossession' is derived from Marx's concept of primitive accumulation, as discussed in Volume I of *Capital*.

27. PAH activists exerted pressure on members of the Spanish government to debate the bill through the use of the *escrache* (a strategy developed in Argentina, where activists show up at a person's house or workplace *en masse* in an attempt to publicly humiliate them). The Initiative was presented to Congress by Ada Colau, the spokesperson for the PAH, in February 2013. The government approved a watered down version of the reform in May 2013, introducing only limited protection to potential evictees (Observatorio DESC, 2013).

28. Unless accompanied with a citation, all data in this paragraph were sourced from the Institut d'Estdística de Catalunya website, http://www.idescat.cat/en, date accessed 29 June 2013.

29. As Gallego and Subirats (2012: 286) confirm, 'Some [Autonomous Communities] that contribute less to the general budget because of their weaker productive capacity end up having a higher per capita budget for their regional government, and see their per capita disposable income levelled up with other [Autonomous Communities]'. The Basque Country and Navarra are both exempted from the 'common' fiscal regime and pay only an agreed quota of taxes to the central state under a distinct '*foral*' system (see Ruiz Almendral, 2004).

30. For an account of the impact of the crisis on nationalist resurgence in the Basque Country's elections in 2012, see Gómez Fortes and Cabeza Pérez (2013). For a materialist critique of nationalism in general, which is consistent with our theoretical approach, see Bonefeld (2004). For a critical analysis of resurgent nationalism in Spain since 2008, see CV (2012b).

31. The demonstration was organised by the non-partisan organisation Assamblea Nacional Catalana (ANC). Created in 2011, the ANC emerged from civic protests in July 2010 under the banner of 'we are a nation, we decide' (Rico, 2012: 220). These protests were in response to the ruling of the Spanish Constitutional Court against many of the reforms contained in a new Statute of Autonomy of Catalonia aimed at granting greater fiscal autonomy and judicial powers to the region. The Court pronounced that the new Statute contravened Articles 1 and 2 of the Constitution: 'National sovereignty belongs to the Spanish people from whom emanate the powers of the state'; and 'the Constitution is based on the indissoluble unity of the Spanish Nation, the common and indivisible homeland of all Spaniards' (Petithomme and Fernández Garcia, 2013: 12). The Generalitat and Spanish Parliament had both previously approved the new Statute, and it had been approved by 70 per cent of voters in a referendum in Catalonia on 18 June 2006 (see Dowling, 2009; Rodon, 2012). For descriptions of political developments in Catalonia since the 1970s, see Nagel (2006; 2009) and Petithomme and Fernández Garcia (2013); for a broader discussion of Statute

reform in the Estados de las Autonomías in recent years, see Keating and Wilson (2009).

32. It was estimated in June 2012 that Spain's households, firms, and government collectively owed almost €1 trillion in foreign debt – more than 90 per cent of GDP (*Economist*, 2012).

33. According to Estefanía (2013), some 65 per cent of Spaniards polled in 2007 expressed confidence in the EU; by the close of 2012 the proportion had fallen to 20 per cent, with 72 per cent 'demonstrating prejudice' toward the EU.

Conclusion

1. See Fouskas and Dimoulas, 2012, for an illustrative discussion of Greece.

2. The relation between the German and Spanish economies epitomised the broader relation between the 'surplus' and 'deficit' countries prior to 2008. As Uxó, Paúl and Febrero (2012: 208) detail, in 2007, Germany's surplus accounted for 71 per cent of the total surplus of the eurozone's lending countries; Spain's deficit was 45 per cent of the total deficit across borrowing countries. They also highlight that the Spanish state's fiscal surplus before the crisis highlights how private and external debt was at the root of the current account deficit. And they also stress that Germany's export-orientated growth was based upon stagnant domestic demand and wages – an 'economic policy that can only succeed, and avoid high unemployment rates, if other countries have large domestic demand and imports growth, and hence a current account deficit' (p. 208).

3. For example, *Porque devemos sair do euro* (*Why we should leave the euro*; Ferreira do Amaral, 2013) was the title of the top-selling book in Portugal in May 2013 (Kowsmann and Walker, 2013). That same month saw the launch of two different pro-drachma parties in Greece, the Plan B party and the Drachma Five Star movement – modelled on the M5S in Italy (*Euronews*, 2013).

4. As Bonefeld (2002: 6–7) emphasizes, within a capitalistically constituted form of social reproduction the 'critique of the euro cannot be a critique for the pound [or the drachma, the peseta, etc.]. The history of "national money" has always been a world market history'.

5. In May 2013, the Greek prime minister, Antonis Samaras, asked the Greek people to 'put on our best face for foreigners', as the country looked set to receive a record 17 million tourists in 2013 (Smith, 2013). Mega-developments designed to draw in huge numbers of tourists have gained much popular attention and criticism in Spain, such as the EuroVegas Madrid project and the planned Barcelona World theme park attraction. Remittances by emigrating workers have also regained significance in the current crisis (for example, 300,000 emigrated from Ireland between 2009 and 2013, according to the *BBC News*, 2013a; 240,000 workers left Portugal in 2011–13, *BBC News*, 2013b).

Bibliography

Aalbers, M. B. (2008) 'The Financialization of Home and the Mortgage Market Crisis', *Competition and Change*, 12:2, 148–66.

Abellán, J., J. Sequera and M. Janoschka (2012) 'Occupying the #Hotelmadrid: A Laboratory for Urban Resistance', *Social Movement Studies: Journal of Social, Cultural and Political Protest*, 11:3–4, 320–6.

Ainger, K. (2013) 'In Spain They Are All Indignados Nowadays', *Guardian*, 28 April, http://www.guardian.co.uk/commentisfree/2013/apr/28/spain-indignados-protests-state-of-mind, date accessed 26 June 2013.

Aizpeolea, L. R. (2011) 'PSOE y PP fijaran por ley un déficit máximo del 0,4% a partir del ano 2020', *El País*, 25 August, http://politica.elpais.com/politica/2011/08/25/actualidad/1314307263_984459.html, date accessed 16 June 2013.

Aláez Aller, R., J. Bilbao Ubillos, V. Camino Beldarrain and J. C. Longás García (1999) 'New Tendencies in Inter-Firm Relations in the Automotive Industry and Their Impact on European Periphery Suppliers: Lessons from Spain', *European Urban and Regional Studies*, 6:3, 255–64.

Albarracín, J. (1987) *La onda larga del capitalismo español* (Madrid: Colegio de Economistas).

Albarracín, J. (1991) 'La extracción del excedente y el proceso de acumulación', in M. Etxezarreta (ed.), *La reestructuración del capitalismo en España, 1970–1990* (Barcelona: Icaria).

Albors, J. and J. L. Hervás (2007) 'CI Practice in Spain: Its Role as a Strategic Tool for the Firm. Empirical Evidence from the CINet Survey Analysis', *International Journal of Technology Management*, 37:3–4, 332–47.

Alcidi, C. and D. Gros (2012) 'The Spanish Hangover', *Centre for European Policy Studies (CEPS) Policy Brief*, 267, 1–3.

Alcorta, L. (1999) 'Flexible Automation and Location of Production in Developing Countries', *The European Journal of Development Research*, 11:1, 147–75.

Allen, K. (2013) 'Protests at ECB as Jobless Rate Hits a High', *Guardian*, 1 June, 32.

Alonso Gil, J. (1982) 'España 1940–60: Crecimiento Económico', *Revista de Estudios Agrosociales*, 121, 81–125.

Álvarez Gil, M. J. and P. González de la Fe (1997) 'La internacionalización de SEAT: De Zona Franca a Martorell pasando por Wolfsburg', Working Paper 97–13, Departamento de Economía de la Empresa, Universidad Carlos III de Madrid, October.

Amin, A. and J. Tomaney (1995) 'The Regional Development Potential of Inward Investment in the Less Favoured Regions of the European Community', in A. Amin and J. Tomaney (eds), *Behind the Myth of the European Union* (London: Routledge).

Anderson, C. W. (1970) *The Political Economy of Modern Spain: Policy-Making in an Authoritarian System* (London: University of Wisconsin Press).

Anduiza, E., I. Martín and A. Mateos (2012) 'Las consecuencias electorales del 15M en las elecciones generales de 2011', unpublished paper, November, http://llet-131-198.uab.es/recercapol/images/publications/anduizaetal.pdf, date accessed 20 June 2013.

Antràs, P. and J. Ventura (2012) 'Dos més dos són mil', *Wilson Initiative*, 23 November, http://www.wilson.cat/en/mitjans-escrits/articles-dels-membres/item/216-dos-més-dos-són-mil-els-efectes-comercials-de-la-independència. html, date accessed 1 July 2013.

Aparicio, L. (2004) 'El cimiento financiero del "boom" inmobiliario', *El País*, 25 April, http://elpais.com/diario/2004/04/25/negocio/1082896881_850215. html, date accessed 2 March 2013.

Arauzo-Carod, J-M. and A. Segarra-Blasco (2005) 'The Determinants of Entry Are Not Independent of Start-up Size: Some Evidence from Spanish Manufacturing', *Review of Industrial Organization*, 27:2, 147–65.

Arestis, P. and E. Paliginis (1995) 'Divergence and Peripheral Fordism in the European Union', *Review of Social Economy*, 53:2, 261–84.

Arocena, P. (2004) 'Privatisation Policy in Spain: Stuck Between Liberalization and the Protection of Nationals' Interests', in M. Köthenbürger, H-W. Sinn and J. Walley (eds), *Privatization Experiences in the European Union* (Cambridge: MIT Press).

Arthur, C. J. (2002) 'Capital, Competition and Many Capitals', in M. Campbell and G. Reuten (eds), *The Culmination of Capital: Essays on Volume III of Marx's Capital* (Basingstoke: Palgrave Macmillan).

Asociación Hipotecaria Española (2006) 'The Spanish Mortgage Market between 1982 and 2006', 17 April, http://www.ahe.es/bocms/images/bfilecontent/2007/04/17/807.pdf?version=3, date accessed 28 February 2012.

Avesani, R. G., A. García Pascual and E. Ribakova (2007) 'The Use of Mortgage Covered Bonds', IMF Working Paper 07/20, Washington DC, January.

Balaguer, J. and M. Cantavella-Jordá (2002) 'Tourism as a Long-run Economic Growth Factor: The Spanish Case', *Applied Economics*, 34:7, 877–84.

Balaguer, J. and M. Cantavella-Jordá (2004) 'Structural Change in Exports and Economic Growth: Cointegration and Causality Analysis for Spain (1961–2000)', *Applied Economics*, 36:5, 473–77.

Ball, M. (1985) 'The Urban Rent Question', *Environment and Planning A*, 17:4, 503–25.

Banco de España (2013) 'Quarterly Report on the Spanish Economy', April, http://www.bde.es/f/webbde/SES/Secciones/Publicaciones/InformesBoletinesRevistas/BoletinEconomico/13/Abr/Files/coye.pdf, date accessed 16 June 2013.

Banyuls, J. and R. Llorente (2010) 'La industria del automóvil en España: Globalización y gestión laboral', *Revista de Economía Crítica*, 9:1, 33–52.

Banyuls, J., E. Cano, J. V. Picher and A. Sánchez (2002) 'El "model" valencià d'ocupació', *Arxius De Ciències Socials*, 7, 83–109.

Banyuls, J., F. Miguélez, A. Recio, E. Cano and R. Lorente (2009) 'The Transformation of the Employment System in Spain: Towards a Mediterranean Neoliberalism?' in G. Bosch, S. Lehndorff and J. Rubery (eds), *European Employment Models in Flux: A Comparison of Institutional Change in Nine European Countries* (Basingstoke: Palgrave Macmillan).

Baquero, A. and C. Márquez Daniel (2012) 'Catalunya clama por independencia', *el Periódico*, http://www.elperiodico.com/es/noticias/diada-2012/manifestacion-diada-barcelona-2202293, date accessed 28 June 2013.

Barciela López, C. (2002) 'Guerra civil y primer franquismo (1936–1959)', in F. Comín, M. Hernández and E. Llopis (eds), *Historia económica de España: Siglos X–XX* (Barcelona; Crítica).

BBC News (2012) 'Valencia Ups Bailout Request from Spain Government', 30 August, http://www.bbc.co.uk/news/business-19422198, date accessed 4 June 2013.

BBC News (2013a) '300,000 Irish People Emigrate in Four Years', 9 May, http://www.bbc.co.uk/news/uk-northern-ireland-22461030, date accessed 5 July 2013.

BBC News (2013b) 'Portuguese Flee Economic Crisis', 25 January, http://www.bbc.co.uk/news/world-21206165, date accessed 5 July 2013.

BBVA (2009) *Spain Watch, March 2009* (Bilbao: BBVA).

BBVA Research (2011) 'Sectors of Future Growth in the Spanish Economy', Spain: Economic Watch, Madrid, 19 January.

Beauregard, R. (1994) 'Capital Switching and the Built Environment: United States – 1970–89', *Environment and Planning A*, 26:5, 715–32.

Becker, G. and R. Posner (2012) 'Breakup of Countries: No Economic Disaster', 12 March, http://www.becker-posner-blog.com/2012/12/breakup-of-countries-no-economic-disaster-becker.html, date accessed 1 July 2013.

Bellofiore, R., F. Garibaldo and J. Halevi (2010) 'The Great Recession and the Contradictions of European Neomercantilism', in L. Panitch, G. Albo and V. Chibber (eds), *Socialist Register 2011: The Crisis This Time* (London: Merlin Press).

Benedikter, R. (2012) 'The European Debt Crisis 2011–12: The Case of Italy', *European Financial Review*, April–May, 1–20.

Benoit, A. (2012) 'EU Sees Spain's Budget Measures Failing to Tackle Deficit', *Bloomberg Businessweek*, 7 November, www.businessweek.com/news/2012-11-07/eu-sees-spain-s-budget-measures-failing-to-tackle-deficit, accessed 13 February 2013.

Benton, L. A. (1992) 'The Emergence of Industrial Districts in Spain: Industrial Restructuring and Divergent Regional Responses', in F. Pyke and W. Sengenberger (eds), *Industrial Districts and Local Economic Regeneration* (Geneva: International Institute for Labour Studies).

Bergareche, B. (2011) 'The Pain in Spain', *World Policy Journal*, 28, 52–9.

Bernardos Domínguez, G. (2009) 'Creación y destrucción de la burbuja inmobiliaria en España', *Información Comercial Española*, 850, 23–40.

Bieler, A. and A. D. Morton (2006) 'Class Formation, Resistance, and the Transnational: Beyond Unthinking Materialism', in A. Bieler, W. Bonefeld, P. Burnham and A. D. Morton (eds), *Global Restructuring, State, Capital and Labour: Contesting Neo-Gramscian Perspectives* (Basingstoke: Palgrave Macmillan).

Bieler, A., W. Bonefeld, P. Burnham and A. D. Morton (eds) (2006), *Global Restructuring, State, Capital and Labour: Contesting Neo-Gramscian Perspectives* (Basingstoke: Palgrave).

Bielsa, J. and R. Duarte (2011) 'Size and Linkages of the Spanish Construction Industry: Key Sector or Deformation of the Economy', *Cambridge Journal of Economics*, 35:2, 317–34.

Binda, V. and A. Colli (2011) 'Changing Big Business in Italy and Spain, 1973–2003: Strategic Responses to a New Context', *Business History*, 53:1, 14–39.

Bini Smaghi, L. (2009) 'A Failure of Capitalism?' lecture delivered on 16 October, Università di Siena, http://www.ecb.int/press/key/date/2009/html/sp091016. en.html, date accessed 20 March 2013.

Blinkhorn, M. (1980) 'Spain: The "Spanish Problem" and The Imperial Myth', *Journal of Contemporary History*, 15:1, 5–25.

Böil, S. and D. Böcking (2011) 'The Myth of a Lazy Southern Europe: Merkel's Clichés Debunked by Statistics', *Spiegel Online International*, 19 May, http://www. spiegel.de/international/europe/the-myth-of-a-lazy-southern-europe-merkel-s-cliches-debunked-by-statistics-a-763618.html, date accessed 25 March 2013.

Boix, C. (1995) 'Building a Social Democratic Strategy in Southern Europe: Economic Policy Under the González Government (1982–93)', *Centro de Estudios Sociales Avanzados Fundación Juan March*, Working Paper 69, May.

Boletín Oficial del Estado (2012) '2076: Real Decreto-ley 3/2012, de 10 de febrero, de medidas urgentes para la reforma laboral', 36, 11 February, http://www. boe.es/boe/dias/2012/02/11/pdfs/BOE-A-2012-2076.pdf, date accessed 16 May 2013.

Bonefeld, W. (1992) 'Social Constitution and the Form of the Capitalist State', in W. Bonefeld, R. Gunn and K. Psychopedis (eds), *Open Marxism: Volume I, Dialectics and History* (London: Pluto).

Bonefeld, W. (1993) *The Recomposition of the British State During the 1980s* (Aldershot: Dartmouth).

Bonefeld, W. (1996a) 'Money, Equality and Exploitation: An Interpretation of Marx's Treatment of Money', in W. Bonefeld and J. Holloway (eds), *Global Capital, National State and the Politics of Money* (Basingstoke: Macmillan).

Bonefeld, W. (1996b) 'Monetarism and Crisis', in W. Bonefeld and J. Holloway (eds), *Global Capital, National State and the Politics of Money* (Basingstoke: Macmillan).

Bonefeld, W. (1998) 'Politics of European Monetary Union: Class, Ideology and Critique', *Economic & Political Weekly*, 33:35, PE55–69.

Bonefeld, W. (2000) 'The Spectre of Globalization: On the Form and Content of the World Market', in W. Bonefeld and K. Psychopedis (eds), *The Politics of Change: Globalization, Ideology and Critique* (Basingstoke: Palgrave Macmillan).

Bonefeld, W. (2002) 'Class and EMU', *The Commoner*, 5, 1–8.

Bonefeld, W. (2004) 'Anti-Globalisation Versus Anti-Capitalism: The Dangers of Nationalism, Racism and Anti-Semitism', in P. Chandra, A. Ghosh and R. Kumar (eds), *The Politics of Imperialism and Counterstrategies* (Delhi: Aakar).

Bonefeld, W. (2006) 'The Capitalist State: Illusion and Critique', in W. Bonefeld (ed.), *Revolutionary Writing: Common Sense Essays in Post-Political Politics* (New York: Autonomedia).

Bonefeld, W. (2008) 'Global Capital, National State and the International', *Critique: Journal of Socialist Theory*, 36:1, 63–72.

Bonefeld, W. (2012a) 'From Humanity to Nationality to Bestiality: A Polemic on Alternatives without Conclusions', *Ephemera*, 12:4, 445–53.

Bonefeld, W. (2012b) 'Neo-Liberal Europe and the Transformation of Democracy: On the State of Money and Law', in P. Nousios, H. Overbeek and A. Tsolakis (eds), *Globalisation and European Integration: Critical Approaches to Regional Order and International Relations* (London: Routledge).

Bonefeld, W., A. Brown and P. Burnham (1995) *A Major Crisis? The Politics of Economic Policy in Britain in the 1990s* (Aldershot: Dartmouth).

Bonefeld, W., R. Gunn and K. Psychopedis (eds) (1992) *Open Marxism* (Volumes I and II) (London: Pluto).

Bonefeld, W., R. Gunn, J. Holloway and K. Psychopedis (1995) *Open Marxism, Volume III: Emancipating Marx* (London: Pluto).

Bonnet, A. (2002) 'The Command of Money-Capital and the Latin American Crises', in W. Bonefeld and S. Tischler (eds), *What Is To Be Done? Leninism, Anti-Leninist Marxism, and the Question of Revolution Today* (Aldershot: Ashgate).

Bordenave, G. and Y. Lung (1996) 'New Spatial Configurations in the European Automobile Industry', *European Urban and Regional Studies*, 3:4, 305–21.

Bote Gómez, V. (1994) 'Turismo y desarrollo económico en España: del insuficiente reconocimiento a la revalorización de su función estratégica', *Papers de Turisme*, 6:14–15, 117–30.

Bote Gómez, V. (1996) 'Research in Spain on Tourism and Economic Development', *The Tourist Review*, 1, 5–11.

Boyer, C. (1988) 'The Return of Aesthetics to City Planning', *Society*, 25:4: 49–56.

Bruegel, I. (1975) 'The Marxist Theory of Rent and the Contemporary City: A Critique of Harvey', in Conference of Socialist Economists (ed.), *Political Economy and the Housing Question* (London: CSE).

Buck, T. (2013a) 'Spain's "Bad Bank" Speeds Up Asset Sales', *Financial Times*, 21 March, http://www.ft.com/cms/s/0/425e44f0-921d-11e2-851f-00144feabdc0.html#axzz2Xc8PMnyU, date accessed 10 May 2013.

Buck, T. (2013b) 'Spain Fights Catalan Push for Secession', *Financial Times*, 1 March, http://www.ft.com/cms/s/0/1dbc93a0-8290-11e2-a3e3-00144feabdc0.html, date accessed 24 June 2013.

Bullain, I. (2013) 'A Basque (and Catalan) Republic Within a Federal Context: Reflections on New Scenarios in the Crisis of the Autonomous State', in A. Lopez-Basaguren and L. Escajedo San Epifanio (eds), *The Ways of Federalism in Western Countries and the Horizons of Territorial Autonomy in Spain: Volume 2* (Berlin Heidelberg: Springer-Verlag).

Burnham, P. (1994) 'Open Marxism and Vulgar International Political Economy', *Review of International Political Economy*, 1:2, 221–31.

Burnham, P. (1996) 'Capital, Crisis and the International State System', in W. Bonefeld and J. Holloway (eds), *Global Capital, National State and the Politics of Money* (Basingstoke: Macmillan).

Burnham, P. (2002) 'Class Struggle, States and Global Circuits of Capital', in M. Rupert and H. Smith (eds), *Historical Materialism and Globalization* (London: Routledge).

Burnham, P. (2011) 'Towards a Political Theory of Crisis: Policy and Resistance Across Europe', *New Political Science*, 33:4, 493–507.

Burriel de Orueta, E. L. (2008) 'La "década prodigiosa" del urbanismo español (1997–2006)', *Scripta Nova: Revista de Geografía y Ciencias Sociales*, XIII:27, 1–28.

Burriel de Orueta, E. L. (2009) 'Los límites del planeamiento urbanístico municipal: El ejemplo valenciano', *Documents d'anàlisi geogràfica*, 54, 33–54.

Cabré, A. and J. A. Módenes (2004) 'Homeownership and Social Inequality in Spain', in K. Kurz and H. Peter-Blossfeld (eds), *Home Ownership and Social Inequality in Comparative Perspective* (Stanford: Stanford University Press).

Cabrero, A., L. A. Maza and J. Yaniz (2007) 'Spain's External Deficit: How Is It Financed?' *ECFIN Country Focus*, IV:7, 1–6.

Calatayud Giner, S. (2011) 'Desarrollo agrario e industrialización: Crecimiento y crisis en la economía valenciana del siglo XX', Unitat d'Història Econòmica Working Paper 2011_9, Universitat de València, 15 February.

Calatayud, S., J. Millán and M. Cruz Romeo (2002/2003) 'Les múltiples cares de la renda: propietaris i arrendataris al País Valencià', *Estudis D'Història Agrària*, 15, 57–86.

Calvo-Gonzalez, O. (2007) 'American Military Interests and Economic Confidence in Spain Under the Franco Dictatorship', *Journal of Economic History*, 67:3, 740–67.

Calvo, K., T. Gómez-Pastra and L. Mena (2011) 'Movimiento 15M: ¿quiénes son y qué reinvindican?', *ZOOMPolítico*, April, 4–17.

Cámara Izquierdo, S. (2007) 'The Dynamics of the Profit Rate in Spain (1954–2001)', *Review of Radical Political Economics*, 39:4, 543–61.

Cambridge Econometrics (2011) 'Study on the Cost Competitiveness of European Industry in the Globalisation Era: Empirical Evidence on the Basis of Relative Unit Labour Costs (ULC) at Sectoral Level', ECORYS Framework Contract Sector Competitiveness Final Report, Cambridge, 28 September.

Cammack, P. (2007) 'RIP IPE', *Papers in the Politics of Global Competitiveness*, 7, Manchester Metropolitan University, e-space Open Repository.

Cammack, P. (2011) 'Knowledge Versus Power in the Field of IPE', in S. Shields., I. Bruff and H. Macartney (eds), *Critical International Political Economy: Dialogue, Debate, Dissensus* (Basingstoke: Palgrave Macmillan).

Cammack, P. (2013) 'Classical Marxism', in T. G. Weiss and R. Wilkinson (eds), *International Organization and Global Governance* (London: Routledge).

Carballo-Cruz, F. (2011) 'Causes and Consequences of the Spanish Economic Crisis: Why the Recovery has Taken So Long?' *Panoeconomicus*, 3, 309–28.

Carchedi, G. (1997) 'The EMU, Monetary Crises, and the Single European Currency', *Capital & Class*, 21:3, 85–114.

Carrasco-Gallego, J. A. (2012) 'The Marshall Plan and the Spanish Postwar Economy: A Welfare Loss Analysis', *The Economic History Review*, 65:1, 91–119.

Carreras, A. and X. Tafunell (1994) 'Spanish Big Manufacturing Firms (1917–1990): Between State and Market', Economics Working Paper, 93, Universitat Pompeu Fabra, Barcelona.

Carreras, A. and X. Tafunell (2003) *Historia económica de la España contemporánea* (Barcelona: Crítica).

Castañeda, E. (2012) 'The Indignados of Spain: A Precedent to Occupy Wall Street', *Social Movement Studies: Journal of Social, Cultural and Political Protest*, 11:3–4, 309–19.

Castany, L. (2010) 'The Role of Size in Firms' Training: Evidence from Spain', *International Journal of Manpower*, 31:5, 563–84.

Catalan News Agency (2013) 'The Catalan Government Posts a Debt of 50.95 Billion at the End of 2012', 14 March, http://www.catalannewsagency. com/news/politics/catalan-government-posts-debt-€5095-billion-end-2012, date accessed 29 June 2013.

Catalan, J. (1995) 'Sector exterior y crecimiento industrial: España y Europa, 1939–59', *Revista de Historia Industrial*, 8: 99–146.

Catalan, J. (2010) 'Strategic Policy Revisited: The Origins of Mass Production in the Motor Industry of Argentina, Korean and Spain, 1945–87', *Business History*, 52:2, 207–30.

Cattaneo, O., G. Gereffi and C. Staritz (eds) (2010) *Global Value Chains in a Postcrisis World: A Development Perspective* (Washington DC: World Bank).

Cebrían Villar, M. (2005) 'La regulación industrial y la transferencia internacional de tecnología en España (1959–1973)', *Investigaciones de Historia Económica*, 3, 11–40.

Charney, I. (2001) 'Three Dimensions of Capital Switching Within the Real Estate Sector: A Canadian Case Study', *International Journal of Urban and Regional Research*, 25:4, 740–58.

Charnock, G. and R. Ribera-Fumaz (2011) 'A New Space for Knowledge and People?' Henri Lefebvre, Representations of Space, and the Production of '22@ Barcelona'. *Environment and Planning D*, 29:2, 613–32

Charnock, G., T. F. Purcell and R. Ribera-Fumaz (2013) 'City of Rents: The Limits to the Barcelona Model of Urban Competitiveness', *International Journal of Urban and Regional Research*, Early View, DOI: 10.1111/1468-2427.12103.

Chilcote, R. H. (1966) 'Spain and European Integration: Heavy Industry in Economic Development', *International Affairs*, 42:3, 444–55.

Chislett, W. (2007) 'Spain's Main Multinationals: An Increasing Force in the Economy', Working Paper 32/2007, Real Instituto Elcano, Madrid, 12 July.

Chislett, W. (2008) *Spain Going Places: Economic, Political and Social Progress, 1975–2008* (Madrid: Telefónica).

Christophers, B. (2010) 'On Voodoo Economics: Theorising Relations of Property, Value and Contemporary Capitalism', *Transactions of the Institute of British Geographers*, 35:1, 94–108.

Christophers, B. (2011) 'Revisiting the Urbanization of Capital', *Annals of the Association of American Geographers*, 101:6, 1347–64.

Cinco Días (2010) 'Sacresa entra en concurso con 1,800 millones de deuda', 29 June, 10.

Clark, E. (1987) 'A Critical Note on Ball's Reformulation of the Role of Urban Land Rent', *Environment and Planning A*, 19:2, 263–67.

Clarke, S. (1978) 'Capital, Fractions of Capital and the State: "Neo-Marxist" Analysis of the South African State', *Capital & Class*, 2:2, 32–77.

Clarke, S. (1988) *Keynesianism, Monetarism and the Crisis of the State* (Aldershot: Edward Elgar).

Clarke, S. (1990) 'State, Class Struggle, and the Reproduction of Capital', in S. Clarke (ed.), *The State Debate* (Basingstoke: Palgrave).

Clarke, S. (1990/1) 'The Marxist Theory of Overaccumulation and Crisis', *Science & Society*, 54:4, 442–67.

Clarke, S. (1992) 'The Global Accumulation of Capital and the Periodisation of the Capitalist State Form', in W. Bonefeld, R. Gunn and K. Psychopedis (eds), *Open Marxism: Volume I, Dialectics and History* (London: Pluto).

Clarke, S. (1994) *Marx's Theory of Crisis* (London: Macmillan).

Clarke, S. (2001) 'Class Struggle and the Global Overaccumulation of Capital', in R. Albritton, M. Itoh, R. Westra and A Zuege (eds), *Phases of Capitalist Development: Boom, Crises and Globalizations* (Basingstoke: Palgrave Macmillan).

Clayburn la Force, J. (1964) 'Royal Textile Factories in Spain, 1700–1800', *The Journal of Economic History*, 24:3, 337–63.

Cobos, T. And C. Kane (2013) 'Spanish Bankruptcies Hit Record in First Quarter of 2013', *Reuters US*, 8 April, http://www.reuters.com/article/2013/04/08/us-spain-bankruptcy-idUSBRE9370PE20130408, date accessed 13 June 2013.

Colau, A. and A. Alemany (2012) *Vidas hipotecadas: De la burbuja inmobiliaria al derecho a la vivienda* (Barcelona: Cuadrilátero de libros).

Colomer, J. M. (1998) 'The Spanish "State of Autonomies": Non-Institutional Federalism', *West European Politics*, 21:4, 50–52.

Comín, F. (2011) 'La crisis económica durante la segunda republica española (1931–1935), *Mediterráneo Económico*, 19, 77–92.

Corsetti, G., M. P. Devereux, J. Hassler, G. Saint-Paul, H-W. Sinn, J-E. Sturm and X. Vives (2011) 'España', IESE Occasional Papers, OP-193, University of Navarra, August.

Cortés-Jiménez, I., M. Pulina, C. Riera i Prunera and M. Artis (2009) 'Tourism and Exports as a Means of Growth', Research Institute of Applied Economics Working Paper 2009/10, Universitat de Barcelona.

Cué, C. E. (2011) 'Rajoy aprueba el mayor recorte de la historia y una gran subida de impuestos', *El País*, 31 December, http://elpais.com/diario/2011/12/31/espana/1325286001_850215.html, date accessed 16 June 2013.

Cué, C. E. (2012) 'Una rectificación total con un argumento: no hay libertad', *El País*, 11 July, http://politica.elpais.com/politica/2012/07/11/actualidad/1341997963_126827.html, date accessed 14 June 2013.

CV (2012a) 'The March 29 Strike Against Labour Law Reform in Spain: Outline of the Conjuncture', *Insurgent Notes: Journal of Communist Theory and Practice*, 6, http://insurgentnotes.com/2012/01/letter-from-spain-the-november-2011-general-elections-in-spain-indignation-trapped-in-the-ballot-box/, data accessed 1 July 2013.

CV (2012b) 'Letter From Spain: The November 2011 General Elections in Spain: Indignation Trapped in the Ballot Box', *Insurgent Notes: Journal of Communist Theory and Practice*, 5, http://insurgentnotes.com/2012/01/letter-from-spain-the-november-2011-general-elections-in-spain-indignation-trapped-in-the-ballot-box/, date accessed 1 July 2013.

de Barrón, I. (2012) 'La codicia de la banca por crecer propició la concesión de hipotecas a insolventes', *El País*, 12 November, 16.

de Carreras, F. (2012) 'The Economics of Catalan Independence Don't Add Up', *Guardian*, 22 November, http://www.guardian.co.uk/commentisfree/2012/nov/22/economics-catalan-independence-dont-add-up, date accessed 29 June 2013.

del Romero Renau, L. and C. Trudelle (2011) 'Mega Events and Urban Conflicts in Valencia, Spain: Contesting the New Urban Modernity', *Urban Studies Research*, 2011:587523, 1–12.

Delgado, C. (2013) 'Más turistas, menos empleos', *El País*, 11 February, http://economia.elpais.com/economia/2013/02/10/actualidad/1360531816_937892.html, date accessed 19 February 2013.

Deutsche Welle (2010) 'Chancellor Merkel Defends Position as Parliament Debates Greece Bailout', 5 May, http://www.dw.de/chancellor-merkel-defends-position-as-parliament-debates-greece-bailout/a-5537752, date accessed 21 March 2013.

Díaz Orueta, F. (2007) 'Madrid: Urban Regeneration Projects and Social Mobilization', *Cities*, 24:3, 183–93.

Dolado, J. J. (2012) 'The Pros and Cons of the Latest Labour Market Reform in Spain', *Spanish Labour Law and Employment Relations Journal*, 1:1–2, 22–30.

Domenech, J. (2008) 'Mineral Resource Abundance and Regional Growth in Spain, 1860–2000', *Journal of International Development*, 20:8, 1122–35.

Domínguez-Mujica, J., R. Guerra-Talavera and J. M. Parreño-Castellano (2012) 'Migration at a Time of Global Economic Crisis: The Situation in Spain', *International Migration*, DOI: 10.1111/imig.12023.

Donges, J. B. (1971) 'From an Autarchic Towards a Cautiously Outward-Looking Industrialization Policy: The Case of Spain', *Review of World Economics*, 107:1, 33–75.

Donges, J. B. (1972) 'Spain's Industrial Exports: An Analysis of Supply and Demand Factors', *Weltwirtschaftliches Archiv*, 108, 191–234.

Dowling, A. (2009) '*Autonomistes, Catalanistes* and *Independentistes*: Politics in Contemporary Catalonia', *International Journal of Iberian Studies*, 22:3, 185–200.

Doz, Y. L. (1986) *Strategic Management in Multinational Enterprises* (Oxford: Pergamon Press).

Drelichman, M. (1995) 'All that Glitters: Precious Metals, Rent Seeking, and the Decline of Spain', *European Review of Economic History*, 9:3, 313–36.

Drelichman, M. and H-J. Voth (2008) 'Institutions and the Resource Curse in Early Modern Spain', in E. Helpman (ed.), *Institutions and Economic Performance* (Cambridge, MA: Harvard University Press).

Duménil, G. and D. Lévy (2004) *Capital Resurgent: The Roots of the Neoliberal Revolution* (London: Harvard University Press).

Duménil, G. and D. Lévy (2011) *The Crisis of Neoliberalism* (London: Harvard University Press).

Dymski, G. A. (2012) 'The Reinvention of Banking and the Subprime Crisis', in M. B. Aalbers (ed.), *Subprime Cities: The Political Economy of Mortgage Markets* (Chichester: Wiley).

Echebarría, G. and J. L. Herrero (1989) 'La evolución de la economía española durante el periodo 1940–1988 a partir de un indicador de la tasa de beneficio del sector industrial', *Información Comercial Española*, 665: 9–23.

Economist (2002) 'House Prices: Going Through the Roof', 28 March, http://www.economist.com/node/1057057?story_id=1057057, date accessed 18 February 2013.

Economist (2007) 'Briefing, Spanish Business: Conquistadors on the Beach', 5 May, 77–9.

Economist (2010a) 'So Hard to Bend: Rigidities in the Labour Market Make Recovery Even Harder', 11 February, http://www.economist.com/node/15503246, date accessed 25 June 2013.

Economist (2010b) 'Zapatero's Cuts', 20 May, http://www.economist.com/node/16167836, date accessed 16 June 2013.

Economist (2011) 'Spain's Indignants: Europe's Most Earnest Protestors', 14 July, http://www.economist.com/node/18959259, date accessed 14 July 2011.

Economist (2012) 'The Euro Crisis: How to Save Spain', 2 June, http://www.economist.com/node/21556238, date accessed 16 June 2013.

Economist (2013a) 'Rajoy Unconfined?' 13 February, www.economist.com/blogs/freeexchange/2013/02/spains-economy, date accessed 13 February 2013.

Economist (2013b) 'The Italian Election: Who Can Save Italy?', 16 February, http://www.economist.com/news/leaders/21571891-europes-most-sluggish-economy-needs-more-mario-montis-reforms-who-can-save-italy, date accessed 25 March 2013.

Edel, M. (1992) *Urban and Regional Economics: Marxist Perspectives* (Chur: Harwood).

Edquist, C. and S. Jacobsson (1987) 'The Diffusion of Industrial Robots in the OECD Countries and the Impact Thereof', *Robotics*, 3, 23–32.

Efe (2013) 'El Govern pagará en octubre los 35 millones que debe a Acciona po el Palau de Congressos', 3 June, http://ultimahora.es/mallorca/noticia/noticias/local/govern-pagara-octubre-millones-debe-acciona-por-palau-congressos.html, date accessed 24 June 2013.

el Economista (2012) 'Una respuesta errónea a los desalojos: Amenaza el crédito', 10 November, 14–15.

El País (2006) 'Ferrovial vende su división inmobiliaria a Habitat por 2.200 millones', 28 December, http://economia.elpais.com/economia/2006/12/28/actualidad/1167294780_850215.html, date accessed 2 June 2012.

El País (2011a) 'Barcelona acumula más de 820.000 metros cuadrados de oficinas vacías, 19 January, 20.

El País (2011b) 'Anti-Eviction Gangs Call Debt into Question', 28 June, http://elpais.com/elpais/2011/06/28/inenglish/1309238442_850210.html, date accessed 28 June 2013.

El País (2012a) 'Seat sufre su cuarto año de pérdidas en 2011 por la caída de las ventas en España', 12 March, http://economia.elpais.com/economia/2012/03/12/actualidad/1331543920_337159.html, date accessed 14 June 2012.

El País (2012b) 'La riqueza de los hogares españoles baja un 18,4%', 11 October, http://economia.elpais.com/economia/2012/10/10/actualidad/1349901592_959130.html, date accessed 21 May 2013.

El País (2012c) 'Así te hemos contado el discurso de Mas', 25 September, http://ccaa.elpais.com/ccaa/2012/09/25/catalunya/1348562619_407567.html, date accessed 29 June 2013.

el Periódico (2011) 'Barcelona agotará la nueva oferta de oficinas en el 2011', 20 October.

Elcano Royal Institute (2006) *20 Years of Spain in the European Union* (Madrid: Real Instituto Elcano and European Parliament – Office in Spain).

Elliott, L. (2013) 'Human and Economic Crisis Threatens to Destroy the Euro', *Guardian*, 1 June, 32.

Encarnación, O. G. (2003) *The Myth of Civil Society: Social Capital and Democratic Consolidation in Spain and Brazil* (Basingstoke: Palgrave Macmillan).

Espinosa Pino, M. (2013) 'Politics of Indignation: Radical Democracy and Class Struggle Beyond Postmodernity', *Rethinking Marxism*, 25:2, 228–41.

Estefanía, J. (2013) 'Mil días de austeridad', *El País*, 5 May, http://economia.elpais.com/economia/2013/05/03/actualidad/1367592834_505488.html, date accessed 5 May 2013.

Estrada, Á. and J. D. López-Salido (2004) 'Understanding Spanish Dual Inflation', *Investigaciones Económicas*, 28:1, 123–40.

Estrada, Á., J. F. Jimeno and J. L. Malo de Molina (2009) 'The Spanish Economy in EMU: The First Ten Years', Documentos Ocasionales 0901, Madrid: Banco de España.

Etchemendy, S. (2004) 'Revamping the Weak, Protecting the Strong, and Managing Privatization: Governing Globalization in the Spanish Takeoff', *Comparative Political Studies*, 37:6, 623–51.

Etxezarreta, M. (1991) 'La economía política del proceso del acumulación', in M. Etxezarreta (ed.), *La reestructuración del capitalismo en España, 1970–1990* (Barcelona: Icaria).

Etxezarreta, M. (2000) 'La vulnerabilidad de los Modelos Económicos Neoliberales', in D. Guerrero (ed.), *Macroeconomía y Crisis Mundial* (Madrid: Editorial Trotta).

Etxezarreta, M. and R. Ribera-Fumaz (2012) 'Nuevos movimientos sociales en tiempo de crisis', in J. L. Calva (ed.), *¡Si se puede! Caminos al desarrollo con equidad* (Mexico City: Consejo Nacional de Universitarios).

EU Commission (2012) *Current Account Surpluses in the EU* (Brussels: European Union).

Euronews (2013) 'Pro-drachma Party Launches Urging Greece to Leave the euro', 19 May, http://www.euronews.com/2013/05/19/pro-drachma-party-launches-urging-greece-to-leave-the-euro/, date accessed 5 July 2013.

Europapress (2002) 'La inversion inmobiliaria en Barcelona alcanzará los 800 millones al cerrar al año', 8 December, http://www.europapress.es, date accessed 1 June 2012.

Europapress (2013) 'Primer año de Gobierno de Rajoy: Más de 36,000 manifestaciones y concentraciones', 12 January, http://www.europapress.es/nacional/noticia-primer-ano-gobierno-rajoy-mas-36000-manifestaciones-concentraciones-20130112120312.html, date accessed 1 July 2013.

European Council (2011) 'Conclusions of the European Council', 24/25 March, http://www.consilium.europa.eu/uedocs/cms_data/docs/pressdata/en/ec/120296.pdf, date accessed 20 July 2011.

European Mortgage Federation (2012) 'Spain: Structure of Housing Industry', EMF Factsheet, March.

Eurostat (2012a) 'At Risk of Poverty or Social Exclusion in the EU27', Press Release 171/2012, 3 December, http://epp.eurostat.ec.europa.eu/cache/ITY_PUBLIC/3-03122012-AP/EN/3-03122012-AP-EN.PDF, date accessed 21 March 2013.

Eurostat (2012b) 'Macroeconomic Imbalances Procedure Scoreboard Headline Indicators, 1 November 2012 Statistical information', European Commission, Luxembourg, 1 November.

Feagin, J. R. (1987) 'The Secondary Circuit of Capital: Office Construction in Houston, Texas', *International Journal of Urban and Regional Research*, 11:2, 172–92.

Fernández Asperilla, A. (1998) 'La emigración como exportación de mano de obra: el fenómeno migratorio a Europa durante el franquismo', *Historia Social*, 30: 63–81.

Fernández de Lis, S. and A. García Herrero (2008) 'The Housing Boom and Bust in Spain: Impact of the Securitisation Model and Dynamic Provisioning', BBVA Working Paper 0806, Madrid.

Fernández-Durán, R. (2006). 'El tsunami urbanizador español y mundial', *Ciudades para un future mas sostenible*, http://habitat.aq.upm.es/boletin/n38/arfer_3.html#fnmark-33, date accessed 21 February 2013.

Fernández-Villaverde, J. and L. Ohanian (2010) 'The Spanish Crisis from a Global Perspective', Working Paper 2010–03, Fundación de Estudios de Economía Aplicada, Madrid, February.

Fernández, F. (2011) 'La internacionalización de las empresas españolas', in Equipo Económico (ed.), *Hacia una nueva política económica española: Diagnóstico, desafíos, estrategias* (Madrid: Alianza Editorial).

Ferreira do Amaral, J. (2013) *Porque devemos sair do euro* (Afragide: Lua de Papel).

Fine, B. (1979) 'On Marx's Theory of Agricultural Rent', *Economy and Society*, 8:3, 241–78.

Fine, B. (2010) 'Locating Financialisation', *Historical Materialism*, 18:2, 97–116.

Flynn, D. O. (1982) 'Fiscal Crisis and the Decline of Spain (Castile)', *The Journal of Economic History*, 42:1, 139–47.

Foster, J. B. (2008) 'The Financialization of Capital and the Crisis', *Monthly Review*, 59:11, http://monthlyreview.org/2008/04/01/the-financialization-of-capital-and-the-crisis, date accessed 10 April 2013.

Fouskas, V. K. and C. Dimoulas (2012) 'The Greek Worship of Debt and the Failure of the European Project', *Journal of Balkan and Near Eastern Studies*, 14:1, 1–31.

Fox Gotham, K. (2009) 'Creating Liquidity out of Spatial Fixity: The Secondary Circuit of Capital and the Subprime Mortgage Crisis', *International Journal of Urban and Regional Research*, 33:2, 355–71.

Fraile, P. and A. Escribano (1998) 'The Spanish 1898 Disaster: The Drift Towards National Protectionism', *Revista de Historia Económica*, 6:1, 265–90.

FROB (2012) 'The Transfer Prices to the Asset Management Company (Sareb) Will Be Sharply Adjusted to Ensure Its Profitability', Press Release, 29 October, http://www.bde.es/f/webbde/GAP/Secciones/SalaPrensa/InformacionInteres/ReestructuracionSectorFinanciero/Archivo/Ficheros/frob291012e.pdf, date accessed 28 June 2013.

Fröbel, F., J. Heinrichs and O. Kreye (1978) 'The World Market for Labor and the World Market for Industrial Sites', *Journal of Economic Issues*, XIII:4, 843–58.

Fröbel, F., J. Heinrichs and O. Kreye (1980) *The New International Division of Labour* (Cambridge: Cambridge University Press).

Galí, J. (2013) 'Estat propi i euro', Wilson Initiative, 19 March, http://www.wilson.cat/en/mitjans-escrits/articles-dels-membres/item/222-estat-propi-i-euro.html, date accessed 1 July 2013.

Gallego, R. and J. Subirats (2012) 'Spanish and Regional Welfare Systems: Policy Innovation and Multi-Level Governance', *Regional & Federal Studies*, 22:3, 269–88.

García, M. (2010) 'The Breakdown of the Spanish Urban Growth Model: Social and Territorial Effects of the Global Crisis', *International Journal of Urban and Regional Research*, 34:4, 967–80.

García Lamarca, M. (2013) 'Resisting Evictions Spanish Style', *New Internationalist*, April, http://newint.org/features/2013/04/01/sparks-from-the-spanish-crucible/, date accessed 28 June 2013.

Garcia-Ramon, M. D. and A. Albet (2000) 'Pre-Olympic Barcelona and Post-Olympic Barcelona: A "Model" for Urban Regeneration Today?' *Environment and Planning A*, 32, 1331–34.

García Ruiz, J. L. (2001) 'La evolución de la industria automovilística española, 1946–1999: una perspectiva comparada', *Revista de Historia Industrial*, 19–20, 133–63.

Girard-Vasseur, M. and L. Quignon (2006) 'What Future for the Spanish Housing Market?' BNP Paribas Conjoncture, Paris, March.

Goldner, L. (2000) *Ubu Saved from Drowning: Worker Insurgency and Statist Containment in Portugal and Spain, 1974–1977* (West Somerville: Queepeg Publications).

Gomes da Silva, E. and A. A. C. Teixeira (2012) 'In the Shadow of the Financial Crisis: Dismal Structural Change and Productivity in South-Western Europe over the Last Four Decades', conference paper, Workshop on European Governance and the Problems of Peripheral Countries, Austrian Institute of Economic Research, 13 July, http://www.foreurope.eu/fileadmin/documents/pdf/Ester_ Silva_and_Aurora_Teixeira_Paper.pdf, date accessed 10 December 2012.

Gómez Fortes, B. and L. Cabeza Pérez (2013) 'Basque Regional Elections 2012: The Return of Nationalism Under the Influence of the Economic Crisis', *Regional and Federal Studies*, 23:4, 495–505.

Gomez Uranga, M. (1991) 'La internacionalización de la industrial española: un proceso acelerado', in M. Etxezarreta (ed.), *La reestructuración del capitalismo en España, 1970–1990* (Barcelona: Icaria).

Gomez Villascuerna, J. And P. Vargas Montoya (2008) 'Explaining the Adoption of Process Technologies in Spanish Manufacturing Firms', Departamento de Economia y Empresa, Universidad de La Rioja, Working Paper 03, May.

Gomez-Mendoza, A. (1988) 'Government and the Development of Modern Shipbuilding in Spain, 1850–1935', *Journal of Transport History*, 9:1, 19–36.

Gómez, J. (2011) 'Trichet pide a Salgado por carta que no pare las reformas', *El País*, http://elpais.com/m/diario/2011/08/13/economia/1313186405_850215.html, date accessed 16 June 2013.

Gómez, J., I. Salazar and P. Vargas (2012) 'La difusión de tecnologías de proceso en la empresa manufacturera española', *Universia Business Review*, primer trimestre, 144–61.

Gómez, M. V. (2013) 'La duración de la crisis y los recortes reducen la factura del paro', *El País*, 7 May, http://economia.elpais.com/economia/2013/05/06/empleo/1367868680_677564.html, date accessed 7 May 2013.

González Ceballos, S. (2005) 'The Role of the Guggenheim Museum in the Development of Urban Entrepreneurial Practices in Bilbao', *International Journal of Iberian Studies*, 16:3, 177–86.

González i Calvet, J. (1991) 'Crisis, transición y estancamiento: la política económica española, 1973–82', in M. Etxezarreta (ed.), *La reestructuración del capitalismo en España, 1970–1990* (Barcelona: Icaria).

González Pérez, J. M. (2010) 'The Real Estate and Economic Crisis: An Opportunity for Urban Return and Rehabilitation Policies in Spain', *Sustainability*, 2, 1571–1601.

Gordon, S. (2013) Spain Remains Shackled by Corporate Debt', 18 January, http://www.ft.com/cms/s/0/1fd11fa0-614b-11e2-9545-00144feab49a.html#axzz2SJZ240fz, date accessed 2 May 2013.

Grinberg, N. (2007) 'The New International Division of Labour and the Differentiated Evolution of Poverty at the World Scale', paper delivered at conference on 'Poverty and Capital', The University of Manchester, 3 July, http://www.sed.manchester.ac.uk/research/events/conferences/povertyandcapital/grinberg.pdf, date accessed 28 November 2011.

Grinberg, N. (2008) 'From the "Miracle" to the "Lost Decade": Intersectoral Transfers and External Credit in the Brazilian Economy', *Brazilian Journal of Political Economy*, 28:2, 291–311.

Grinberg, N. (2013) 'The Political Economy of Brazilian (Latin American) and Korean (East Asian) Comparative Development: Moving Beyond Nation-Centred Approaches', *New Political Economy*, 18:2, 171–97.

Grinberg, N. and G. Starosta (2009) 'The Limits of Studies in Comparative Development of East Asia and Latin America: the Case of Land Reform and Agrarian Policies', *Third World Quarterly*, 30:4, 761–77.

Grinberg, N. and G. Starosta (2013) 'Revisiting the Debate over the New International Division of Labour: The Case of the Steel Industry', unpublished research paper.

Guadalupe, M., O. Kuzmina and C. Thomas (2012) 'Innovation and Foreign Ownership', *American Economic Review*, 102:7, 3594–627.

Guardian (2011) 'Greek Unemployment: How Bad Is It for Youths?', 4 August, http://www.guardian.co.uk/news/datablog/2011/aug/04/greece-youth-unemployment-rate#data, date accessed 21 March 2013.

Guardian (2012a) 'Greek Elections: The Replay Deepens the Divide', 17 June, http://www.guardian.co.uk/commentisfree/2012/jun/17/greek-elections-replay-deepens-divide, date accessed 26 march 2013.

Guardian (2012b) 'Spanish Miners in Mass Protest Against the Cuts', 11 July, http://www.guardian.co.uk/world/2012/jul/11/spanish-miners-protest-cuts, date accessed 16 June 2013.

Guerrero, D. (2003) 'Capitalist Competition and the Distribution of Profits', in A. Saad-Filho (ed.), *Anti-Capitalism: A Marxist Introduction* (London: Pluto).

Guerrero, D. (2009) 'Economía franquista y capitalismo: una interpretación alternativa a la del antifranquismo liberal postfranquista', unpublished research paper, http://www.correntroig.org/IMG/pdf/Economia_franquista_y_capitalismo.pdf, date accessed 26 September 2012.

Hadjimichalis, C. (1987) *Uneven Development and Regionalism: State, Territory and Class in Southern Europe* (Croom Helm: London).

Hadjimichalis, C. (1994) 'The Fringes of Europe and EU Integration: A View from the South', *European Urban and Regional Studies*, 1:1, 19–29.

Hadjimichalis, C. (2011) 'Uneven Geographical Development and Socio-Spatial Justice and Solidarity: European Regions after the 2009 Financial Crisis', *European Urban and Regional Studies*, 18:3, 254–74.

Haila, A. (1988) 'Land as a Financial Asset: The Theory of Urban Rent as a Mirror of Economic Transformation', *Antipode*, 20:2, 79–101.

Haila, A. (1991) 'Four Types of Investment in Land and Property', *International Journal of Urban and Regional Research*, 15:3, 343–65.

Halpin, P. (2012) 'Irish Unemployment Rate Hits Crisis-High 14.8 Per Cent', *Reuters*, 7 June, http://uk.reuters.com/article/2012/06/07/uk-ireland-economy-unemployment-idUKBRE8560OX20120607, date accessed 26 March 2013.

Hamann, K. (2001) 'The Resurgence of National-Level Bargaining: Union Strategies in Spain', *Industrial Relations Journal*, 32:2, 154–172.

Hampton, M. (2006) 'Hegemony, Class Struggle and the Radical Historiography of Global Money Standards', *Capital & Class*, 30:2, 131–64.

Harrison, J. (1978) *An Economic History of Spain* (Manchester: Manchester University Press).

Harrison, J. (1985) *The Spanish Economy in the Twentieth Century* (Beckenham: Croom Helm).

Harrison, J. and D. Corkill (2004) *Spain: A Modern European Economy* (Hampshire: Ashgate).

Harvey, C. and P. Taylor (1987) 'Mineral Wealth and Economic Development: Foreign Direct Investment in Spain, 1851–1913', *Economic History Review*, 40:2, 185–207.

Harvey, D. (1973) *Social Justice and the City* (London: The Johns Hopkins University Press).

Harvey, D. (1974) 'Class-Monopoly Rent, Finance Capital and the Urban Revolution', *Regional Studies*, 8:3–4, 239–55.

Harvey, D. (1976) 'The Marxian Theory of the State', *Antipode*, 8:2, 80–9.

Harvey, D. (1982) *The Limits to Capital* (Oxford: Blackwell).

Harvey, D. (1985a) 'The Geopolitics of Capitalism', in D. Gregory and J. Urry (eds), *Social Relations and Spatial Structures* (Basingstoke: Palgrave).

Harvey, D. (1985b) *The Urbanization of Capital: Studies in the History and Theory of Capitalist Urbanization 2* (Oxford: Blackwell).

Harvey, D. (1988) 'The Geography of Class Power', in L. Panitch and C. Leys (eds), *The Socialist Register 1998: The Communist Manifesto Now* (London: Merlin Press).

Harvey, D. (1989) 'From Managerialism to Entrepreneurialism: The Transformation in Urban Governance in Late Capitalism', *Geografiska Annaler. Series B, Human Geography*, 71:1, 3–17.

Harvey, D. (1990) *The Condition of Postmodernity: An Enquiry into the Origins of Cultural Change* (Oxford: Blackwell).

Harvey, D. (2000) *Spaces of Hope* (Edinburgh: Edinburgh University Press).

Harvey, D. (2001) 'The Art of Rent: Globalization and the Commodification of Culture', in D. Harvey (ed.), *Spaces of Capital: Towards a Critical Geography* (New York: Routledge).

Harvey, D. (2003) *The New Imperialism* (Oxford: Oxford University Press).

Harvey, D. (2005) *A Brief History of Neoliberalism* (Oxford: Oxford University Press).

Harvey, D. (2010a) *A Companion to Marx's* Capital (London: Verso).

Harvey, D. (2010b) *The Enigma of Capital and the Crises of Capitalism* (London: Profile Books).

Harvey, D. (2012) 'History Versus Theory: A Commentary on Marx's Method in *Capital*', *Historical Materialism*, 20:2, 3–38.

Heinrich, M. (2012) *An Introduction to the Three Volumes of Karl Marx's* Capital (New York: Monthly Review Press).

Heinrich, M. (2013) 'Crisis Theory, the Law of the Tendency for the Rate of Profit to Fall, and Marx's Studies in the 1870s', *Monthly Review*, 1 April, http://monthlyreview.org/2013/04/01/crisis-theory-the-law-of-the-tendency-of-the-profit-rate-to-fall-and-marxs-studies-in-the-1870s, date accessed 9 April 2013.

Heneric, O., G. Licht, S. Lutz and W. Urban (2005) 'The European Automotive Industry in a Global Context', in O. Heneric, G. Licht and W. Sofka (eds), *Europe's Automotive Industry on the Move: Competitiveness in a Changing World* (Heidelberg: Physica-Verlag).

Hidalgo, A., J. Molero and G. Penas (2010) 'Technology and Industrialization at the Take-off of the Spanish Economy: New Evidence Based on Patents', *World Patent Information*, 32:1, 53–61.

Holloway, J. (1992) 'Crisis, Fetishism, Class Composition', in W. Bonefeld, R. Gunn and K. Psychopedis (eds), *Open Marxism: Volume II, Theory and Practice* (London: Pluto).

Holloway, J. (1996a) 'Global Capital and the National State', in W. Bonefeld and J. Holloway (eds), *Global Capital, National State and the Politics of Money* (Basingstoke: Macmillan).

Holloway, J. (1996b) 'The Abyss Opens: The Rise and Fall of Keynesianism', in W. Bonefeld and J. Holloway (eds), *Global Capital, National State and the Politics of Money* (Basingstoke: Macmillan).

Holman, O. (1996) *Integrating Southern Europe: EC Expansion and the Transnationalization of Spain* (London: Routledge).

Hopkin, J. (2012) 'A Slow Fuse: Italy and the EU Debt Crisis', *The International Spectator: Italian Journal of International Affairs*, 47:4, 35–48.

Hughes, N. (2011) '"Young People Took to the Streets and All of a Sudden All of the Political Parties Got Old": The 15M Movement in Spain', *Social Movement Studies: Journal of Social, Cultural and Political Protest*, 10:4, 407–13.

Husson, M. (2012) 'A Radical Strategy for Europe: From the Endless Bailout of Europe to Taking Leave from Neoliberalism', in E. Chiti, A. J. Menéndez and P. G. Teixeira (eds), *The European Rescue of the European Union? The existential Crisis of the European Political Project* RECON Report 19, ARENA Report 3/12, Oslo, February.

Huxley, J. (2009) *Value Capture Finance: Making Urban Development Pay its Way* (Washington DC: Urban Land Institute).

Idoate, E., F. Zamorano, N. Caicedo and J. Junyent (2008) 'Políticas de vivienda el Estado español', in Seminario de Economía Crítica TAIFA (ed.), *Auge y crisis de la vivienda en España*, Informes de economía 5 (Barcelona: Seminari d'Economia Crítica TAIFA).

IMF (2009) 'Hard Landing for Spain', *IMF Survey Magazine: Countries and Regions*, 24 April, http://www.imf.org/external/pubs/ft/survey/so/2009/car042409b.htm, date accessed 15 March 2010.

IMF (2011) 'Spain: Selected Issues' IMF Country Report No. 11/216, Washington DC, July.

Iñaki Oliden, A., A. Requena Aguilar and J. Luis Sánchez (2013) 'Los hijos del 15-M ya andan solos', *el diario*, 12 May, http://www.eldiario.es/politica/hijos-andan-solo_0_130887633.html, date accessed 27 June 2013.

INE (2012a) 'Encuesta de Condiciones de Vida: Año 2012, Datos provisionales', Press Release, 22 October.

INE (2012b) 'Encuesta de las personas sin hogar: Avance de resultados, Año 2012', Press Release, 21 December.

INE (2013) 'Encuesta de la Población Activa (EPA): Primer trimestre de 2013', Press Release, 25 April.

Iñigo Carrera, J. (2006) 'Argentina: The Reproduction of Capital Accumulation through Political Crisis', *Historical Materialism*, 14:1, 185–219.

Iñigo Carrera, J. (2007) *La formación económica de la sociedad argentina. Volumen I: Renta agraria, ganancia industrial y deuda externa, 1882–2004* (Buenos Aires: Imago Mundi).

Iñigo Carrera, J. (2008) *El capital: razón histórica, sujeto revolucionario y conciencia* (Buenos Aires: Imago Mundi).

Intermón Oxfam (2012) 'Crisis, desigualdad y pobreza: Aprendizajes desde el mundo en desarrollo ante los recortes sociales en España', *Informe de Intermón Oxfam*, 32.

Jerez Darias, L. M. and V. O. Martín Martín (2011) 'La renta de la tierra: los precios del suelo y la especulación inmobiliaria en España', *Nimbus*, 27/28, 41–61.

Jiménez, F. (2009) 'Building Boom and Political Corruption in Spain', *South European Society and Politics*, 14:3, 255–72.

Jimeno, J. F. and L. Toharia (1994) *Unemployment and Labour Market Flexibility: Spain* (Geneva: ILO).

JP Morgan Chase Bank (2012) 'Catalan Challenge Asks Real Questions of Europe', *Economic Research Global Data Watch*, London, 26 October.

Juamotte, F. and P. Sodsriwiboon (2010) 'Current Account Imbalances in the Southern Euro Area', IMF Working Paper 10/139, Washington DC, June.

Kamen, H. (1978) 'The Decline of Spain: A Historical Myth?', *Past & Present*, 81, 24–50.

Kaplanis, Y. (2011) 'An Economy that Excludes the Many and an "Accidental" Revolt', in A. Vradis and D. Dalakoglou (eds), *Revolt and Crisis in Greece: Between a Present Yet to Pass and a Future Still to Come* (London: AK Press and Occupied London).

Kaplinsky, R. (1989) '"Technological Revolution" and the International Division of Labour in Manufacturing: A Place for the Third World?' in R. Kaplinsky and C. Cooper (eds), *Technology and Development in the Third Industrial Revolution* (London: Frank Cass).

Karamessini, M. (2008) 'Still a Distinctive Southern European Employment Model?' *Industrial Relations Journal*, 39:6, 510–31.

Katseli, L. K. (2001) 'The Internationalization of Southern European Economies', in H. D. Gibson (ed.), *Economic Transformation, Democratization and Integration into the European Union: Southern Europe in Comparative Perspective* (Basingstoke: Palgrave).

Keagan, W. (1989) *Mr Lawson's Gamble* (London: Hodder & Stoughton).

Keating, M. and A. Wilson (2009) 'Renegotiating the State of Autonomies: Statute Reform and Multi-Level Politics in Spain', *West European Politics*, 32:3, 536–58.

Kerr, D. (1996) 'The Theory of Rent: From Crossroads to the Magic Roundabout', *Capital & Class*, 20:1, 59–88.

Kerr, D. (1998) 'The Private Finance Initiative and the Changing Governance of the Built Environment', *Urban Studies*, 35:12, 2277–2301.

King, R. J. (1989) 'Capital Switching and the Role of Ground Rent: 1. Theoretical Problems', *Environment and Planning A*, 21:4, 445–62.

Kirby, P. (2010) *Celtic Tiger in Collapse: Explaining the Weaknesses of the Irish Model* (Basingstoke: Palgrave Macmillan).

Kitchin, R., C. O'Callaghan, M. Boyle, J. Gleeson and K. Keaveney (2012) 'Placing Neoliberalism: The Rise and Fall of Ireland's Celtic Tiger', *Environment and Planning A*, 44: 1302–26.

Köhler, C. and J. Woodward (1997) 'Systems of Work and Socio-Economic Structures: A Comparison of Germany, Spain, France and Japan', *European Journal of Industrial Relations*, 3:1, 59–82.

Kowsmann, P. and M. Walker (2013) 'Idea of Euro Exit Finds Currency in Portugal', *Wall Street Journal*, 27 May, http://online.wsj.com/article/SB10001 424127887323336104578503253715866368.html, date accessed 4 July 2013.

Krempel, L. and T. Plümper (1999) 'International Division of Labor and Global Economic Processes: An Analysis of the International Trade in Automobiles', *Journal of World Systems Research*, V:3, 487–98.

Lagendijk, A. and B. van der Knapp (1995) 'Spatial Effects of Internationalisation of the Spanish Automobile Industry', *Tijdschrift voor Economische en Sociale Geografie*, 86:5, 426–42.

Lapavitsas, C. (2009a) 'Financialised Capitalism: Crisis and Financial Expropriation', *Historical Materialism*, 17:2, 114–48.

Lapavitsas, C. (2009b) *El capitalismo financiarizado: Expansión y crisis* (Madrid: Maia Ediciones).

Lapavitsas, C. et al. (2010) 'Eurozone Crisis: Beggar Thyself and Thy Neighbour', *RMF Occasional Report*, March, http://researchonmoneyandfinance.org/media/reports/eurocrisis/fullreport.pdf, date accessed 23 January 2013.

Lauria, M. (1984) 'The Implications of Marxian Rent Theory for Community-Controlled Redevelopment Strategies', *Journal of Planning Education and Research*, 4:1, 16–24.

La Vanguardia (2009) 'SEAT pierde 78 milliones de euros en 2008', 12 March, http://www.lavanguardia.com/ocio/20090312/53659140951/seat-pierde-78-millones-en-2008-la-unica-marca-de-volkswagen-en-numeros-rojos.html, date accessed 7 July 2013.

Lawlor, T. and M. Rigby (1986) 'Contemporary Spanish Trade Unions', *Industrial Relations Journal*, 17:3, 249–65.

Leitner H. and E. Sheppard (1989) 'The City as Locus of Production', in R. Peet and N. Thrift (eds), *New Models in Geography: The Political-Economy Perspective* (London: Unwin Hyman).

Lieberman, S. (1982) *The Contemporary Spanish Economy: A Historical Perspective* (London: Allen & Unwin).

Lieberman, S. (1995) *Growth and Crisis in the Spanish Economy 1940–93* (London: Routledge).

Llamazares, I. (2005) 'The Popular Party and European Integration: Re-elaborating the European Programme of Spanish Conservatism', *South European Politics and Society*, 10:2, 315–32.

López Garrido, D. (2012) 'Introduction: Twelve Months of Economic Despair', in D. López Garrido et al. (eds), *The State of the European Union: The Failure of Austerity* (Madrid: Fundación Alternativas and Friedrich-Ebert-Stiftung).

López, I. (2007) 'Sin los pies en el suelo. Acumulación de capital y ocupación de territorio en la Comunidad de Madrid', in Observatorio Metropolitano (ed.), *Madrid: ¿la suma de todos? Globalización, territorio, desigualdad* (Madrid: Traficantes de Sueños).

López, I. and E. Rodríguez (2010) *Fin de ciclo: Financiarización, territorio y sociedad de propietarios en la onda larga del capitalismo hispano (1959–2010)* (Madrid: Traficantes de Sueños).

López, I. and E. Rodríguez (2011) 'The Spanish Model', *New Left Review*, 69, 5–28.

López, J. G. (2006) 'Spanish Unemployment: Balance of Payments–Constrained Growth and Structural Change', *International Journal of Political Economy*, 35:3, 3–22.

Lucarelli, B. (2011) 'German Neomercantilism and the European Sovereign Debt Crisis', *Journal of Post Keynesian Economics*, 34:2, 205–24.

Luis Sánchez, J. (2013) 'Partido X: "Queremos desarrollar un método, no una ideología"', *el diario*, 8 January, http://www.eldiario.es/politica/Partido_X-entrevista-programa-anonimos-15m_0_87841344.html, date accessed 1 July 2013.

Maravall, J. M. (1997) *Regimes, Politics and Markets: Democratization and Economic Change in Southern and Eastern Europe* (Oxford: Oxford University Press).

Margaronis, M. (2008) 'How Police Shooting of a Teenage Boy Rallied the "700 euro Generation"', *Guardian*, 13 December, http://www.guardian.co.uk/world/2008/dec/13/athens-greece-riots, date accessed 21 March 2013.

Martín, C. (2000) *The Spanish Economy in the New Europe* (London: Macmillan).

Martín-Marcos, A. and J. Jaumandreu (2004) 'Entry, Exit and Productivity Growth: Spanish Manufacturing during the Eighties', *Spanish Economic Review*, 6, 211–26.

Martínez Hinojal, F. (2004) 'Mentiras sobre suelo y vivienda: Diez típicas falacias sobre el suelo y la vivienda protegida', *Boletín Ciudades para un Futuro mas Sostenible*, 29/30, http://habitat.aq.upm.es/boletin/n29/afmar.html, date accessed 11 May 2013.

Martínez Lucio, M. and P. Blyton (1995) 'Constructing the Post-Fordist State? The Politics of Labour Market Flexibility in Spain', *West European Politics*, 18:2, 340–60.

Martínez Ruiz, E. (2001) 'Sector exterior y crecimiento en la España autárquica', *Revista de Historia Económica*, 14:extraordinario, 229–51.

Martínez Sánchez, A. (1992) 'Regional Innovation and Small High Technology Firms in Peripheral Regions', *Small Business Economics*, 4:2, 153–68.

Martínez Sánchez, A. (1994) 'FMS in Spanish Industry: Lessons from Experience', *Integrated Manufacturing Systems*, 5:4, 48–63.

Martínez Sánchez, A., M. Pérez Pérez and I. Alonso Nuez (2000) 'Las tecnologías de automatización flexible en España', *Boletín económico de ICE*, 2654, 7–16.

Martínez Zarzoso, I. (1999) 'Competitividad internacional de la industria española', *Cambio tecnológico y competitividad*, 781, 143–56.

Martínez-Alier, J. and J. Roca (1987) 'Spain after Franco: From Corporatist Ideology to Corporatist Reality', *International Journal of Political Economy*, 17:4, 56–87.

Martínez, G. (ed.) (2012) *CT o la Cultura de la Transición: Crítica de 35 años de cultura española* (Barcelona: Debols!llo).

Martínez, M. (2007) 'The Squatters' Movement: Urban Counter-Culture and Alter-Globalization Dynamics', *South European Society and Politics*, 12:3, 379–98.

Marx, K. (1976) *Capital: A Critique of Political Economy, Volume One* (Harmondsworth: Penguin).

Marx, K. (1978) *Capital, Volume Two* (Harmondsworth: Penguin).

Marx, K. (1981) *Capital, Volume Three* (Harmondsworth: Penguin).

Marx, K. and F. Engels (1997) *The Communist Manifesto* (London: Pluto).

Mas, M. and J. Quesada (2005) 'ICT and Economic Growth in Spain, 1985–2002', EUKLEMS Working Paper, 1, http://www.euklems.net/pub/no1(online).pdf, date accessed 10 April 2013.

Mason, P. (2012) 'Valencia: A Spanish City Without Medicine', 23 September, http://www.bbc.co.uk/news/magazine-19682049, date accessed 4 June 2013.

Mathieson, D. (2007) *Spanish Steps: Zapatero and the Second Transition in Spain* (London: Policy Network).

Matsaganis, M. (2012) 'Social Policy in Hard Times: The Case of Greece', *Critical Social Policy*, 32:3, 406–21.

Mayals, D. and J. Iglesias Fernández (2008) 'El negocio de la construcción-inmobiliario', in Seminario de Economía Crítica TAIFA (ed.), *Auge y crisis de la vivienda en España*, Informes de economía 5 (Barcelona: Seminari d'Economia Crítica TAIFA).

Mayayo, G. (2007) 'The Spanish Mortgage Market and the American Subprime Crisis', December, http://www.ahe.es/bocms/images/bfilecontent/2007/12/18/2146.pdf?version=4, date accessed 7 July 2013.

McMillion, C. W. (1981) 'International Integration and Intra-National Disintegration: The Case of Spain', *Comparative Politics*, 13:3, 291–312.

McNeill, D. (1999) *Urban Change and the European Left: Tales from Barcelona* (London: Routledge).

Meardi, G., A. Martín and M. Lozana Riera (2012) 'Constructing Uncertainty: Unions and Migrant Labour in Construction in Spain and the UK', *Journal of Industrial Relations*, 54:1, 5–21.

Medina Albaladejo, F. J. (2010) 'External Competitiveness of Spanish Canned Fruit and Vegetable Businesses During the Second Half of the Twentieth Century', *Business History*, 52:3, 417–34.

Minder, R. (2012) 'Car Factories Offer Hope for Spanish Industry and Workers', *New York Times*, 27 December, http://www.nytimes.com/2012/12/28/business/global/car-factories-offer-hope-for-spanish-industry-and-workers.html?page wanted=all&_r=0, date accessed 17 April 2013.

Ministerio de Economia y Hacienda (2011) 'Private Indebtedness: Some Highlights', Madrid, 20 December, http://www.thespanisheconomy.com/SiteCollectionDocuments/en-gb/Financial%20Sector/111220_Private_debt.pdf, date accessed 15 May 2013.

Miranda Montero, M. J. (2007) 'Transformaciones urbanas en Valencia: La Copa del América', *Estudios Geográficos*, LXVII:263, 709–24.

Moix, L. (2010) *Arquitectura milagrosa: Hazañas de los arquitectos estrella en la España del Guggenheim* (Barcelona: Anagrama).

Molero, J. (ed.) (1995) *Technological Innovation, Multinational Corporations and New International Competitiveness: The Case of Intermediate Countries* (London: Harwood)

Molero, J. (1998) 'Multinational and National Firms in the Process of Technology Internationalization: Spain as an Intermediate Case', Working Paper 9, Instituto de Análisis Industrial y Financiero, Complutense University of Madrid.

Molinas, C. (2012) 'España, capital Madrid', *El País*, 4 March, http://economia.elpais.com/economia/2012/03/02/actualidad/1330712282_179577.html, date accessed 25 June 2013.

Molinas, C. and L. Prados de la Escosura (1989) 'Was Spain Different? Spanish Historical Backwardness Revisited', *Explorations in Economic History*, 26:4, 385–402.

Molinero, C. and P. Ysás (2003) 'El malestar popular por las condiciones de vida. ¿Un problema político para el régimen franquista?, *Ayer*, 52, 255–80.

Montes, P. (1991) 'La integración el la Comunidad Económica Europea en el proceso de la internacionalización del capitalismo español', in M. Etxezarreta (ed.), *La Reestructuración del capitalismo en España, 1970–1990* (Barcelona: Icaria).

Montgomery, C. and I. Sabate (2010) 'The Steel Industry and the Spanish Economy', Country Profile prepared for the Medea Project, www.medeasteelproject.org/sites/medea.localhost/files/National%20trajectories%20-%20Spain.pdf, date accessed 12 March 2012.

Moseley, F. (2002) 'Hostile Brothers: Marx's Theory of the Distribution of Surplus-Value in Volume III of *Capital*', in M. Campbell and G. Reuten (eds), *The Culmination of Capital: Essays on Volume III of Marx's Capital* (Basingstoke: Palgrave).

Moseley, F. (2009) 'The Development of Marx's Theory of the Distribution of Surplus-Value in the Manuscripts of 1861-63', in R. Bellofiore and R. Fineschi (eds), *Re-Reading Marx: New Perspectives After the Critical Edition* (Basingstoke: Palgrave).

Muñoz de Bustillo, R. and J. Ignacio Antón (2010) 'From Sending to Host Societies: Immigration in Greece, Ireland and Spain in the 21st Century', *Industrial Relations Journal*, 41:6, 563–83.

Muñoz Gielen, D. and W. K. Korthals Altes (2007) 'Lessons from Valencia: Separating Infrastructure Provision from Land Ownership', *The Town Planning Review*, 78:1, 61–79.

Muñoz Gielen, D. and T. Tasan-Kok (2010) 'Flexibility in Planning and the Consequences for Public-Value Capturing in UK, Spain and the Netherlands', *European Planning Studies*, 18:7, 1097–1131.

Muñoz, R. (2001) 'La construcción registra el mayor ritmo de crecimiento en los últimos anos en España', *El País*, 2 November, http://elpais.com/diario/2001/11/02/economia/1004655613_850215.html, 22 February 2013.

Muñoz, J. and M. Guinjoan (2012) 'Accounting for Internal Variation in Nationalist Mobilization: Unofficial Referendums for Independence in Catalonia (2009–11)', *Nations and Nationalism*, 19:1, 44–67.

Murado, M-A. (2011) 'What Next for Spain's "Angry Ones"?' *Guardian*, 20 May, http://www.guardian.co.uk/commentisfree/2011/may/20/spain-protesting-angry-ones, date accessed 21 July 2011.

Nagel, K-J. (2006) '25 Years of Catalan Autonomy', *Scottish Affairs*, 54, 22–38.

Nagel, K-J. (2009) 'The Nationalism of Stateless Nations And Europe: The Catalan Case', Grup de Recerca en Teoria Política working paper, 6, Universitat Pompeu Fabra, Barcelona, December.

Naredo, J. M., O. Carpintero and C. Marcos (2007) *Patrimonio inmobiliario y balance nacional de la economía española (1995–2007)* (Madrid: Fundación de las Cajas de Ahorros).

Navarro, M. (1984) 'Cédulas sin identificación fiscal', *El País*, 10 June, http://elpais.com/diario/1984/06/10/economia/455666415_850215.html, date accessed 2 March 2013.

Nieto Ferrández, M. (2007) 'Tendencias de la rentabilidad y la acumulación en el capitalismo español', *Revista de economía institucional*, 8: 15, 185–206.

Nogueira, J. M. (2005) 'El suelo y la vivienda', *Boletín Ciudades para un Futuro mas Sostenible*, 34, http://habitat.aq.upm.es/boletin/n34/ajnog.html, date accessed 27 April 2013.

O'Brien, P. (1975) 'Foreign Technology and Industrialization: The Case of Spain', *Journal of World Trade*, 5, 525–52.

O'Brien, P. K. and L. Prados de la Escosura (1998) 'The Costs and Benefits for Europeans from Their Empires Overseas', *Revista de Historia Económica (Second Series)*, 16:1, 29–89.

Observatorio DESC (2013) 'El abismo entre la ILP por la dación en pago y la ley "antidesahucios" aprobada por el PP', 22 May, http://www.observatoridesc.org/es/abismo-entre-ilp-dacion-pago-y-ley-antidesahucios-aprobada-pp, date accessed 1 July 2013.

OECD (2005) 'Economic Survey of Spain 2005: Stabilising the Housing Market', http://www.oecd.org/spain/34586052.pdf, date accessed 22 February 2011.

OECD (2008) *OECD Economic Surveys: Spain* (Paris: OECD).

OECD (2009) *Promoting Entrepreneurship, Employment and Business Competitiveness: The Experience of Barcelona*, LEED Programme Local Development Agency Review Series (Paris: OECD).

OECD (2010) *OECD Economic Surveys: Spain, 2010* (Paris: OECD).

O'Grady, S. and J. Lichfield (2010) '"Very Real" Threat that Greek Contagion Could Spread to Britain', *Independent*, 7 May, http://www.independent.co.uk/news/business/news/very-real-threat-that-greek-contagion-could-spread-to-britain-1965610.html, date accessed 21 March 2013.

Ó Riain, S. (2012) 'The Crisis of Financialisation in Ireland', *The Economic and Social Review*, 43:4, 497–533.

Ortiz-Villajos, J. M. (2010) 'Aproximación a la historia de la industria de equipos y componentes de automoción en España', *Investigaciones de Historia Económica*, 6:16, 135–72.

Pack, S. D. (2006) *Tourism and Dictatorship: Europe's Peaceful Invasion of Franco's Spain* (Basingstoke: Palgrave).

Pallarès Barberà, M. (1997) 'El sistema de producción flexible, el just-in-time y la transformación espacial: las empresas del automóvil en España', *Boletín de la Asociación de Geógrafos Españoles*, 24, 53–71.

Pallarès Barberà, M. (1998) 'Changing Production Systems: The Automobile Industry in Spain', *Economic Geography*, 74:4, 344–59.

Pascual-Molinas, N. and R. Ribera-Fumaz (2009) 'Retail Gentrification in Ciutat Vella, Barcelona', in L. Porter and K. Shaw (eds), *Whose Urban Renaissance? An International Comparison of Urban Regeneration Strategies* (London: Routledge).

PCE (2013) 'Manifiesto del PCE para el 1º de mayo frente a las políticas que están arruinando a la mayoría de nuestro país', 1 May, http://www.pce.es/docpce/pl.php?id=5284, date accessed 24 May 2013.

Pellicer Mateu, L. (2013) 'La vivienda sufre ahora su mayor caída', *El País*, 14 June, http://economia.elpais.com/economia/2013/06/13/vivienda/1371156470_964853.html, date accessed 14 June 2013.

Pérez-Amorós, F. and E. Rojo (1991) 'Implications of the Single European Market for Labour and Social Policies in Spain', *International Labour Review*, 130:3, 359–72.

Pérez, F. et al (2004) *La competitividad de la economía española* (Barcelona: La Caixa).

Peréz, S. A. (1997) *Banking on Privilege: The Politics of Spanish Financial Reform* (Ithaca: Cornell University Press).

Peréz, S. A. (1999) 'From Labor to Finance: Understanding the Failure of Socialist Economic Policies in Spain', *Comparative Political Studies*, 32:6, 659–89

Pérez, S. A. (2000) 'From Decentralisation to Reorganisation: Explaining the Return to National Bargaining in Italy and Spain', *Comparative Politics*, 32:4, 437–58.

Petithomme, M. and A. Fernández Garcia (2013) 'Catalonian Nationalism in Spain's Time of Crisis: From Asymmetrical Federalism to Independence?', The Federal Idea: A Quebec Think Tank on Federalism, March, http://ideefederale.ca/documents/Catalonia.pdf, date accessed 24 June 2013.

Phillips, N. (2009) 'Migration as Development Strategy? The New Political Economy of Dispossession in the Americas', *Review of International Political Economy*, 16:2, 231–59.

Piccione, S. and F. Cerezo (2012) 'Pioneros en flexibilidad', *El Mundo*, 1 April, 6.

Polo, C. (2013) 'Efectos de la "eurización" de la economía catalana', in O. Amat et al. (eds), *La cuestión catalana, hoy* (Madrid: Instituto de Estudios Económicos).

Powell, C. (2003) 'Spanish Membership of the European Union Revisited', in S. Royo and C. Manuel (eds), *Spain and Portugal in the European Union: The First Fifteen Years* (London: Frank Cass)

Prados de la Escosura, L. (2003) *El progreso económico de España (1850–2000)* (Bilbao: Fundación BBVA).

Prados de la Escosura, L. and J. C. Sanz (1996) 'Growth and Macroeconomic Performance in Spain, 1939–93', in N. Crafts and G. Toniolo (eds), *Economic Growth in Europe Since 1945* (Cambridge: Cambridge University Press).

Prados de la Escosura, L., J. R. Rosés and I. Sanz Villarroya (2010) 'Stablilization and Growth under Dictatorship: The Experience of Franco's Spain', Working Papers in Economic History, 10–2, Universidad Carlos III de Madrid.

Preston, P. (1994) *The Coming of the Spanish Civil War: Reform, Reaction and Revolution in The Second Republic*, second edition (London: Routledge).

Prytherch, D. L. (2006) 'Narrating the Landscapes of Entrepreneurial Regionalism: Rescaling, "New" Regionalism and the Planned Remaking of València, Spain', *Space and Polity*, 10:3, 203–27.

Prytherch, D. L. and J. V. Boira Maiques (2009) 'City Profile: Valencia', *Cities*, 26, 103–15.

Prytherch, D. L. and L. Huntoon (2005) 'Entrepreneurial Regionalist Planning in a Rescaled Spain: The Cases of Bilbao and València', *GeoJournal*, 62, 41–50.

Radice, H. (2010) 'The Idea of Socialism: From 1968 to the Present-day Crisis', *Antipode*, 41:S1, 27–49.

Radice, H. (2013) 'Reshaping Fiscal Policies in Europe: Enforcing Austerity, Attacking Democracy', *The Bullet*, 772, http://www.socialistproject.ca/bullet/772.php#fn1, date accessed 16 June 2013.

Rama, R., D. Ferguson and A. Melero (2003) 'Subcontracting Networks in Industrial Districts: The Electronics Industries of Madrid', *Regional Studies*, 37:1, 71–88.

Ramos Barrado (1986) 'La industria española de automoción: Cambios tras la crisis', *Estudios sobre Consumo*, 8: 56–80.

Rand Smith, W. (1998) *The Left's Dirty Job: The Politics of Industrial Restructuring in France and Spain* (Pittsburgh: University of Pittsburgh Press).

Reinert, E. S. and S. A. Reinert (2011) 'Mercantilism and Economic Development: Schumpeterian Dynamics, Institution Building, and International Benchmarking', *OIKOS*, 10:1, 8–37.

Rico, G. (2012) 'The 2010 Regional Election in Catalonia: A Multilevel Account in an Age of Economic Crisis', *South European Society and Politics*, 17:2, 217–38.

Rigby, M. and T. Lawlor (1994) 'Spanish Trade Unions 1986–1994; Life After National Agreements', *Industrial Relations Journal*, 25:4, 258–71.

Roca Cladera, J. and M. C. Burns (2000) 'The Liberalization of the Land Market in Spain: The 1998 Reform of Urban Planning Legislation', *European Planning Studies*, 8:5, 547–64.

Rodon, T. (2012) 'The Next Independent State in Europe? Catalonia's Critical Juncture and the Conundrum of Independence', *Godišnjak FPN*, 6:8, 129–47.

Rodrigues, J. and Reis, J. (2012) 'The Asymmetries of European Integration and the Crisis of Capitalism in Europe', *Competition and Change*, 16:3, 188–205.

Rodríguez López, E. (2007a) 'La ciudad global o la nueva centralidad de Madrid', in Observatorio Metropolitano (ed.), *Madrid: ¿la suma de todos? Globalización, territorio, desigualdad* (Madrid: Traficantes de Sueños).

Rodríguez López, E. (2007b) 'Nuevos diagramas sociales: Renta, explotación y segregación en el Madrid global', in Observatorio Metropolitano (ed.), *Madrid: ¿la suma de todos? Globalización, territorio, desigualdad* (Madrid: Traficantes de Sueños).

Rogers, C. (2012) *The IMF and European Economies: Crisis and Conditionality* (Basingstoke: Palgrave Macmillan).

Román, M. (1971) *The Limits of Economic Growth in Spain* (New York: Praeger).

Román, M. (1997) *Growth and Stagnation of the Spanish Economy: The Long Wave, 1954–1993* (Aldershot: Avebury).

Román, M. (2002) *Heterodox Views of Finance and Cycles in the Spanish Economy* (Aldershot: Ashgate).

Rosés, J. R. (2003) 'Why Isn't the Whole of Spain Industrialized? New Economic Geography and Early Industrialization, 1797–1910', *The Journal of Economic History*, 63:4, 995–1022.

Roxburgh, C. et al. (2012) 'Debt and Deleveraging: Uneven Progress on the Path to Growth', McKinsey Global Institute: Updated research, January.

Royo, S. (2009a) 'Reforms Betrayed? Zapatero and Continuities in Economic Policy', *South European Society and Politics*, 14:4, 435–51.

Royo, S. (2009b) 'After the Fiesta: The Spanish Economy Meets the Global Financial Crisis', *South European Society and Politics*, 14:1, 19–34.

Royo, S. (2013) 'How Did the Spanish Financial System Survive the First Stage of the Global Crisis?' *Governance: An International Journal of Policy, Administration, and Institutions*, 26:4, 631–656.

Rubenstein, J. M. (2001) *Making and Selling Cars: Innovation and Change in the US Automotive Industry* (Baltimore: The Johns Hopkins University Press).

Ruiz Almendral, V. (2004) 'The Asymmetric Distribution of Taxation Powers in the Spanish State of the Autonomies: The Common Systems and the *Foral* Tax Regimes', *Regional and Federal Studies*, 13:4, 41–66.

Rutland, T. (2010) 'The Financialization of Urban Redevelopment', *Geography Compass*, 4:8: 1167–78.

Salmon, K. (1990) *The Modern Spanish Economy: Transformation and Integration into Europe* (London: Pinter).

Salmon, K. (1995) *The Modern Spanish Economy: Transformation and Integration into Europe*, second edition (London: Pinter).

Salmon, K. (2002) 'The Spanish Economy from Maastricht to the Millennium: Integration into Europe and Transition to an Open Market Economy', conference paper, University of Bath, 6 December.

Salmon, K. (2010) 'Boom to Bust: Reconstructing the Spanish Economy', *International Journal of Iberian Studies*, 23:1, 39–52.

Samaniego, F. (1997) 'La ciudad frente "todo será urbanizable"', *El País*, 16 March, http://elpais.com/diario/1997/03/16/cultura/858466801_850215.html, date accessed 7 February 2013.

Sánchez-Pedreño Kennaird, A. and G. Arranz Pumar (2009) 'Covered bonds y su impacto en el Sistema Financiero', Asociación de Mercados Financieros, Madrid, 29 June, http://www.asociacionmercadosfinancieros.com/actividades/cursos/2009%20Covered%20Bonds%20AMF.pdf, date accessed 15 February 2013.

Sánchez, M. (2012) 'Losing Strength? An Alternative Vision of Spain's Indignados', *ROAR Magazine*, 23 June, http://roarmag.org/2012/06/losing-strength-an-alternative-vision-of-the-indignados/, date accessed 19 June 2013.

Santamaría, A. (2012) 'La apuesta soberanista de Artur Mas', *El Viejo Topo*, 298, 7–11.

Santiso, J. (2007). 'The Emergence of Latin Multinationals', OECD Emerging Markets Network Working Paper, OECD Development Centre, Paris.

Santos Preciado, J. M. (1997) 'La segmentación del mercado laboral juvenil y su especialización ocupacional por edad y sexo', *Anales de geografía de la Universidad Complutense*, 17, 153–71.

Sassen, S. (2009) 'When Local Housing Becomes an Electronic Instrument: The Global Circulation of Mortgages – A Research Note', *International Journal of Urban and Regional Research*, 33:2, 411–26.

Sastre-Jiménez, L. (2002) 'Simultaneidad e interdependencia entre los flujos de ingresos por turismo e inversión extranjera en inmuebles en España', *Información Comercial Española*, 802, 129–40.

Schaeffer, P. V. and R. S. Mack (1997) 'The Conceptual Foundations of the New International Division of Labour', *Journal of Planning Literature*, 12:1, 3–15.

Schrijver, F. J. (2006) *Regionalism after Regionalisation: Spain, France and the United Kingdom* (Amsterdam: Universiteit van Amsterdam).

Scobie, H. M. et al. (1998) *The Spanish Economy in the 1990s* (London: European Economics Financial Centre and Routledge).

Seminari d'economia Crítica TAIFA (2010) *La crisis en el estado español: el rescate de los poderosos*, Informes de economía crítica 7 (Barcelona: Seminari d'economia Crítica TAIFA).

Serrano Sans, J. M. and E. Pardos (2002) 'Los años de crecimiento del franquismo (1959–1975)', in F. Comín, M. Hernández and E. Llopis (eds), *Historia económica de España: Siglos X–XX* (Barcelona: Crítica).

Serrano, I. (2013a) 'Just a Matter of Identity? Support for Independence in Catalonia', *Regional and Federal Studies*, 23:5, 523–545.

Serrano, I. (2013b) *De la nació a l'estat* (Barcelona: Angle Editorial).

Share, D. (1988) 'Dilemmas of Social Democracy in the 1980s: The Spanish Socialist Workers Party in Comparative Perspective', *Comparative Political Studies*, 21:3, 408–35.

Shields, S., I. Bruff and H. Macartney (eds) (2011) *Critical International Political Economy: Dialogue, Debate, Dissensus* (Basingstoke: Palgrave Macmillan).

Simpson, J. (1995) *Spanish Agriculture: The Long Siesta, 1765–1965* (Cambridge: Cambridge University Press).

Simpson, J. (1997) 'Economic Development in Spain, 1850–1936', *Economic History Review*, 50:2, 348–59.

Smith, H. (2013) 'Greece Asked to Welcome Tourists Who Are Bound for Nation in Record Numbers', *Guardian*, 14 May, http://www.guardian.co.uk/world/2013/may/14/greeks-welcome-record-number-of-tourists/print, date accessed 4 July 2013.

Smith, N. (1984) *Uneven Development: Nature, Capital, and the Production of Space* (Oxford: Blackwell).

Smyth, S. (2013) '"A Tide of Squatters" Spreads in Spain in Wake of Foreclosures', *Bloomberg News*, 17 April, http://business.financialpost.com/2013/04/17/a-tide-of-squatters/, date accessed 10 May 2013.

Smyth, S. and R. Urban (2013) 'Spain Braces for Tsunami of Bankruptcies as Banks Pull Plug on Zombie Developers', *Bloomberg News*, http://business.financial post.com/2013/03/20/spain-braces-for-tsunami-of-bankruptcies-as-banks-pull-plug-on-zombie-developers/?__lsa=a07a-9ecc, date accessed 24 May 2013.

Spiegel Online (2011) 'German Chancellor on the Offensive: Merkel Blasts Greece over Retirement Age, Vacation', 18 May, http://www.spiegel.de/inter national/europe/german-chancellor-on-the-offensive-merkel-blasts-greece-over-retirement-age-vacation-a-763294.html, date accessed 25 March.

Standing, G. (1997) 'Globalization, Labour Flexibility and Insecurity: The Era of Market Regulation', *European Journal of Industrial Relations*, 3:1, 7–37.

Starosta, G. (2008) 'The Commodity-Form and the Dialectical Method: On the Structure of Marx's Exposition of Chapter 1 of Capital', *Science & Society*, 72:3, 295–318.

Starosta, G. (2010a) 'The Outsourcing of Manufacturing and the Rise of Giant Global Contractors: A Marxian Approach to Some Recent Transformations of Global Value Chains', *New Political Economy*, 15:4, 543–63.

Starosta, G. (2010b) 'Global Commodity Chains and the Marxian Law of Value', *Antipode*, 42:2, 433–65.

Stein, S. J. and B. H. Stein (2000) *Silver, Trade, and War: Spain and America in the Making of Early Modern Europe* (Baltimore: The Johns Hopkins University Press).

Stevens, L. and E. Henning (2012) 'State of Europe's Banks: Safe and Stressed – Germany's Leaders Find Fortunes Tied to Spanish Peers', *Wall Street Journal*, 24 September.

Stücklin, M. (2013) 'Spanish Housing Stock Increases 24pc in a Decade', *Spanish Property Insight*, 12 April, http://www.spanishpropertyinsight.com/2013/04/12/spanish-housing-stock-increases-24pc-in-a-decade/, date accessed 15 May 2013.

Studer-Noguez, I. (2002) *Ford and the Global Strategies of Multinationals: The North American Auto Industry* (London: Routledge).

Sturgeon, T. and R. Florida (2004) 'Globalization, Deverticalization, and Employment in the Motor Vehicle Industry', in M. Kenney and R. Florida (eds), *Locating Global Advantage: Industry Dynamics in the International Economy* (Stanford: Stanford University Press).

Suárez, J. (2010) 'The Spanish Crisis: Background and Policy Challenges', Centro de Estudios Monetarios y Financieros (CEMFI), working paper 1005, Madrid, July.

Swyngedouw, E. (2010) 'Rent and Landed Property', in B. Fine, A. Saad-Filho and M. Boffo (eds), *The Elgar Companion to Marxist Economics* (London: Elgar).

Taibo, C. (2013) 'The Spanish Indignados: A Movement with Two Souls', *European Urban and Regional Studies*, 20:1, 155–58.

Tamames, R. (1986) *The Spanish Economy: An Introduction* (London: C Hurst & Co).

Tejedor, E. (2013) 'Aniversario para militantes', *El País*, 15 May, http://politica.elpais.com/politica/2013/05/15/actualidad/1368632102_221970.html, date accessed 16 May 2013.

Tirado, D. A., E. Paluzie and J. Pons (2002) 'Economic Integration and Industrial Location: The Case of Spain before World War I', *Journal of Economic Geography*, 2:3, 343–63.

Tokatli, N. (2008) 'Global Sourcing: Insights from the Global Clothing Industry – The Case of Zara, a Fast Fashion Retailer', *Journal of Economic Geography*, 8:1, 21–38

Toral, P. (2008) 'The Foreign Direct Investments of Spanish Multinational Enterprises in Latin America, 1989–2005', *Journal of Latin American Studies*, 40, 513–44.

Tornabell, R. (2012) 'Spain's 90s Greed is at the Root of its Banking Crisis', *Guardian*, 8 June, http://www.guardian.co.uk/commentisfree/2012/jun/08/spain-90s-greed-banking-crisis, date accessed 23 April 2013.

Tortella, G. (2000) *The Development of Modern Spain: An Economic History of the Nineteenth and Twentieth Centuries* (London: Harvard University Press).

Tortella, G. and S. Houpt (2000) 'From Autarky to the European Union: Nationalist Economic Policies in Twentieth-Century Spain', in A. Teichova, H. Matis and J Pátek (eds), *Economic Change and the National Question in Twentieth-Century Europe* (Cambridge: Cambridge University Press).

Tremlett, G. (2011) 'How Corruption, Cuts and Despair Drove Spain's Protestors onto the Streets', *Guardian*, 21 May, http://www.guardian.co.uk/world/2011/may/21/spain-reveals-pain-cuts-unemployment, date accessed 21 July 2011.

Tremlett, G. (2012a) 'Valencia's Hopes Remain Grounded as It Bids for Bailout', *Guardian*, 29 August, http://www.guardian.co.uk/world/2012/aug/29/valencia-hopes-remain-grounded-bailout, date accessed 4 June 2013.

Tremlett, G. (2012b) 'Spanish Government Rescues Fourth Largest Lender, Bankia', *Guardian*, 10 May 2012, http://www.guardian.co.uk/business/2012/may/10/spanish-government-rescues-fourth-largest-bank-bankia, date accessed 16 June 2013.

Tremlett, G. (2013) 'Pay Pain', *Guardian*, 1 June, 32.

Truett, L. J. and D. B. Truett (2001) 'The Spanish Automotive Industry: Scale Economies and Input Relationships', *Applied Economics*, 33, 1503–13.

Tusell, J. (2007) *Spain, From Dictatorship to Democracy: 1939 to the Present* (Oxford: Blackwell).

Uriel, E., C. Albert, E. Benages, and V. Cucarella (2009) *El stock de capital en viviendas en España y su distribución territorial, 1990–2008* (Madrid: Fundación BBVA).

Uxó, J., J. Paúl, and E. Febrero (2010) 'Current Account Imbalances in the Monetary Union and the Great Recession: Causes and Policies', *Panoeconomicus*, 5:Special Issue, 571–92.

Uxó, J., J. Paúl, and E. Febrero (2012) 'European Economic Policy and the Problem of Current Account Imbalances: The Case of Germany and Spain', in J. Jesperson and M. Ove Madsen (eds), *Keynes's General Theory for Today: Contemporary Perspectives* (Cheltenham: Edward Elgar).

Vallespín, I. (2013) '500 personas de PAH de toda Cataluña ocupan la sede de BBVA en Sabadell', *El País*, 21 June, http://ccaa.elpais.com/ccaa/2013/06/21/catalunya/1371829064_130026.html, date accessed 28 June 2013.

Viñas, A., J. Viñuela, F. Eguidazu, C. Fernández-Pulgar and S. Florensa (1979) *Política Comercial Exterior en España, 1931–1975*, volumen 1 (Madrid: Banco Exterior de España).

Viñals, J. et al. (1990) 'Spain and the "EC cum 1992" Shock', in C. Bliss and J. Braga de Macedo (eds), *Unity with Diversity in the European Economy: The Community's Southern Frontier* (Cambridge: Cambridge University Press).

Vives Miró, S. (2011) 'Producing a "Successful City": Neoliberal Urbanism and Gentrification in the Tourist City – The Case of Palma (Majorca)', *Urban Studies Research*, 2011:989676, 1–13.

Vlachou, A. (2012) 'The Greek Economy in Turmoil', *Rethinking Marxism: A Journal of Economics, Culture & Society*, 24:2, 171–200.

Walker, R. (2006) 'The Boom and the Bombshell: The New Economy Bubble and the San Francisco Bay Area', in G. Vertova (ed.), *The Changing Economic Geography of Globalization: Reinventing Space* (London: Routledge).

Walt, V. (2013) 'Meet Amancio Ortega: The Third-Richest Man in the World', *CNNMONEY*, 8 January, http://management.fortune.cnn.com/2013/01/08/zara-amancio-ortega, date accessed 1 May 2013.

Weeks, J. (2013) 'Euro Crisis and Euro Scams: Trade Not Debt and Deficits Tell the Tale', http://jweeks.org/2012%20Euro%20Crisis_Weeks%20Rope.pdf, date accessed 18 November 2013.

Whelan, K. (2012) 'Macroeconomic Imbalances in the Euro Area', Directorate General for Internal Policies, European Parliament, April.

Williams, A. M. (2001) 'Tourism as an Agent of Economic Transformation in Southern Europe', in H. D. Gibson (ed.), *Economic Transformation, Democratization and Integration into the European Union: Southern Europe in Comparative Perspective* (Basingstoke: Macmillan).

Wölfl, A. and J. S. Mora-Sanguinetti (2011) 'Reforming the Labour Market in Spain', *OECD Economics Department Working Papers*, 845, 17 February.

World Policy Journal (2011) 'Anatomy of a Crisis: Ireland's Agony', 25:1, 16.

Wright, A. (1977) *The Spanish Economy, 1959–1976* (London: Macmillan).

Wright, V. and G. Pagoulatos (2001) 'The Comparative Politics of Industrial Privatization: Spain, Portugal and Greece in European Perspective', in H. D. Gibson (ed.), *Economic Transformation, Democratization and Integration into the European Union: Southern Europe in Comparative Perspective* (Basingstoke: Palgrave).

Yaniz Igal, J. (2006) 'The Spanish Housing Market: Are We in for a Soft Landing?' *ECFIN Country Focus*, 3:1, 1–6.

Žižek, S. (2013) 'The Cyprus Crisis is a Symptom of What Is Rotten in the EU', *Guardian*, 8 April, http://www.guardian.co.uk/commentisfree/2013/apr/08/cyprus-crisis-symptom-rotten-eu, date accessed 8 April 2013.

Index

Printed and bound in the United States of America